Internationalizing
a School of Education

Internationalizing
a School of Education
INTEGRATION AND INFUSION IN PRACTICE

John Schwille

Michigan State University Press | *East Lansing*

Michigan State University Press
East Lansing, Michigan 48823-5245

Printed and bound in the United States of America.

25   24   23   22   21   20   19   18   17   1   2   3   4   5   6   7   8   9   10

LIBRARY OF CONGRESS CATALOGING-IN-PUBLICATION DATA
Names: Schwille, John, author.
Title: Internationalizing a school of education : integration and infusion in practice / John Schwille.
Description: East Lansing, Michigan : Michigan State University Press, 2016. | Series: International race
and education series | Includes bibliographical references and index.
Identifiers: LCCN 2016000402| ISBN 9781611862157 (pbk. : alk. paper) | ISBN 9781609175023 (pdf)
ISBN 9781628952759 (epub) | ISBN 9781628962758 (kindle)
Subjects: LCSH: International education. | Michigan State University. College of Education. | Teachers—
Training of—Michigan—Lansing. | International education. | Comparative education. |
Comparative and International Education Society. | Knowledge, Sociology of.
Classification: LCC LB2193.M38 S35 2016 | DDC 370.1/16—
dc23 LC record available at http://lccn.loc.gov/2016000402

Book design by Charlie Sharp, Sharp Designs, Lansing, Michigan
Cover design by Shaun Allshouse, www.shaunallshouse.com

Michigan State University Press is a member of the Green Press Initiative and is
committed to developing and encouraging ecologically responsible publishing
practices. For more information about the Green Press Initiative and the use of
recycled paper in book publishing, please visit www.greenpressinitiative.org.

Visit Michigan State University Press at www.msupress.org

Contents

vii   Preface

xi   Acknowledgments

xv   Introduction

PART 1. The Landscape of Internationalization in U.S. Schools of Education

3   CHAPTER 1. Toward a Sociology of Comparative and International Education

9   CHAPTER 2. Differing Approaches to Comparative and International Education in Schools of Education

19   CHAPTER 3. The Changing Landscape of Internationalization in a New Era of MSU History

PART 2. Convergent and Divergent Channels of Internationalization

29   CHAPTER 4. Faculty to Develop and Explore the Main Channels of Internationalization

43 CHAPTER 5. Creating and Benefiting from New Channels of International Research

79 CHAPTER 6. Building New Channels for International Development Work

113 CHAPTER 7. The Fragility of International Partnerships Needed to Feed Channels of Internationalization

129 CHAPTER 8. Preparing the Ground for Channels of International Content and World Languages in K–12 and Teacher Education

169 CHAPTER 9. Engaging Internationally Oriented Students to Create New Channels and Broaden Existing Ones

197 CHAPTER 10. Two Streams Less Connected with the Main Channels of Internationalization

207 CHAPTER 11. International Visiting Scholars, a Source of Internationalization That Could Exceed Expectations but Often Did Not

219 CHAPTER 12. Finding Enough Money and Support Staff to Feed and Expand Channels

231 CHAPTER 13. Connecting to the Channels of Other Institutions through the CIES

235 CHAPTER 14. Summing Up

241 APPENDIX 1. Development of International Strengths among MSU College of Education Faculty, 1984–2012

249 APPENDIX 2. Thirty-Two International Books Authored or Edited by MSU College of Education Faculty, 1994–2012

255 APPENDIX 3. Timeline: MSU Integration-Infusion Policy in Practice

263 Notes

275 References

285 Index

Preface

I n 2011–12 I decided to write a paper for the annual meetings of the Comparative and International Education Society (CIES), explaining our distinctive approach to internationalization at Michigan State University. Instead of a separate degree program in comparative and international education, after 1984 we tried to put our international strengths into the development of an international dimension throughout the College of Education—in its outreach, its teaching, and especially its research. It was what in this book is called an integration-infusion approach. Years later, it seemed that our colleagues in the other universities who were well known for international work in education did not really understand what we were up to, and I wanted them to know. When I finished the first version of this CIES paper, it was forty-some pages single spaced, far too long for publication as a journal article and not easily delivered in a short conference presentation. Nevertheless, I sent the paper out to colleagues around the country and asked for their feedback. I especially welcomed suggestions for shortening the paper. The feedback was diverse. Some colleagues immediately responded that they were not convinced by my arguments and did not agree with our position. Other colleagues responded more positively. And a few said, don't shorten it, this is good, it should be a book. At first I was skeptical that anyone would be interested in this book, but I allowed myself to be convinced since it was in fact a story I yearned to tell. This book is the result.

Since the book features profiles of other faculty members and students who were leaders of this integration-infusion approach in our college, I will start by saying something about myself as well. My career in international research on education now stretches back more than fifty years, starting as a doctoral student at the University of Chicago in 1963. Since 1972, after initial research on France and French education, one of my primary interests has been in cross-national studies of educational achievement, primarily in civic education and mathematics. Late in my career I ended my work on these studies as codirector of a large-scale international study of teacher education—the first international assessment of student learning in higher education based on national samples. I also worked extensively on international development in education, primarily in Africa, with major projects first in Burundi, then Guinea, and finally Tanzania. At the same time, I was the college administrator who for twenty-nine years after 1984 had special responsibility for implementing a comprehensive integration-infusion approach. This book is based largely on that experience and the lessons my colleagues and I learned from it.

How did this happen—coming to MSU, staying so long, and focusing so much of my life on Erickson Hall and the MSU International Center, the two buildings that sit side by side on the banks of the Red Cedar River and are home to the College of Education, on the one hand, and international units serving the whole campus, on the other? Although I was lucky enough to do my undergraduate and graduate studies at two of our country's most elite universities (Harvard and the University of Chicago), I always had had a secret hankering to be at a Big Ten school. Perhaps this was because I was born in a family of upstate New York dairy farmers where the word from land-grant Cornell was always treated with respect. Or maybe it was because of that record of Big Ten fight songs I got when I was in grade school. In the thinking of an eleven-year-old, with music like that, those universities had to be good. But it was only in 1977, after studying and working in other wonderful places—Boston, Chicago, San Antonio, Paris, and Stockholm—that I actually got a chance to come to MSU and be part of those Big Ten universities I had long admired. I jumped at it. Soon thereafter we pulled our U-Haul up at a rather nondescript (though patriotic MSU green and white) house in the Flowerpot neighborhood right next to campus, and we've been there ever since.

What I didn't quite realize at that time was how fabulous the MSU College of Education would turn out to be for me. The College was at the beginning of an era in which it became the place to be if you wanted to join a school of education with great ambitions for the quality of its research and practice as well as its influence on K–12 education. By the time I arrived in 1977, the leadership to do this was already emerging, starting with Judy Lanier, Lee Shulman, Andy Porter, Phil Cusick, Henrietta Barnes, Bill Schmidt, and others. After that we had the good fortune to continue to recruit many other outstanding people, with extraordinary gifts, right up to the present day.

In 1993 it was a new dean, Carole Ames, who brought the same determination, toughness, and shrewdness to maintain and increase the quality of our faculty as had her predecessor. For thirty years we had only two permanent deans, Lanier and Ames—both extraordinarily strong, smart, competent, and unforgettable women in all sorts of ways. While they had very different visions for the College, they were both absolutely committed to bring their school of education up to the highest standard of scholarship, teaching, and service. Both played an important role in supporting the integration-infusion approach across the College, as described in this book.

I spent my first seven years at MSU (1977–84) as a regular faculty member, doing collaborative research in the Institute for Research on Teaching, while continuing to work on international assessment research for the International Association for the Evaluation of Educational Achievement (IEA). Otherwise I had no mandate to work on international matters, and truth be told, at the time my perspective on international and comparative education was pretty conventional—looking on a degree program as what it was all about. Having earned my PhD at the University of Chicago, where comparative education was purely and simply the application of social sciences to the study of education in other countries (see chapter 2 in this book), I saw teaching in such a program as part of my mission in life, but one that I had not yet had a chance to put into practice in a university environment. Nevertheless, I already thought that comparative education had a lot to say to researchers and practitioners who had not studied in that field. And yet, up to that point, comparative education scholars were doing little to make good on that opportunity. I, too, had not made my views known. I would start to do that later.[1]

It was in 1984, after adoption of the integration-infusion approach, that my approach to this field started to change in a big way. I was selected to be assistant dean for international studies in education for the College of Education. The title was not impressive, but it was a great opportunity for me to return to my roots in comparative and international education and to the obsessive interest I have had in other countries since I was in grade school. I took this job as a mandate to get the College interested and committed to the education of *all* the world's children—an ambition even Judy Lanier, as ambitious as she was to transform education, considered way over the top. Nevertheless, in the years since I got this job, I have seen a lot of progress at MSU in pursuing the internationalization that has become the prerequisite for excellence in all of today's higher education and a way to emphasize education for all.

I have loved all aspects of this job—continuing to do international research, using this research in my courses, working on international development projects, and developing relationships with educators and institutions around the world— but most of all what gave me satisfaction was working with my internationally active colleagues in the college and across the university, and giving support and guidance to internationally minded students in all the programs of our college.

It was a college full of smart, stimulating, and productive people—more than one could reasonably hope for, and when I started working so closely with International Studies and Programs in 1984 I found other such people in the international units across the campus. It was therefore especially fulfilling for me to collaborate with people like this in research, teaching, proposal writing, international projects, recruitment of internationally oriented faculty and students, as well as support and mentoring of faculty and students once recruited—anything at all to advance the mission of a great university. I came to feel that the international students and the American students with international interests were one of the greatest blessings in my life, as was the chance to work with inspiring people in Africa and throughout the world.

Since MSU quickly became the source of my closest friends and colleagues, I never seriously considered leaving. I knew I could not replicate the advantages of colleagues like this, especially if I wanted to be in an excellent school of education and a university with exceptional international capabilities where I could find a special niche. My mentor at the University of Chicago once asked if I wouldn't like to come back to be on the faculty at Chicago—an outcome I thought very unlikely to occur even if it was what I wanted. But, setting this impediment aside, I must have shocked him when I said without hesitation, "No, I wouldn't." Although one of the greatest universities in the world, Chicago is one of the least likely places to take an integration-infusion approach seriously and to work on internationalization as broadly and deeply as described in this book.

Acknowledgments

I n one sense this whole book can be seen as a series of acknowledgments. Nothing could have been done without the accomplishments of all the faculty, students, and staff mentioned and discussed within these pages. In working on the book, I have enjoyed remembering the importance of all of them. While the persons profiled in these pages are among the most notable, they are not the only ones who deserve credit. Not to be overlooked are all of the people who made the college not only a great place to work but also a good place for innovation. I give some indications of what this meant in the Foreword to this book. But it's important to acknowledge that the influence of two very strong, long-serving deans can hardly be overstated—Judith Lanier and Carole Ames, the only permanent deans of the college between 1980 and 2011.

Even when the focus is on internationalization, the persons named in the book are but the tip of the proverbial iceberg. Many, many more made significant contributions. Supposing that I had the space in the book to list them all, my memory would no doubt fail in attempting this task. But what I can do is single out for special thanks the support staff who worked with me over the years. Of particular note are the persons who had administrative and clerical responsibilities in my office, including Anne Schneller, who is profiled in the book, as well as Gretchen Neisler and Cheryl Bartz. The clerical-technical staff who were so important in making the college more of a supportive and pleasant community for internationally oriented students and faculty included Christine Caster, Marlene Green, Chery Moran, Kate Baird, and Jan Grider.

Others who made my life so much easier with the competence and dedication they brought to international work were the leaders of the Graduate Studies in Education Overseas program. Sandy Bryson in particular, as program manager, brought four decades of expertise in managing MSU international efforts to our office. Susan Melnick and Bruce Burke were likewise key as the senior faculty leaders of this program.

Michigan State University has an unequalled record for leadership in giving scholarship, teaching, and outreach an international scope. The university-wide dean of international studies and programs and the directors and staffs of all of the international units on campus were important sources of support in virtually everything we attempted. Ralph Smuckler, John Hudzik, David Wiley, David Horner, Brett Berquist, and John Metzler, in particular, deserve to be thanked for their exceptionally supportive and positive relationships with our college.

Across the university in still other units and departments many other individuals made the work of integration-infusion more feasible and productive. Let me cite one example: Carl Eicher, longtime international leader in agricultural economics. He took me in hand and helped me learn the ropes in dealing with USAID when I started my job in 1984 and was still naive about the university role in international development.

Going back to the College of Education, much appreciation is due to Assistant Dean Gail Nutter, Building Manager Eric Mulvany, and others for their tolerance of my pack-rat tendencies in keeping as many of my papers as possible (most of which have been turned over to the MSU Archives). Not that any of my friends and colleagues thought this obsession was worthwhile. They were generally convinced that no good could come of storing such a huge, personal, and, to a great extent, unsorted archive. With the exception of Anne Schneller—who got rid of stuff that, when confronted with it, even I had no desire to keep—none of my wonderful associates made much of an effort to get me to clean house. Their hands-off attitudes made this book possible.

I would like to apologize to those I should have singled out in the book but did not, and also make clear that none of the people mentioned bears any responsibility for shortcomings and errors in the book itself.

My wife and partner for the whole MSU experience and more, Sharon Schwille, surely deserves more credit for everything I have accomplished in these years than I can adequately express. The fact that she, too, played an important role in the college, becoming director of teacher education before she retired, made these contributions that of a valued colleague as well as leader of our family and the person I love most of all. And I'm sure the fact that we both devoted ourselves to the college made it easier for some people to overlook my shortcomings as they recognized the grace and class with which Sharon did her job.

Introduction

This book is an analysis of what it can take to internationalize a university school of education. It contrasts an integration-infusion approach with one centering on more or less self-contained degree programs in international and comparative education. The integrated approach is an attempt to break down boundaries between academic specialties in education in order to challenge the ethnocentric orthodoxy of most fields of educational inquiry in the United States and thereby create the space needed for international and comparative perspectives to influence education research, policy, and practice as widely as possible. As a case study in the sociology of knowledge and academic work, this book discusses the strategies or channels of internationalization used in the College of Education at Michigan State University in its integration-infusion approach since 1984, when this approach was adopted in replacement of separate comparative and international education degree programs as well as a separate Institute of International Education. These channels included building faculty strengths that can break through the barriers between international and domestic research and practice; undertaking international multicountry team research that will attract the interest of scholars outside the comparative education community as currently understood; maintaining space for international development work; forming institutional partnerships to connect with educational research and practice in other countries; breaking down ethnocentric barriers to international content and world languages in k–12 schools and teacher education; engaging internationally oriented students as major assets in this work; seeking out international visitors who can contribute to this work; finding sufficient funds and leadership staff to make this challenge to the status quo viable; and using the capabilities gained from the integration-infusion approach to inform and strengthen the Comparative and International Education Society (cies), which has been the main body of scholars in comparative education and related fields.

At the beginning, the integration-infusion approach at msu was just a vision and, moreover, a vision that could be pursued only opportunistically. It called for a school of education where all faculty members and students would not only become knowledgeable, while still continuing to learn, about the educational state of the world in all its diversity, where their aspirations for themselves as educators would be influenced by international research and experience, and where they would reach out to educators in other countries in collaborative efforts to do good research, inform policy, and improve practice. It was a vision extremely difficult to realize comprehensively and deeply in practice. To explain why it was so difficult, the book builds on the work of French sociologist Pierre Bourdieu in highlighting the boundaries and authority of established fields that at any one time may be impossible to surmount.[1] Instead, these obstacles can be overcome only gradually, incrementally, and opportunistically in moving toward the vision. To be sure, opportunism alone can be a trap that leads to actions and outcomes that do not fit well together and therefore do little to advance the vision. In international education, this trap often takes the form of projects that are not sufficiently tied to faculty strengths and the generic or domestic priorities of a school of education, projects that therefore do not offer advantageous venues for faculty and student learning, and projects that in the end may increase rather than decrease resistance to internationalization.

Nevertheless, at the same time there are pivotal opportunities for creating new or changing old channels to bring them into better alignment with our vision in the landscape of internationalization. To allow this to happen at msu, a single degree program in comparative and international education had to give way to make way for the new channels that were needed. The experience of msu over twenty-eight years proves that this approach is a viable alternative to a more traditional comparative education degree program.

PART I

The Landscape of Internationalization in U.S. Schools of Education

Priestliness is not our trade.
—Edmund King, 1990

CHAPTER 1

Toward a Sociology of Comparative and International Education

The discourse and literature on comparative and international education have been the subject of much commentary over the last five decades as interest has grown in this field. These commentaries have brought to light a domain that is fragmented, incoherent, and able to accommodate schools of thought that have little or nothing in common with one another. Even so, much remains unexplored. In particular, it's important to examine in depth the sociology of this field of knowledge and to explain the institutionalized channels and obstacles on which the nature of the discourse in large part depends. As a case study in the sociology of knowledge and academic work, this book attempts in a small way to deal with this gap. It largely follows Pierre Bourdieu in his analyses of intellectual work in general and sociology in particular.[1] Bourdieu built his complex conceptual apparatus around three central concepts: field, habitus, and capital, none of which, according to him, is primary or dominant over the others. Instead they are in continual interaction with one another, in part to reproduce the social worlds that they embody and in part to change these worlds. *Field* in Bourdieu refers to the social space within which this interaction takes place. Roughly speaking, it is analogous to a playing field on which a sport is played. But Bourdieu's fields are never level. Instead they favor certain players or teams above others because of the influence of the rules of the game, its history, positioning of star players in shaping the field, and so on. Since the concept of field was developed by Bourdieu in analyses of educational institutions and practices, among others, it is not surprising that the concept of field is superficially at least a good fit with university disciplines as organized within schools or faculties. This fit is reflected, both within and among fields and subfields, by the struggles of individual scholars and the units to which they belong for status and recognition.

These specialized scholars bring to the field their *habitus*, which is Bourdieu's term for the set of *dispositions* with which an individual enters a field and which subsequently evolve in interaction with the field. Bourdieu points out that a habitus includes far more than an individual's scholarly agenda; it extends even to nonverbal communications. "The habitus manifests itself continuously, in oral examinations, in seminar presentations, in contacts with others, and, more simply, in a bodily hexis, a way of tilting the head, a posture of the body."[2] "A posture that might be perceived as a superficial lightness ('is it really serious?') may also be seen as a promising 'ease' if it has in some sense found its 'natural home,' in other words a region of the field occupied by people predisposed by their position and their habitus to apprehend positively and appreciate favourably the behaviours in which [another person's] habitus is unveiled."[3]

Within the university, the habitus of practitioners immersed in interaction with a field embodies a strong tendency to develop, transmit, and control the status culture of a particular specialty. In each field the habitus of participants predisposes them toward erecting barriers against outsiders. Nevertheless, the boundaries between fields often remain fuzzy and contested. The most the players can expect is, not a perfect understanding of the field, but rather a "feel for the game."[4] Thus, in contrast to Thomas Kuhn, in whose theories scientific change takes the form of a relatively disinterested process of solving puzzles in ways that have proven to be productive until the anomalies in this process are considered important enough to address,[5] Bourdieu describes a struggle of self-interest in which the norms of science that appear to be disinterested are in fact mixed with vested interests, resulting in status systems and boundaries that remain to a considerable extent arbitrary, without this being acknowledged.

Successful scholars acquire a sort of *capital* in the form of valued knowledge that determines their place in the system, their access to resources and status. This capital accrues to institutional units as well as individual scholars. "Scientific capital is a particular kind of symbolic capital, a capital based on knowledge and recognition. It is a power which functions as a form of credit, presupposing the trust or belief of those who undergo it because they are disposed (by their training and by the very fact of their belonging to the field) to give credit, belief." Distribution of this capital shapes the power relations within this field. "Possession of a large quantity (and therefore a large share) of capital gives a power over the field and therefore over agents (relatively) less endowed with capital."[6]

This struggle and competition brings change, as orthodoxies call forth, in dialectical fashion, challenges from heterodox critics who attempt to change the field.

Using a Channeling Metaphor to Represent Fluidity in the Field

Bourdieu effectively challenges views that see intellectual work as the free and detached pursuit of knowledge. Faced with the idea that internationalization in higher education is a discourse socially constructed by scholars who more or less freely follow their chosen intellectual journey, Bourdieu provides an excellent antithesis: from his position, the view that ideas are freely chosen is an illusion. However, since Bourdieu's perspective can seem overly deterministic and without allowance for human agency,[7] it can be difficult to see how changes in the knowledge valued by higher education institutions could ever occur. According to him, capital in the form of knowledge is accumulated within a powerful, hierarchical status system that can be thought virtually impervious to change. From this perspective, therefore, it is hard to understand how the royal classic track of Greek and Latin in French lycées (the object of much of Bourdieu's analysis), dominant for so many years, could ever give way to mathematics and science as the highest-status course of study, and yet it did. This change illustrates the need to find a middle way between determinism and agency.

With a middle way, change can be difficult, but not impossible, to bring about. Francisco P. Pérez advances such a formulation that, according to him, is compatible with Bourdieu. "Agency in social life is seen as a 'menu' from which you can choose on the basis of your social background and available capital rather than as a free-will game, thus taking into account, although to different degrees, both the enabling and constraining sides of structure and agency."[8]

In this book this middle way is represented by a metaphor of multiple streams of thought and work, sometimes coming together, sometimes remaining separate

—images of change that sooner or later can wear through obstacles and create new currents of ideas. Internationalization is pictured as channels, streams that grow and add to an emerging river of internationalization. However, the image that these words conjure up, of one mighty river with tributaries and subtributaries, does not perfectly fit the observed phenomena in education. Channels do at times converge and combine, but they also diverge and separate; and sometimes remain separate from other channels flowing in a similar direction. Thus, instead of tributaries feeding a single river, a more appropriate metaphor is a delta with multiple channels flowing together and breaking apart, making it possible for more than one of these channels to feed separately into the sea of internationalization. Moreover, as with a delta, the channels of internationalization are not stable over time; instead they can fill up, clog up, and cease to be channels of internationalization, while other new channels emerge to cut through earlier barriers of resistance. In our thinking about this metaphor, it is especially instructive to recall that there are, in the world of nature, inland deltas, such as the Ovakango Delta in Botswana, that never reach the sea directly, but either evaporate or soak into the ground, where their influence persists in underground aquifers.

When taken together, Bourdieu's point of view and this metaphor offer different perspectives on change and resistance to change in fields like comparative education. Bourdieu's perspective shows how fields of knowledge, seemingly products of human thought that stand on their own logic, can in fact be bastions of resistance to change owing to competition within and between them for status and power through accumulation of academic capital. However, the metaphor of a delta and its changing streams makes clear that in a field where knowledge claims are contested, change does take place, as different schools of thought seek to displace one another and advance their own ideas and projects.

This is not as far from Bourdieu as it might seem. In the insightful book edited by Michael Grenfell on Bourdieu's key concepts, the concept of habitus is illustrated by a metaphor similar to that of a delta in its emphasis on life as a journey through channels or pathways.

> Where we are in life at any one moment is the result of numberless events in the past that have shaped our path. We are faced at any moment with a variety of possible forks in that path or choices of actions and beliefs. This range of choices depends on our current context (the position we occupy in a particular social field), but at the same time which of those choices are visible to us and which we

do not see as possible is the result of our past journey, for our experiences have helped shape our vision.[9]

The author emphasizes that the structures of the habitus are not fixed, nor are they in constant flux. Rather the dispositions that form one's habitus continue to evolve. They are durable but not immutable. At the same time the fields with which habitus interacts are themselves changing. "Habitus is the link not only between past, present and future, but also between the social and the individual, the objective and the subjective, and structure and agency."[10] Bourdieu explains the respective importance of structure and agency by making clear that, while habitus is not completely shaped by the field, the field does in large part determine whether a habitus can find a position with the field. That is, in an exceptionally autonomous scientific field, where the aggregate capital of accumulated resources is enormous, "it is the field that 'chooses' the habitus." But in a field like sociology or education whose autonomy is continually challenged, the habitus of practitioners can make a greater difference, especially when others in the field are not prepared to exercise special vigilance to ensure that practices are consistent with its existing contours.[11]

Differing Approaches to Comparative and International Education in Schools of Education

Traditionally, in U.S. schools of education, the dominant orthodoxies have taken the form of a lack of interest in and rewards for the study and practice of education in other countries (with the partial exception of the English-speaking countries). Degree programs in comparative and international education have had little success in challenging these dominant orthodoxies. Instead they have generally occupied a marginal space. Thus, while their academic and intellectual capital has been recognized and valued internally within the relatively small network of university academics identifying themselves with comparative education, outside this space, comparative education capital has been much less valued than within.

Pierre Bourdieu provides a good explanation of why this is so. Dominant scientists are able to impose, without making any special effort, "the representation of science most favorable to their interests." They are the ones who set the rules of the game, the correct, "legitimate way to play." Since their interests are aligned with the established state of the field, they are the "natural defenders of the normal science of the day." For these reasons, they enjoy decisive advantages in scientific competition and they become an obligatory point of reference for other scientists, forcing the latter to explain their work in relationship to that of the dominant scientists.[1]

From this perspective, although much has been written and said in recent decades about the need to internationalize education, including schools of education, it stands to reason that, for the most part, ethnocentricity remains entrenched not only in academic systems of power and prestige, but also in what is taken for granted about the policies and practices of education[2]—an aspect that Bourdieu developed at length in his analyses of cultural capital and reproduction in French education.[3] Bourdieu's perspective helps make clear that internationalizing is not just a process of professional development to help faculty members and their students acquire new knowledge but also an assault on accepted norms of what constitutes legitimate knowledge in education, on the vested interests of scholars who have invested in and benefited from the capital they acquire in the status quo, and on the boundaries that have substantially sealed off international studies in education so they do not challenge or undermine the accumulation of more "legitimate" intellectual capital (e.g., in educational psychology or school administration applied to the United States) and the existing streams that channel the work and lay out the boundaries and content of particular fields.

This concern for channels and boundaries in and around the domain of comparative education is long-standing, with scholars both challenging and defending existing or proposed boundaries. As a result, there has been wide agreement in the literature on the fluidity and impermanence of comparative education channels and boundaries as well as debate over whether and how much to stick to them. For example Jesse Foster, Nii Antiaye Addy, and Joel Samoff in a 2012 article, based on their analysis of the content of journal articles in the field, reiterate this emphasis on diversity and lack of agreement among approaches to this domain of study: "Notwithstanding periodic calls for a common body of theory and a standardized, shared methodology, comparative and international education research reflects far more diversity than convergence in approach, theory, and methodology."[4]

Some four decades ago, my PhD adviser at the University of Chicago, C. Arnold Anderson, the fourth president of the Comparative and International Education Society (CIES), then in his later years, wrote an article vigorously defending his long-held view that comparative education properly understood is the application of the different and distinct social science disciplines to education—and nothing more.[5] A corollary of this position was that comparative education cannot be considered in any sense a discipline on its own—an argument also made by Phil

Altbach,[6] who like me got his start at the University of Chicago. Altbach, however, went much further than Anderson in giving credit to new epistemological and substantive alternatives to positivism that were changing the field. Other scholars had different ideas about how comparative education functioned beyond well-established disciplines. Few agreed with Anderson. Andreas Kazamias, who had been a colleague of Anderson at the University of Chicago Comparative Education Center for a short time in the 1960s, weighed in with a CIES presidential address about ten years later to say that frameworks that viewed education simply in terms of application of social science disciplines were reductionistic and limited the questions that could be asked.[7]

My predecessor at MSU, Cole Brembeck, the fourteenth president of CIES, wrote another article that appeared in the *Comparative Education Review* in 1975.[8] He, too, argued that comparative education should not be limited to the disciplines as traditionally understood. Instead, he made a case for stronger ties between comparative education and another loosely defined domain, teacher education.

By the year 2000 Michael Crossley went still further in crossing the borders surrounding and traversing comparative education. He noted that mainstream educational researchers were increasingly engaged in comparative and international education, an observation that led him to advocate more cross-fertilization between comparativists and those he refers to as "mainstream."[9] In a related article Leon Tikly and Crossley also dealt with the options of specialized comparative education versus integration with other specialties of educational research, before introducing a third option, characterized as transformation:

> Exponents of integration argue that the boundaries between comparative and international education and other parts of education studies are increasingly blurred and that, as such, it is problematic to talk of a distinct comparative and international education specialism. They argue that there is now less need for comparative and international education to exist as a separate field of study and that teachers with comparative and international education expertise could best use their energies in developing international and comparative perspectives within other programs of study in their institutions.[10]

In effect he was arguing for the integration-infusion approach, such as has been applied at MSU.

More recently Foster, Addy, and Samoff, in their review of articles published in four journals from 2004 to 2008, found that approaches to comparative education were far from reaching consensus:

> Our mapping effort shows clearly the permeability of field, disciplinary, and methodological boundaries. The community of comparative and international education researchers moves in multiple directions simultaneously, does not feel constrained by the walls that commonly separate, say, economists from anthropologists or survey research from textual analysis, and regularly insists that understanding education requires studying not only what happens within schools' walls but also where the schools sit and who enters their doors.[11]

Whereas from this perspective, this emphasis on understanding context can be seen as a strength, it can also be a weakness if understanding of the context of education comes at the expense of understanding the content and substance of education. And, indeed, according to these same three authors, in the comparative and international education literature, "education's context continues to attract more attention than its content, a trend noted by several analysts. While curriculum, pedagogy, and instructional materials remain of interest, the concentration appears to have shifted increasingly toward the economic, political, and social context of education, especially education policy."[12]

In fact, their content analysis of journals in international and comparative education reveals major shortcomings in terms of coverage of substance and domains internal to education:

> Perhaps surprisingly, teaching and learning, that is, education content, received the least attention among the three thematic categories, 22% of the journals' total thematic focus. The individual topics within this category receiving the least attention across the journals include special education and textbooks, each less than 1% of the journals' thematic focus. The next lowest ranked topics include examinations and ICT (1%). Also infrequently addressed across the journals was literacy (2%). Subject matter topics received limited attention across the journals.[13]

According to this analysis, these journals are not dealing with many of the issues with which schools of education are faced, and cannot therefore serve as a sufficient basis for internationalization of the programs offered by these schools—especially if internationalization were to be based on an integration-infusion approach. Similarly, a 2016 book *Teaching Comparative Education*, which discusses various points of view, has almost nothing to say about an approach that calls for teaching comparative and international education in integrated and infused forms throughout the coursework of doctoral programs in education.[14]

The systematic and thorough analyses by Rosalind Latiner Raby of the bibliography listings published by the Center for Education Reform over many years substantiate this critique and further demonstrate the changing nature of the domains of comparative education.[15] These analyses showed that, as the years passed, authors were not only writing about subjects not coded so frequently before, but about topics not previously included in the classification. In order to fill in such gaps in content, bibliographers had to add journals to the target population of journals covered as well as to revise the classification scheme for coding articles thematically.

Thus, there has been wide agreement in the literature on the fluidity and impermanence of comparative education boundaries in discussion of whether and how these boundaries should be crossed. A 2011 book by Maria Manzon, *Comparative Education: The Construction of a Field*, is perhaps the best and most comprehensive attempt to bring some conceptual order to all this disarray—a true tour de force in its coverage of a multitude of disparate sources. To make sense of this domain, Manzon also draws on Bourdieu in a major way. Her apt summary of Bourdieu's project applies both to this book and to hers: "Theoretical definitions of a field can be understood comprehensively if they are examined in the light of the positions and interests held by those who produce them within the intellectual field, which is where *habitus* and the external field of power—academic-institutional, national, and international—intersect and interact."[16]

Manzon's work, however, does not include the case studies that, in my mind, would be required for a full-blown application of Bourdieu to comparative education. Given how much she had to do in just analyzing written attempts to define the domain of comparative education, it would not be reasonable to expect her to attempt that application. To go further with case studies would require specifics on the struggles, the pursuit of exclusivity, the blindness and the resistance to views outside the habitus of high-status scholars, and so on. Bourdieu is clear that these specifics do not fit neatly into predetermined scenarios. Thus, to fully understand what Bourdieu means for comparative education and similar fields of study, in-depth analysis would be needed of how the professional lives of individual scholars have been shaped by the competition for status, the value of different schools of knowledge, the resistance encountered—in short by showing how the interaction of habitus, field, and capital has worked in particular cases, changing not only the careers of these scholars, but also the field in which they work. This, neither she nor I have been able to do in a fully adequate way.

When it comes to Bourdieu, Manzon's book, surprisingly, also turns out to be something of a paradox. The book has excellent explanations of Bourdieu's theory and how it applies to comparative education. And yet her book itself is open to a Bourdieuian critique that she does not discuss. Instead of showing how the interaction of habitus, field, and capital has produced a comparative education with questionable boundaries in which many practices that could be considered comparative education are not fully valued within the comparative education status system, she more or less accepts at face value a map that privileges academic comparative education and marginalizes and even excludes the major efforts outside academic programs which have institutionalized comparative education in a different way (e.g., International Association for the Evaluation of Educational Achievement [IEA], Program for International Student Assessment [PISA], Board on International Comparative Studies in Education [BICSE], Association of International Educators [NAFSA]). Thus, her framework leads her to minimize the importance of facts on the ground such as the IEA international assessment studies, which have had a major influence on the development of comparative and international education (in terms of habitus, field, and capital alike), not just as illustrated in the case of MSU, but also in many of the sixty-plus countries that have participated in the IEA.

In contrast to Manzon, this book takes the most inclusive view possible of what might be considered comparative and international education at a single university. To be sure, like Manzon's book, it does not present a full Bourdieuian perspective on the field of comparative and international education. Without more fully developed professional biographies of important scholars, without entering more deeply into their habitus, and without finding what happens when habitus is forced to deal with the contours of particular fields, one can do only limited justice to Bourdieu. To provide such an analysis in depth would require a sequel to this one, in which participants would speak from their positions about their evolving habitus and changing field. This would permit, as Bourdieu explains, identifying "families of trajectories, with . . . opposition between on the one hand 'the central' players, the orthodox, the continuers of normal science, and, on the other hand, the marginal, the heretics, the innovators, who are often situated on the boundaries of their disciplines (which they sometimes cross) or who create new disciplines on the boundaries of several fields."[17]

To see what Bourdieu would expect from such an inquiry, one has only to examine how he analyzes his own intellectual and social life, the changes in his habitus when confronted with ongoing changes in the fields in which he engaged. His "Sketch for Self-Analysis,"[18] full of complexities and idiosyncrasies, is a strong warning against anyone who wants to apply Bourdieu's ideas in a mechanical, deterministic, and fully generalizable fashion.

With research on the lack of conceptual consensus among scholars of comparative education in mind, one can compare these conceptual analyses with institutional perspectives on existing graduate programs in international and comparative education. There is much more variation among these programs than is apparent in what Manzon says about them. When Timothy Drake[19] reported on data from thirty-five institutions using websites and institutional questionnaires (61 percent responded to the questionnaires), the questions he attempted to answer were the following:

1. Why is comparative and international education a relevant field of study?
2. What will I learn in the program?
3. How will I learn it?

He goes on to discuss the implications of diverse conceptions of comparative education for the organization and content of international and comparative education degree programs as follows: "Comparative and international education (CIE) has been characterized as having a schizophrenic disposition—split between those who consider it a legitimate academic discipline and those who consider it a mode of inquiry."[20]

In order to make sense of competing and overlapping points of view, Drake starts by examining *globalization* and *development* as two phenomena deemed by many as most important in understanding education across countries. He infers from his data that programs at eleven universities emphasize globalization, even though they may not use this term in their website. In discussing their programs, Drake, for example, treats training in cross-cultural communication and exchange as part of the emphasis on globalization. Six institutions in his database emphasize such exchange programs. Finally, Drake predicts that this emphasis on globalization "may take the form of a more general infusion of international content throughout schools and colleges of education, perhaps at the expense of an autonomous Comparative and International Education program of study."[21]

Drake pursues a similar line of analysis with regard to the importance of *international development* in comparative and international education, calling attention to departments and centers of development education that have taken this route, including Chicago, Harvard, Pittsburgh, Stanford, Syracuse, and Teachers College, Columbia. In his database are eighteen universities that have "development" as an important part of their degree program. This development orientation is associated with a strong emphasis on social justice and equity.

In addition to these concerns with globalization and development, Drake goes on to categorize programs in terms of seven different areas in the study of education: *education leadership, policy, practice, reform, research, systems,* and *theory*. Educational reform and to a lesser extent policy, for example, he finds most salient in the programs of Harvard, Kent State, Wisconsin, and Vanderbilt. In a related article Stephen Heyneman defends the Vanderbilt approach in more detail. He criticizes the work of comparative education scholars whom he regards as ideological or impractical, and calls for a more exclusive focus on the relevance of comparative education to policymaking:

> There is a guiding principle which determines the degree of relevance in work on Comparative Education, and that is the degree to which it appears to respond to questions of practitioners and policy-makers. It may be particularly helpful if those policy-makers are domestic as well as international.[22]

Heyneman goes on to say that, because of these concerns, comparative education at Vanderbilt is different from comparative education programs at other universities:

> The organizing principle is derived not from the imagination of theorists but by the priorities determined by policy and practice. Course content is decided on the basis of questions which arise from ministers of education, from school teachers, from policy analysts and parents. If it is considered to be a problem in the eyes of these groups it becomes relevant to our course of study.

Likewise "theories and problems emanating from domestic sources are considered to be important foci for anyone studying comparative education." Thus,

Vanderbilt expects comparative education students to study domestic educational issues, while students with primarily domestic concerns take coursework in comparative education. Even so, in spite of Heyneman's heavy emphasis on addressing issues of concern to policymakers, his 2009 article makes no mention of a need to study educational practice in terms of what actually happens in schools and classrooms.

Another dimension used by Drake[23] to compare comparative education programs is disciplinary focus. Although the reliance of comparative and international education on the social sciences and humanities has been much discussed and advocated, a number of universities make no explicit reference to disciplinary specialty or emphasis in their websites. In contrast, some universities, such as Lehigh, NYU, and Teachers College, Columbia, require that students concentrate in one discipline. More commonly, institutions are committed to a multi- or interdisciplinary approach. Ten of the institutions sampled use the word *interdisciplinary* and six institutions use the word *multidisciplinary*. Drake notes that Penn State, while maintaining a separate program, takes a distinctive approach to the integration of disciplinary studies by allowing for dual graduate degrees in comparative and international education, on the one hand, and another specialized area of educational research, on the other.

Teachers College, Columbia, instead of combining fields in a dual degree offers its students a choice of two tracks—Comparative and International Education (CIE) and International Educational Development (IED). The website for its overall Program in International and Comparative Education distinguishes between these two tracks as follows: "The major difference . . . is that CIE is based on an academic discipline in the social sciences, while IED is based on a professional specialization of education."

Finally, Drake (2011) also acknowledges the fundamental difference between MSU and the other institutions he examined (with the exception of South Carolina): "Michigan State University (MSU) views the global processes of internationalization as reason to 'infuse' the entire graduate school of education with international and comparative education content. . . . As a result, MSU has no separate program of study but rather attempts to have an international dimension in teaching, research, and outreach throughout the four departments of the College of Education."[24]

Overall, this analysis of the positions taken by various comparative education degree programs, when combined with the theoretical perspectives discussed above, shows that not only is there an absence of agreement on what comparative education entails across institutions, but even within institutions the boundaries between comparative education and other fields of study are weak, somewhat arbitrary, and hard to defend. Whatever is done in degree programs in comparative and international education and in the research produced by scholars in these programs could easily be done elsewhere, were it not for the barriers maintained by those scholars whose status and ability to control curricular matters could be threatened by change. This book reports on Michigan State's effort to lower and ultimately remove these barriers by a policy of integration and infusion to graft comparative and international education on to other fields and thereby create an international dimension throughout its studies of education.

CHAPTER 3

The Changing Landscape of Internationalization in a New Era of MSU History

nder the leadership of John Hannah, for thirty years MSU's president (1941–69) and architect of its future, MSU was one of the first public universities to commit heavily to international work. Before the end of World War II, on February 25, 1945, President Hannah talked about this commitment on the university radio station, WKAR: "The good will and civic intelligence which can deal with international questions wisely and humanly will have to be developed, not only in the schools and colleges of America but in the schools and colleges of all the nations of the world. . . . Michigan State College as a public institution financed by the people of Michigan has a responsibility to provide some leadership in this direction."[1] As a result, by the 1960s MSU had undertaken a number of important international development projects—including the assistance in Vietnam that was considered a blot on the university's record by opponents of the Vietnam War.[2]

For the College of Education, the most significant of these initiatives was MSU's role in the founding of the University of Nigeria at Nssuka, which was intended to introduce a land-grant model as an alternative to the British-style universities to which the Nigerians were accustomed. A number of MSU College of Education faculty were assigned there on a long-term basis. All this created space for the beginnings of substantial internationalization at MSU, and challenged the education faculty to rationalize and justify these efforts in academic terms.[3]

An integration-infusion approach to internationalization was even proposed and endorsed at that time.[4] A little over fifty years ago, in May 1962, a College of Education committee submitted a "charter" for international programs to the whole faculty for possible adoption. The introduction asserts the following and shows that the term *internationalize* was already in use:

> The Education Faculty believes that the proper exercise of its profession demands that its attention be devoted to education in all its aspects or forms, in all its relationships to the human condition, and in all lands and languages. . . .
>
> The Faculty therefore believes that this approach must pervade College of Education activities in all aspects of the multiple tasks that traditionally are deemed appropriate to a university: teaching, research, publication, and service. . . . A balance must be maintained between and among domestic and international activities: without in any way diminishing its concern for local conditions, the Faculty must escape provincialism and must so broaden its outlook as to "internationalize" itself, the College of Education, and the personnel, programs and clientele of the College.

When a new era for the college began in the early 1980s under the revolutionary leadership of Dean Judith Lanier, it was clear that such internationalization had not been attempted in a broad form, much less reached. The international interests of the college, though substantial and important, were still largely bounded by its Institute for International Studies in Education (under the leadership of Associate Dean Cole Brembeck, former CIES president), by its separate MA and PhD programs in comparative education, by the professional interests of the small number of faculty who chose to make this a high priority, and by a program to offer professional development to teachers in American overseas schools.

These international efforts remained fragmented and, in terms of competition for status and resources, at a disadvantage compared to the "mainstream" programs of the college. At the national level, in work on international development, this was the era of nonformal education, favored by the US Agency for International Development and based on a critique of formal education as unsuited to the mass of unschooled families in poor regions of developing countries. In general, however, the MSU College of Education, except for a small number of internationalists, continued to concentrate more or less exclusively on formal education. The USAID funded the Nonformal Education Information Center, which, though organizationally within the college, functioned separately on its own. In addition, another major weakness in the international work of the college limited progress in internationalization: the college's internationally minded faculty were producing very little empirical research or publications in peer-reviewed journals. Thus, when a new era began in 1976 with the establishment of a federally funded MSU Institute for Research on Teaching, and the college began to make its mark nationally in educational research by taking a more programmatic approach to integration of research, program development, and practice,[5] the internationalist generation among the faculty was more and more marginalized and, in any case, nearing retirement. Hence, in the early 1980s, when the university faced major budget cuts, the Institute for International Studies in Education was abolished, the graduate programs in comparative and international education were eliminated, and Associate Dean Brembeck retired. A task force chaired by one of the college's star researchers and leaders, Andy Porter, was appointed to rethink the role of international education within the college. In 1984, this task force finished its work and published a report recommending a comprehensive effort to deal with international students, visitors, scholars, and alumni; international content in college programs and courses; international research in education; education courses, degree programs, and teaching sites overseas; development assistance and international service; faculty development and utilization; and management of international activities.[6] The changes this effort would require were made clear in observations like the following:

> If the College is to fulfill its responsibilities in a world in crisis and if it is to seize the opportunities and enjoy the strengths that come through international participation, the ultimate responsibility for doing so must be accepted by the departments and by all faculty members. No small body of "international experts" can, or should, be chosen exclusively to represent this commitment and carry out this responsibility.

Finally, the report recommended the appointment of an assistant dean to work on its recommendations for a completely different approach to comparative and international education, one that emphasized the development of an international dimension in research, teaching, and service throughout the college—in short, implementation of what in this book is called the *integration-infusion approach.*

Accepting this recommendation, Dean Lanier appointed me to this position in 1984 and created a special office that still exists. In the beginning, the agenda laid out in the task force report seemed overwhelming to me. But now, thirty years later, it is possible to assess what was done, what was not done, and find out what progress, if any, has been made.

Breaking Out of an Academic Ghetto

The various positions taken by advocates of comparative and international education paved the way for this book's account of the attempt by one university to push out the boundaries of the fields in question. The aim has been to see if these diverse perspectives can be better accommodated and institutionalized within a single institution as a whole than when largely confined to individual departments or programs.[7] In other words, through this undertaking, now lasting over twenty-five years, MSU has been gradually trying to break out of the academic ghetto in which comparative education has too often found itself. This integration-infusion approach has given scholars in all the specialties of educational research the chance to earn capital with value in comparative education, and in so doing, to rework the fields or social spaces of education specialties to accommodate international and comparative concerns.

However, given the lack of consensus in comparative and international education and the obstacles posed by the existing structure of educational studies, there was no clear map to guide this work. Instead, the 1984 college task force report, *Report of the Task Force on International Activities*,[8] gave this endeavor direction by making four arguments to show the importance and relevance of international study throughout the college:

1. *Crisis of understanding argument.* The U.S. will face a growing inability to solve problems resulting from the fact that its citizens have little understanding of the rest of the world on which our future in large part depends. If the College of Education is to be a leader in educational studies, it must take steps to counter this deficiency.
2. *Ethical argument.* International concern is a moral obligation for educators. Just as well-to-do suburbanites have a moral obligation to be concerned with the education of inner-city children, as U.S. citizens, we have an obligation

to be concerned with the education of all the world's children, not just those who, by accident of birth, have a call on the United States' disproportionate share of the world's resources.

3. *Comparative education argument.* By learning about educational systems in other countries, we can better understand our own.

4. *Intrinsic interest argument.* Knowledge is valuable in its own right: "If we want to know as much as we can about education as a field of study, our domain is arbitrarily limited and impoverished by the exclusion of education as practiced in other countries" (1–2).

Taken seriously, these arguments open the door to a more inclusive field of comparative and international education. From this perspective, the field is defined more on the basis of what is done in practice than on theory. Instead of imposing a definition of comparative education that would shut out much that is actually or potentially international in schools of education, MSU has gone in the opposite direction. Comparative and international education is defined primarily by what is or could be done by college faculty and students that is international in nature. Comparative education is what self-styled comparative educators do, and international education is what people who identify with international education do. In other words, if anyone in a school of education or if constituents and stakeholders believe that the school should be concerned with something international, then knowledge acquired in that endeavor may count as valued knowledge. In Bourdieu's terms, this approach changes the nature of the field, what faculty members or students do to acquire capital, and opens the field to individuals with a habitus that differs from what otherwise would be required.

This line of reasoning shows why a graduate degree program in comparative education, which has been rejected by MSU, would run counter to such inclusiveness. Such programs are an attempt to establish a Bourdieuian field with clearer boundaries, criteria for what knowledge is most valued and which sorts of habitus would be most welcome and rewarded. In other words, such a program typically amounts to taking a stand on what counts as knowledge in recruiting and retaining faculty, on what research will receive the most credit, and on what curriculum is most appropriate for students in the program. What counts as knowledge is also embodied in course and program requirements, and especially in the examinations that students are required to take. Faculty members with the most capital in valued knowledge earn the highest status and acquire the most influence on the program, creating a disincentive for them to support or undertake other forms of less valued international education, such as working closely with international students in other graduate programs. Faculty participation in study abroad and efforts to internationalize K–12 and teacher education would also be unlikely to appeal strongly to program faculty or to produce the most valued knowledge. As the boundaries between inside and outside the program become clearer, barriers may be raised to prevent students outside the program from taking program courses. Likewise, there would be disincentives for faculty to design and teach courses with international content outside the program, in order to increase the concentration of faculty efforts on production of knowledge valued by the program. In short, any effort to share international knowledge and increase international involvement on the part of those not in the program could be seen as less valuable and therefore discouraged. Bourdieu's field in such a case would be far more restricted than it would be without a program, and the habitus of those recruited as faculty and students would likewise tend to be relatively narrow in order to obtain a better fit with the reduced domain.

Efforts to move in the opposite direction, to open up a college's international domain to more inclusiveness, would most likely meet with resistance, since inclusiveness would mean less clarity on boundaries, status, and criteria for admission to the field. Inclusiveness could therefore reduce the autonomy of comparative and international education within a school of education; understood in this light, this domain would no longer be a field in the strict Bourdieuian sense, but simply a form of capital valued in other educational specialties. In that case, those whose habitus tends to favor the more traditional forms of comparative education could still acquire capital, but this capital would not give them undue status and power over what others count as capital in comparative education. An inclusive agenda opens up the possibility of valuing comparative education capital across a wide range of educational specialties, making it possible for comparative education to more easily influence the study and practice of education in general.

Consistent with this argument for inclusiveness, the 1984 MSU task force report was not a doctrine intended to limit faculty choices as far as internationalization was concerned. Quite the contrary, MSU faculty members were encouraged in their scholarly work and in teaching to follow whatever approach to international-comparative education they thought appropriate (e.g., emphasis on area studies or global education, application of social sciences to education in other countries, exploration of critical theory and postmodernism as applied to international studies). The integration-infusion approach has aimed to make allies of these often contending forms of international-comparative education and likewise to co-opt other fields, making these domains less subject to the zero-sum game of university power and politics. Insofar as we can tell, during the period covered by this book, MSU has tried to push further and more widely in this direction than other U.S. schools of education, even though other universities are now making similar moves.[9]

This book is an account and analysis of what the policy of integration and infusion has meant at MSU, discussing the history of this effort so that readers can not only understand what has occurred, but also better answer the following instrumental questions: Can such an approach work—is it viable? How does it work, and how well does it work? Is it the most desirable approach to academic study in comparative and international education, and should other universities move in this direction? Or should they attempt some sort of mixed approach, in which a more traditional degree program is combined with the broader goals of internationalization?[10]

PART II

Convergent and Divergent Channels of Internationalization

Recollected conversation of recent years:

Distinguished colleague from prestigious university: "Jack, you have the best international education faculty of any university in the country, but you ought to have a program."

My response: "But, my friend, the reason we have the best faculty is because we don't have a program."

CHAPTER 4

Faculty to Develop and Explore the Main Channels of Internationalization

nderlying the new integration-infusion era at MSU was the assumption that without a great deal of faculty strength in international education, there could be no major internationalization channels. Absent that strength, the channels would remain small and marginal. Therefore, the 1984 task force report contained this call to action:

> The College should give priority to developing and utilizing the international expertise of its faculty as a whole rather than developing a separate internationalist faculty, not only by using international expertise and interests as relevant criteria in the selection of new faculty but by developing the international experience of its existing faculty.[1]

Successful internationalization depends primarily on recruitment, engagement, and rewarding of faculty in whatever way possible—faculty already prepared as specialists in international and comparative education, faculty born and educated in other countries, and faculty given the opportunity to take on international responsibilities in spite of not having any such experience before. As it turned out, more strength was needed and ultimately acquired than we could have imagined at the start.

To jump start this new approach to international work in the college in the 1980s, Dean Judith Lanier and other administrators approved two new faculty positions, combining international studies with disciplinary strength: one for sociology of education and international studies and the other for economics of education and international studies. Each position was defined as a mix of international and domestic responsibilities. Each called for strengths in a particular region of the world without specifying the region. Luckily for us, both of these search committees came up with candidates who had extraordinary strengths with respect to China, as well as disciplinary knowledge of importance to domestic policy and practice. One of the searches resulted in the appointment of Lynn Paine, whose exemplary faculty career is the focus of the first in a series of leadership profiles that highlight the accomplishments of individuals who were instrumental in making the integration-infusion approach work.

Taking a College-Wide Perspective

When the 1984 task force report called for developing international strengths in research, teaching, and service across the whole college instead of in specialized comparative and international education programs, it implied hiring faculty with international strengths throughout the college. Implementing the report's recommendations would mean that the college would have faculty members working in all the populated continents, especially in major countries like China, India, Brazil, and South Africa. Ideally, these internationally oriented faculty members would be competent in major world languages, cover all the disciplines of education, embody the diversity of American educators, include scholars from other countries, and be willing to address the educational problems of both the United States and other countries. Although it has come closer and closer to this goal, at the end of the era covered by this book MSU still did not have all areas, languages, and disciplines adequately covered.

Once these goals were accepted, it followed that international qualifications should be desirable in all faculty searches. This idea emerged early on, but from the start many faculty and administrators were not convinced that it was a good idea, and this practice therefore was slow to take hold. As predicted by Bourdieu, this

LYNN PAINE

The search for the international sociology of education position, which I chaired, proved difficult to fill. It was only after we had brought candidates to the campus to find out how well suited they were (they were found lacking) that we heard about Lynn Paine, a Stanford student whom no one at MSU knew at the beginning of the search. We learned that she had combined sociology of education with a focus on China and a specialization in teacher education research—exactly fitting what the position called for. Still there was a problem. When we found out about her, Lynn was far off in China, doing dissertation research. She was located in what was formerly known as Manchuria—well off the beaten tracks. For some time we had no way of getting in touch with her and finding out how well she would fit our position, or even if she was interested in it.

My fear at the time was that, since Lynn had developed such a highly specialized research agenda, plus the fluency in Mandarin needed to do good work in China, she would probably want a comparative education position where she could concentrate exclusively on China. Why would she want a position designed for our new integration-infusion approach, which combined a call for international research with the overall quest for general research on teacher education and ways to improve our MSU teacher education programs. Fortunately, these fears turned out to be groundless. When we finally had a chance to talk to Lynn, we found she did not want to be pigeonholed as a China specialist and welcomed research and teaching in other countries as well as in the United States. She already had a sophisticated understanding of the complexities of teaching and teacher education that was likely to stand in good stead, in the United States or whatever country she worked in. This settled the matter as far as we were concerned, especially since the search committee for the position in international studies and economics of education had selected Mun Tsang, whose research interests were also focused on China. These two hires put us on the map for research on Chinese education in a way that our peer institutions could not match.

So how did Lynn Paine end up doing her research on teacher education in an area of China virtually unknown to other Americans at the time, and where she lived the life of a Chinese student in an unheated dormitory in the coldest parts of the year? Unlike many Americans who speak and read Chinese, Lynn has no Chinese ancestry, nor did she grow up in a Chinese-speaking area. Quite the contrary, she grew up in a St.

Louis family in circumstances unlikely to produce a person with so much knowledge of China and its language.

Lynn's passion for Chinese studies started with a middle school enrichment course on China. Fascinated, she developed a passion for China and ultimately became an undergraduate at Princeton with a major in Asian studies. By the end of her undergraduate experience, she had not only acquired a good foundation for contemporary Mandarin, but was also able to read classical Chinese. After graduation, she took a teaching position in Taiwan, where she spent two years immersed in a Chinese-speaking environment. Next she spent two more years as a high school English teacher near Chicago, acquiring the "wisdom of practice" that has served her well since then. Her career then took a decisive turn when she enrolled to do a master's and PhD at the Stanford International Development Education Center (SIDEC), where she developed the research competence for a dissertation. All of this indicated that she was the ideal person for our position.

This assessment turned out to be right on target. At MSU since 1985, Lynn has played a key role in developing our international research strengths, as well as other channels of internationalization. She, together with Teresa Tatto, became a pioneer in international research on teacher education. Drawing on her dissertation, she wrote a classic article titled "Teaching as Virtuoso Performance."* In this article she

response was symptomatic of resistance to changes in the qualifications for faculty work. Nevertheless, in some instances the policy was in fact followed: for example, in 1997, faculty positions were advertised for learning and cognition in education, measurement, and quantitative methods; language and literacy education; and mathematics education. In each of these cases, the following language was included in the announcements published in the *Chronicle of Higher Education* and other venues: "The College is interested in recruiting individuals who will contribute to existing strengths in teaching and learning, educational policy, comparative and international perspectives."

In 2007 the following wording was used to search for open-rank senior scholars with a focus on learning, development, and teaching:

The College of Education at Michigan State University is seeking senior scholars with a focus in learning, development, teaching, learning to teach, educational analyzed the paradoxical finding that teacher education students in China completed practicums with very little time in classrooms. Instead, they devoted most of their practicum time to mastering the model of teaching that Lynn characterized as "virtuoso performance."

Lynn's work also brought to the attention of Americans the fact that teachers in China are not isolated in their classroom; they do not go in, shut the door, and do their own thing. Some American analyses had misled readers into believing that this isolation was more or less true of teaching throughout the world. But Lynn's research showed that Chinese teachers work together in many ways.[†] Much of what Lynn brought to our attention has since become more common knowledge among scholars, but at the time these findings were surprising, and important for American researchers and educators to learn.

Judged as a whole, the research produced by Lynn Paine and her colleagues over the past quarter-century has been one of the best demonstrations that international research, combined with domestic research, is needed to understand and be in a position to improve education in general—exemplifying the integration-infusion approach.

NOTES

[*] Paine, 1990.
[†] Paine & Ma, 1993.

reform, or urban education to provide leadership within the College of Education, conduct research and inquiry, teach undergraduate and graduate courses, and collaborate with other faculty in program development and research projects. *Candidates with a record of international research are encouraged to apply.*[2]

Over the years we drew on three sources to increase international strengths among faculty: (1) persons with a degree in comparative education or other specialization in international studies; (2) faculty originally from other countries; and (3) faculty with neither of those two backgrounds who nonetheless were involved in international activity and had gained the needed strength through on-the-job experience.

As far as the first source was concerned, Lynn Paine and Mun Tsang were only two of the instances in which MSU was the beneficiary of other PhD programs in comparative and international education. Lynn was an advisee of Joel Samoff, and

Mun was a student of Hank Levin, both at Stanford. Others with a comparative education background in the early years included Teresa Tatto, who studied under Noel McGinn at Harvard; Richard Navarro, whose adviser was George Spindler at Stanford; Susan Peters, another Hank Levin student; David Plank, whose mentor was Mary Jean Bowman at the University of Chicago; while I studied under C. Arnold Anderson, director of the University of Chicago Comparative Education Center. Gilbert Valverde, who followed later, was one of the last PhD students at the Chicago Comparative Education Center, with John Craig as his major advisor. Later in 2011 Riyad Shahjahan joined our faculty after obtaining his degree from the Ontario Institute for Studies in Education (OISE), University of Toronto.

Cumulative success in recruitment was documented in 2008–9 when the whole faculty was surveyed to check on the state of interest in and commitment to the international dimension of the college.[3] The response was one of great enthusiasm and interest, as well as special qualifications for international work—more than we anticipated.[4] To be more specific, 55 respondents (52 percent of the 106 who answered the questionnaire) said they wanted to be identified as a faculty member with special international interests, qualifications, and/or experience, and 46 (42 percent) wanted to be listed on the college website as a faculty member willing and able to advise doctoral students on how to integrate an international dimension in their program of study. Seventy-six (72 percent) said they would be willing to engage at least once a semester in discussions of what internationalization and globalization mean for college research, teaching, and outreach programs. Twenty-seven (25 percent) reported teaching courses with significant international content. Thirty-four (32 percent) were willing to organize and lead a study abroad program. Fifty-eight (55 percent) reported that they were currently active in an international project or organization. Responses to the latter question included seventeen references to international research, fourteen to international development efforts, sixteen to participation in other international organizations, and eleven to other international outreach. Fifty-four respondents (51 percent) reported working in or publishing about countries outside the United States in the past five years. In response to that question, fifty-one different countries were listed. Thirty-seven faculty members (35 percent) listed ideas for international projects they would like to pursue. Thirty-three (31 percent) said they could identify international alumni with whom they continued to be in contact.

How was the college able to recruit these people for international work and to facilitate their international work? As can be seen in appendix 1, which features some of the MSU faculty best known for international work, they did indeed come into this work from very diverse backgrounds.

Building Community among Faculty and Developing Our Vision

Recruiting highly qualified faculty to lead an integration-infusion approach would be for naught if the members of this group continued to function as independent scholars having relatively little to do with one another, or even dyads and triads working together but only for limited periods of time on an ad hoc basis. For the college to be successful in integration and infusion, it was important for faculty to have continuing relationships not only with their own individual students but also with the larger body of international and internationally oriented students and faculty across the college. This did not happen spontaneously. The pressures to stick to individual agendas were huge for faculty who wanted to be rewarded with merit pay, promoted as soon as possible, and recognized nationally and internationally. Creating more of an international community within the college required continued effort and special measures.

Whereas recruiting and developing faculty with international strengths proved easier than I expected, building this community of shared understanding and intentions continued to be difficult. Some faculty could be counted on to contribute continually, while others made extraordinary contributions on their own but never worked simply for the common good of our international cause. And whatever efforts we made were unevenly spread out across the college.

Among these efforts were organizing study groups, retreats, social gatherings; preparing responses to university drives for internationalization; participating in CIES and other relevant conferences; helping to host international visitors. Some of these measures stand out as exceptional for what they did or how long they lasted. Notable among them were the international teacher education study group of the latter half of the 1980s, the college-wide committee the dean commissioned to deal with the aftermath of 9/11, the international theme group formed in response to another invitation from Dean Ames to the whole faculty to create special interest groups, and finally the seminars organized in recent years in response to the greatly increased emphasis on internationalization of research and teaching in the college.

Other measures met with limited success as far as faculty were concerned. For example, faculty contributed very little to the listservs established in 1993, one for internationally oriented students and faculty and the other for internationally oriented faculty alone. Few faculty attended our monthly breakfasts, although many turned out once a year for the one to mark the beginning of the academic new year. Another and bigger disappointment was that we could never get faculty to participate regularly in LATTICE, the professional development group for MSU international students and area K–12 teachers. Generally, they came to LATTICE only when invited as guest speaker in their area of specialization.

Special Interest and Study Groups

One of the most successful efforts was also one of the earliest. The international teacher education and research study group met regularly for some years after 1985 with intellectually meaningful discussions and outreach to researchers in other countries, all before we had the funding needed to support this work. For example, in November 1988, after the group was well established, an invitation went out to internationalist faculty in the college, proposing to meet every two to three weeks at Lynn Paine and Brian Delany's house. By fall 1989, under the leadership of Margret Buchmann, the group was taking a tour of what Margret called "nineteenth-century sages" and studying texts by Friedrich Schiller, John Stuart Mill, and John Ruskin, among others. The intellectual quality of the group was strikingly illustrated by two memos to the group, one from former faculty member Margret Buchmann in 1989 and the other from Lynn Paine in 1990.[5] These memos show how in developing an international perspective on teacher education research, Margret and Lynn drew on intellectual resources far outside the usual purview of teacher-educators, giving colleagues a sense for how much the integration-infusion approach could enrich the intellectual life of the college.

Margret's memo of October 17, 1989, was meant to give the group a preview of upcoming readings assigned to the group. The very language she used was a reminder of the intellectual, social, and cultural borders she had crossed from her youth in Germany, moving to Stanford as a student and then on to MSU. This journey, together with many additional forays into the world of ideas, made it possible for her to contribute to the college in very special ways and in what Bourdieu could see as a revealing interaction of habitus and field:

> Having brooded over paragraphs and words, pondered ineffable Germanisms and
> seen how Schiller never gets down to talking about education as an activity and

actual experience, we will now turn to an account of an educational experience (that of J. S. Mill) and the lessons drawn from that experience, his later life, learning and reflections in thinking about the meaning, compass and ultimate purposes of a university education. . . .

Pursuing the themes of *utility* (suggested by Schiller, taken up, in a refined version, by Mill) and of *liberal learning* (exemplified in Schiller's concept of art as play, considered in autobiographical and curricular terms by Mill), we will turn [in a subsequent session] to a work referenced by Mill: Cardinal Newman's *Idea of a University*. We should try to visualize, and allow ourselves to be moved, by Newman's ideal of the educated person, while appreciating (as we did for Schiller) the historical moment and the steps of his argument in the discourse on liberal learning and professional skill.

Be warned: we will execute a more mystical turn soon in studying Simone Weil's "Reflections on the Right Use of School Studies with a View to the Love of God."

Lynn Paine in a February 19, 1990, memo offered another appealing preview, orienting the group to readings from a very different tradition, stretching from ancient times to the last century in China:

We're moving from England in the 19th century to China, where we'll dabble in the 6th century B.C., the 20th century A.D., and some centuries in between. This act of hubris can only be forgiven by the sincerity of our motives—to consider what classical Chinese philosophy, particularly that of Confucius, has to say to us about the questions we've been considering in our Victorian musings—what knowledge is important to learn, who should learn what, and how this learning should be undertaken. To consider these questions in the Chinese context, I've chosen some key passages from the Confucian Analects, selections from two later classics of Confucian tradition . . . as well as memoirs from an early 20th century rural teacher and 'Kong Yiji," a short story by China's most important 20th century writer. . . .

Li Wei, Ma Liping, and I will all try to give some background to this core text in Chinese philosophy and education when we get together. What I've done in preparation is select passages from the Analects that speak directly to three central themes in Confucius which we care about: learning, teaching and the educated person (that is, the goal of education, what Confucius calls *junzi* and which is often translated as "the gentleman").

This group met regularly in 1990–91, but then faded away as the demands of not just talking, but doing international research, increased and absorbed more and more faculty time. It was only toward the end of the 1990s that we returned to another sort of study or special interest group, one commissioned with a more pragmatic intent than the preceding one. This group was formed in response to a general invitation from the dean in 1996 for the faculty to form such groups to cultivate their areas of research interest and search for external funding. If judged promising, these groups were eligible to receive college funds to support their work. Since this invitation was especially well fitted to support our infusion-integration approach to internationalization, internationally oriented faculty came together to propose such a group.[6] It decided to use its money in a small competition for faculty to get seed money to pursue their international goals. For example, one year this international theme group sponsored competition for seven seed grants as well as four colloquiums and two visits by international scholars, and one strategic retreat attended by twenty-five members. While this approach worked well initially, the group ran into a snag when the dean discovered that one of the grants had gone to a faculty member she considered undeserving and unproductive. Shortly thereafter, she cut the group off from further funding, and it was dissolved.

It was only later that the dean herself developed a passion for international work and made internationalization a top priority for the college. Her increased interest and support enabled us to put much more emphasis on the internationalization of research and coursework, making clear that these efforts were no longer just a matter of individual faculty agendas or limited to the work of my office. To move forward, the dean asked Lynn Paine to take the lead on the learning goals end and me on the international research side. My charge was to find ways to help faculty who had not done international research get started. We organized a series of noontime seminars with this end in view. We also planned a course for faculty members to work on internationalization projects for their courses, but for lack of funding this was never done.

Crisis Response

After 9/11 another very different and deeply felt concern for the international community was invoked by the dean. She was among the MSU leaders who reacted most strongly to the attack and had the most adamant views about how the university should respond. The day of the attack on the World Trade Center in New York, she immediately sent out a message to college faculty and staff supporting President McPherson in saying that there was no reason to think the campus was in immediate danger and adding the following example of the community building called for in the integration-infusion approach: "This is a tragic day for everyone, please reach out to those colleagues and students who may need help." Two days later, she followed up with another message as follows: "I urge all of us to reach out to our international colleagues and students and help them feel secure. . . . Our Islamic students and other international students abhor this attack as much as everyone else. Please do everything you can to encourage students to reach out and to not tolerate private or public expressions of bigotry and prejudice."

Within the college, she came to me and gave me instructions, indicating that the matter was not open for discussion: "Jack, I want you to form a committee to figure out how the college should respond to 9/11 and take a lead in carrying out these plans." One of our school psychologists, the late Jean Baker, was designated to cochair this committee with me.[7] The committee that Jean and I organized sponsored two open evening sessions in the fall, one an evening of "artistic response" and the other a panel session on the role of educators in the aftermath of September 11. A website was also set up by colleagues Punya Mishra and Smita Sawai to keep the college informed about the committee's work and to link interested educators to resources they could use in teaching about the events of 9/11.[8]

Conclusion

The foundation of internationalization in our college was the cultivation of faculty strengths, either through recruitment from the outside or helping faculty already at MSU to develop international strengths. Over the years since 1984 an extraordinary array of faculty talent has been assembled, and this in turn has been the key to opening up channels of internationalization.

Some colleagues, even those at MSU, have challenged the long-term viability of an approach that asks faculty members to do both domestic and international work. Critics question whether it is possible for junior faculty members to meet these expectations and also achieve the status of a leader in comparative education as the field is generally understood within CIES. From this point of view, those who wish to specialize as much as possible in teaching comparative education courses, publishing in comparative education, and achieving status in comparative education are at a decided disadvantage, forced into work that will reduce their academic success. This is what a Bourdieuian perspective would lead one to expect, but the more important question in my view is whether such expectations are good for internationalizing a school of education in general.

Let's look at these matters more carefully. Up until now MSU has in fact been able to find professors who excel in the integration-infusion approach and who still exercise national or international leadership through their work, even though we have no separate degree program. The leadership profiles in this book are examples. Lynn Paine, Bill Schmidt, Teresa Tatto, Chris Wheeler, Punya Mishra, Mike Leahy, and Yong Zhao have all done work that is nationally and internationally recognized. Other examples can be found in appendix 1 among those who have made contributions at MSU and then moved on or retired (e.g., David Plank, Susan Peters, Reitu Mabokela). Some have been active in CIES, and some have not.

But, critics may ask, what about the junior faculty members who face more and more rigid promotion demands for peer-reviewed journal publication, making international work at the junior level still more difficult? Does this justify a separate degree program? Wouldn't it be better to give such persons special consideration and support for international work, support that currently is more the exception than the rule? If we had a separate comparative education degree program, some internationally oriented faculty might have an easier time of it. But if one asks the persons named above if they would have been more satisfied with their career at MSU if they had done less of what is documented in this book and more of the work of building a degree program, what would they say? Would they have been happier if they had been forced to give up much of what this book shows they have accomplished because of the demands of a separate program? I doubt it.

And even though the grass in a separate degree program may seem greener, one can question whether that is the case, given that the total number of tenure-stream positions in a school of education is limited and that programs compete in a zero-sum game for resources. Comparative education is not well placed to compete with the powerful constituencies who lobby education schools to expand the work these constituencies are invested in (e.g., special education, literacy education, STEM areas, and school administration). Comparative educators may be better off with the integration-infusion approach, which calls for influencing faculty recruitment and converting faculty in other programs. If this is done, an integration-infusion approach may produce more new knowledge in comparative education than a school with a separate degree program, and, moreover, this knowledge could be of more importance to the field of education as a whole than the research coming from separate degree programs. At the same time, an integration-infusion approach should be in a better position to influence students across a school of education than is a more traditional degree program.

Although there are those who say a school of education should do both integration infusion and a separate degree program, this book argues that from the Bourdieu framework, there is an inherent tension between a separate degree program and the integration-infusion approach; this tension tends to undermine the integration-infusion approach; all things considered, the integration-infusion approach is better suited to achieving the broad goals of a research-oriented and professional school of education than is a separate program; and therefore instead of devoting resources to a separate degree program, it would be better to modify policy and positions in schools of education to make fulfillment of aims of integration-infusion more feasible, with appropriate incentives and expectations for those faculty members who choose to devote a good deal of time to this approach. The rest of this book, which details MSU's experience with such an approach, provides a basis for each reader to judge for him- or herself, in comparison with other universities where comparative and international education is emphasized, whether the benefits and costs of such an approach are justified, and to think about whether there are other ways to keep all the channels of internationalization open and effective in creating and sustaining international dimensions to the research, teaching, and service of schools of education.

CHAPTER 5

Creating and Benefiting from New Channels of International Research

International research takes faculty from a state of interest in and willingness to work on internationalization, to having the capabilities to do this work they otherwise would lack. Simply put, international research is the primary engine producing the knowledge upon which successful internationalization depends. The profiles of Bill Schmidt and Teresa Tatto illustrate two desired trajectories that made the integration-infusion approach possible, trajectories that link international work to specialties in which international matters did not commonly play a role. These trajectories can move either into or out from international research in education. In Bill's case, he moved from specializing in cutting-edge psychometrics to becoming one of the most influential advocates of the United States teaching more ambitious mathematics and science in light of the international assessment research that he had done so much to shape and analyze. Teresa Tatto moved in the other direction, from a Harvard doctorate in education, program evaluation, and international development toward expertise in teacher education domestically as well as internationally.

BILL SCHMIDT

When Bill Schmidt got his PhD from the University of Chicago only three years after his bachelor's degree in 1969—a very young, precocious psychometrician—there was nothing in his record to predict that he would later become known throughout the world for his international research and his commitment to the reform of curricula and teaching in science and mathematics. Instead, he came immediately to MSU as an assistant professor specializing in quantitative methodologies of research and on this basis had already become a full professor by 1978.

It was shortly thereafter in early 1979 that I made one of my most important contributions to the international work of MSU (although I certainly did not know it at the time). I recruited Bill to go to New Zealand to work for a couple of months on the design of the IEA Second International Mathematics Study (SIMS) for the consortium that had originated such studies, namely, the International Association for the Evaluation of Educational Achievement (IEA). Bill's talents as a sophisticated statistician and very productive researcher were already well known. So not surprisingly, it did not take very long after this trip for Bill to become a key continuing member of the SIMS leadership team.

After that study was finished, Bill took leave from MSU for the years 1986 to 1988 to become head of the Office of Policy Studies and Program Assessment in the Education Division of the U.S. National Science Foundation. In that position he became one of the early leaders in the planning and conduct of the Third International Mathematics and Science Study (TIMSS) of 1995. In fact, Bill had a lot to do with the initial discussions that led IEA to attempt to do two subjects (mathematics and science) simultaneously with data collection at two points in time. This plan was so ambitious that many assumed it could not work.

To help make it work, MSU under Schmidt's leadership played a role in TIMSS at both international and national levels. Internationally, Schmidt's team received a grant from NSF titled Survey of Mathematics and Science Opportunity (SMSO) to develop and validate instruments for TIMSS based on preliminary research on classrooms in six countries.* Bill was also selected in a widely advertised competition as the U.S. national research coordinator for TIMSS. As a result, throughout the initial planning and conduct of this study, Bill met frequently in Washington with the other national leaders of the study: one was the project officer from the National Center for Educational Statistics, and the other, Gordon Ambach, was the influential executive director of the Council of Chief State School Officers (ccsso) who had become the U.S. member of the IEA General Assembly, the policymaking body for TIMSS and other IEA studies.

As the results of TIMSS became available, Bill became still more highly visible and active in U.S. arenas of educational reform—more than any other professor in our college. He reached out to both domestic and international audiences as called for in the integration-infusion approach. During this period he spent more and more of his time discussing the results of TIMSS and their implications with policymakers and educators. He was an invited speaker at conferences on educational policy in countries as diverse as England, Portugal, Greece, and Japan. He was the first author of the U.S. TIMSS national report.[†] This report and its extensive press coverage were the origin of the well-known sound bite characterizing the U.S. curriculum in mathematics as "a mile wide and an inch deep." After this report was released, articles quoting Schmidt appeared in the *Los Angeles Times, Arizona Republic, Philadelphia Inquirer, San Francisco Chronicle, Boston Globe, Cincinnati Enquirer, Star Tribune* (Minneapolis), *Chicago Sun-Times, St. Petersburg Times*, and other newspapers too numerous to mention.[‡]

Schmidt not only worked closely with key education policymakers in Washington, but also met directly with many governors, top education officials at the state level, and CEOs of business. On one such trip he was invited to share a plane with Governor Engler of Michigan. During one single year (2000–2001) Schmidt gave thirty-eight speeches in twelve states on implications of TIMSS, with audiences as diverse as state school boards in Illinois and Idaho, the Ohio School Boards Association, the Pennsylvania Science Teachers Association, the Miami Dade Secondary Principals, the Council of Great City Schools, and the City Club of Cleveland. During these same years Schmidt was also widely featured on broadcast media, including C-Span, CNN, and National Public Radio. In February 1998, he was one of two featured guests on *ABC Prime Time Live* to discuss TIMSS results.[§]

Bill's ability to make educational research results meaningful to policymakers, business people, and education leaders was no accident. When preparing for the release of TIMSS 1995 results, he got a public relations firm to train him on how to communicate better with nonresearchers. What he learned helped him gain the wide access to the media and policymakers that he later enjoyed.

At the national level, TIMSS became a matter of interest to the White House. President Clinton himself briefed the press on the TIMSS 1995 fourth-grade results in a White

House press conference on March 5, 1997. And when the president came to Lansing to speak to the Michigan legislature the following day (March 6), he thanked Schmidt and MSU by name for all this work.[||] Bill's transformation was complete—from specialized psychometrician to educational leader and reformer with expertise not only in research methods but also in education policy and practice in mathematics and science. This extraordinary record was later recognized in Bill's election to the National Academy of Education. For our purposes here, it is especially important to note that he had opened a major breach in the ethnocentrism and vested interests of U.S. educational research.[#]

NOTES

[*] For results of this research on classrooms in six countries, see Schmidt et al., 1996.
[†] Schmidt, McKnight, Raizen, et al. 1997.
[‡] Nomination of Schmidt for R. H. Smuckler Award, 1998.
[§] The specifics of this paragraph were retrieved from AR ISP 1996–97, 1997–98, 1998–99, 2000–2001.
[||] AR ISP 1996–97; reported in more detail in *College of Education Update Newsletter* 6 (2), March 11, 1997.
[#] Schmidt also played a key role in bringing the first IEA international study of teacher education to a successful conclusion, including a developmental study of six countries reported in Schmidt et al., 2007; Schmidt et al., 2011.

LEADERSHIP PROFILE

MARIA TERESA TATTO

Starting in 2000 and continuing for more than ten years, Maria Teresa Tatto took the lead in what became the college's most important and difficult research project. Known as the Teacher Education and Development Study in Mathematics (TEDS-M), it was a seventeen-country project for research on the preparation of students in teacher education to teach mathematics in primary and secondary school. Nothing quite like it had ever been done before. Since these prospective teachers were tested on knowledge of mathematics and mathematics pedagogy, TEDS-M was the first international assessment of learning outcomes in higher education based on representative national samples in any field. Thus it perfectly embodied the integration-infusion goal of having both domestic and international importance, making it relevant to educational researchers who had previously not looked beyond the borders of their own country.

The challenges Teresa faced in TEDS-M, working in collaboration with colleagues at MSU and many other institutions across the world, included getting funding, recruiting countries, satisfying all sorts of stakeholder groups, coordinating the TEDS-M work of a large consortium of research organizations, hiring and managing staff, writing and publishing an in-depth conceptual framework document, solving methodological issues, developing and piloting instruments in participating countries, designing and implementing sampling plans, supporting national efforts to get cooperation from sampled institutions, their teaching staffs and students, working out instructions for administering instruments, doing the data analyses, and finally writing up and publishing what had been learned in seven voluminous volumes.

Leadership in Teresa's case was not about her being right on every issue, and certainly not about always getting her way. Her capabilities and drive were tested to the limit by difficult colleagues and unprecedented research issues as well as the usual tensions that arise in projects in which decision-making and doing the work are shared within a consortium of powerful organizations far removed from one another in location and often in their points of view as well. Passionate about educational research in general and teacher education research in particular, Teresa worked at TEDS-M with relentless determination, tremendous energy, and a willingness to think through the issues as many times as necessary. In the end, TEDS-M could not have been done without her.

Important as it was, TEDS-M was by no means Teresa's only major research accomplishment. Another tour de force was the collaborative study she led over twenty years ago on the cost-effectiveness of three teacher education programs in Sri Lanka. Ahead of its time, demonstrating the methodology used for the first time in a developing country, this very ambitious study included data on program characteristics, tested knowledge of program graduates and their subsequent performance in classrooms (data collected by trained observers), tested performance of their pupils, and obtained data on program costs, institutional as well private.* At the time, I was the overall director of the MSU project in which the Sri Lanka work was embedded; I remember when Teresa first came to tell me what she proposed to do. "Totally unrealistic," I told her. "You can't possibly do all that." But she did, giving me my first real understanding that Teresa could manage what I considered impossible.

The Sri Lanka project also exemplified how determined she was to overcome the obstacles that stood in her way. Much of her work in Sri Lanka took place during the civil war and in the midst of conditions that were far from conducive to research. After her last trip, she reported that she had been at our collaborating research institute when conditions in Colombo were so dangerous that her Sri Lankan collaborators were afraid to come to work. When I remonstrated that I did not want her to be at a research site with so much violence, her response was that she wished she could have stayed a few more days—how much more she could have accomplished. Teresa is fearless.

In line with our philosophy of integration-infusion, Teresa has done domestic as well as international work at MSU. In fact, the domestic work was key to giving her a specialization in teacher education that had not been a part of her graduate education at Harvard or in Mexico. A major part of her MSU assignment in her early years was to work for MSU's National Center for Research on Teacher Education. Among other things, her research examined the influence of teacher education on teachers' values and beliefs about teaching diverse students.[†]

Outside MSU, Teresa is known for her extensive publications, her presentations at conferences, and her leadership in the association most relevant to her work, the Comparative and International Education Society (CIES). She was elected to the presidency of the CIES in 2008, with duties spread out over four years, meaning that she had her presidential duties in addition to directing TEDS-M.

While becoming a tenured faculty member and expert on U.S. teacher education, Teresa has remained strongly linked to her home country and very proud of the Mexican part of her identity. She has published periodically on research and program evaluations she has done in Mexico, including the Mexican component of an international study of values education and studies of decentralization policy and community approaches to teacher education.

In an outward sign of her loyalties and bicultural persona, Teresa has been vigilant against any tendency to lose her Mexican accent, which also makes for an appealing part of her sociability. Teresa grew up in Mexico City, attending public schools and the National Autonomous University of Mexico (UNAM). Then in 1981 she went to Harvard as a graduate student in education. Noel McGinn, a longtime leader in comparative education who became Teresa's advisor at Harvard, tells a story of her determination and ability to do great things. He had initially met her in in Mexico when she took the initiative to seek him out and get application forms for Harvard. Her plan was to work with the noted program evaluation expert Carol Weiss. And characteristically, she did just that, in spite of the fact that she had felt slighted because, according to her, male members of her department had received the forms from McGinn earlier than she. She had to ask McGinn for them herself, even though she was already working at a UNAM research center where she had used the program evaluation approach advocated by Weiss in a study of the Mexican National Health Services.

In her first terms at Harvard, her ability to speak English was limited, and therefore she needed help from Spanish-speaking classmates to know what was going on. In return, she helped classmates with statistics, in which she felt more proficient than they. Once this phase of acculturation was over, Teresa, true to type, moved on to tackle a very ambitious dissertation that took her to multiple Latin American countries to collect data. She had a grant to assess the effectiveness of a scholarship program that had brought Latin American students to the United States. She could have worked on this full-time until it was finished, but this was not Teresa's style of work. When the thesis was becoming tiresome and frustrating, she went out and found more work to do on top of her dissertation, and having done so, she felt much better.

The same not-to-be-deterred attitude characterized Teresa's arrival at MSU in 1987. Having no job, she came to my office to talk about her plans and discuss her desire to join our faculty. Although there was no suitable position open at the time, she was not to be stymied by any such bureaucratic obstacle. She explained that she wanted to come to MSU because she knew its reputation as an education school of extraordinary strengths and aspirations and also because her spouse was a pilot whose home base was Detroit. In this first meeting, she reminded me that we had already got to know each other briefly when she was a graduate assistant on the BRIDGES project, in which MSU collaborated with Harvard in research on primary education in multiple developing countries. Although I was not in a position then to offer her a job, I was delighted when she managed to get hired, and even more so when we found a way for her to work again on BRIDGES, this time as an MSU faculty member. This was the beginning of her exceptional performance on the BRIDGES Sri Lanka project and in other projects since then in support of our integration-infusion approach.

NOTES

* Tatto et al., 1993.
† Tatto, 1996, 1998, 1999.

Taking a College-Wide Perspective

The most important change called for after 1984 in how international education was conceived and organized at MSU was to make international research a top priority. Without international research, one cannot recruit, prepare, and keep faculty who have the capabilities required for other aspects of the integration-infusion approach. And without research strengths, international education would have been out of step with the college's efforts to be more competitive with other schools of education in the United States in terms of research.

To contribute effectively to the new approach to international-comparative education, international research had to be more than the sum of its parts and had to have an institutional dimension and impact. That is, for this approach to succeed, it would not be enough to have individual scholars publishing solely in the areas of personal interest, as has often been the case in comparative education more generally. Instead what was needed were international research studies of relevance to domestic U.S. research in a variety of fields, multicountry research, and research carried out by teams, not just one individual researcher. In addition, the integration-infusion approach called for a close relation and interplay between international research and domestic research such that the knowledge generated in international research informs domestic research and vice versa. Research on teacher education at MSU has been a prime example of this.

But it was not teacher education faculty who carried out the one event at MSU that most perfectly exemplified this point. It was a conference held in March 2000 and organized by David Plank, Barbara Markle, and Gary Sykes to examine school choice reforms from international, national, and Michigan perspectives. The first day of the conference focused on case studies of school choice in eight countries in which MSU had taken the lead, while the remaining two days looked at the same issues, first in national perspective and then with special attention to Michigan. The eight case studies on different countries were then published in a book edited by Plank and Sykes.[1]

Research in multiple countries was considered important because comparative education had long been criticized for relying too much on single-country studies and not enough on truly comparative research. Typically this criticism is cast in terms of pointing out that *comparison* implies that there is more than one nation to compare. But if one considers what Bourdieu would see as issues in crossing boundaries, the implications of doing such multicountry studies go far deeper than that. For example, a project involving multiple countries has to focus on issues of general interest, thus minimizing the idiosyncratic characteristics of any one country that make it difficult for educational researchers without international experience to see relevance or find any meaning that applies in their own specialties.

In addition, the individual researcher in a single country usually does not have to face a challenge to what he or she sees as the legitimate nature and methods of research. In contrast, in a multicountry study, complexities and contrasts abound that call for collaboration among diverse researchers from different countries and often representing different specialties. This draws in scholars in with no previous international experience who learn much about the other countries that they can apply to their own specialty. Optimally, this process challenges what researchers would otherwise take for granted in their own specialty. Committing to such collaboration thus ultimately requires the understanding and compromise that enable crossing disciplinary and national boundaries.

By 1984–85 MSU was on the verge of breaking into major international research in education, much of it comparative across multiple nations. During the first ten years after 1984, three major channels of international research were carved out: USAID BRIDGES research on primary education in developing countries, especially Thailand, Sri Lanka, and Burundi; leadership in channels of the Third International Mathematics and Science Study (TIMSS), extending what MSU had already done in the IEA second mathematics study; international teacher education research (starting mainly with Teresa Tatto's study in Sri Lanka and Lynn Paine's work on mentoring and induction) before ending with Teacher Education and Development Study in Mathematics (TEDS-M), the pioneering seventeen-country study of teacher education done in collaboration with IEA. The first two channels were brought to a successful conclusion at the beginning and end of the 1990s, leaving a gap that we were fortunate to fill with the IEA TEDS-M.[2]

Channels of International Research at MSU: Navigating IEA, MSU's Main Channel

When I left Washington and the National Institute of Education (NIE) in 1977 to take a job at Michigan State University, I was the only person at MSU who had played a substantial role in earlier IEA international assessment research. With a lot of IEA experience already behind me, I was by then heavily involved in the IEA

Second International Mathematics Study (SIMS). My work on SIMS lasted about ten years. By October 1986, when I attended my last SIMS meeting in Los Angeles, I had participated in more than thirty working meetings on the second mathematics study. As a result, among other things, the classy Georgian-style student union at the University of Illinois, Champaign-Urbana, which was a SIMS international study center, had become one of my favorite places to stay. By then I was no longer the only MSU researcher to be so involved and not even the most important as far as SIMS was concerned. MSU had become an important vessel in the IEA armada.

In SIMS, controversy over the design and execution of the study split its leadership in ways that ultimately had a major impact on MSU. The root of this tension was a perennial problem in the design of IEA studies, namely, how to handle the fact that any measure of student achievement represents cumulative learning throughout the student's lifespan and throughout his or her school experience—not just what occurred close to the time of data collection. This was not a problem as long as student achievement scores were reported without any attempt to account for these scores. But if one wanted to analyze the impact of teacher variables, classroom characteristics, and other measures that affect learning, it was important to find a way to control for earlier achievement. To deal with this problem, the leaders of SIMS proposed to do the first IEA longitudinal study with a pretest and posttest, to permit computing measures of growth in achievement. In the first plans for the study, it was expected that all countries would take this approach, but this design was resisted by many of the study's national research coordinators (NRCS), who thought the logistical difficulties of collecting longitudinal data far outweighed the benefits. Gradually two separate camps emerged within the second mathematics study, one willing to conduct a true longitudinal study[3] and the other sticking to a cross-sectional survey as in earlier IEA studies.[4]

The faction promoting a longitudinal design coalesced around the University of Illinois, Champaign-Urbana, under the leadership of mathematics education professor Ken Travers. Illinois was one of two main international centers for the study. Gradually an informal kitchen cabinet formed around Travers, composed of North American researchers who advised him on methodological issues, a group that came to include Richard Wolfe from OISE, Leigh Burstein from UCLA, Bill Schmidt from MSU, Skip Kifer from the University of Kentucky, and myself. The existence of this group fed the perception that Americans were too dominant in the study, contributing to the split opening up between the study's leaders. The resistance to a longitudinal design and to the views of the U.S. kitchen cabinet came together around Neville Postlethwaite, then professor of comparative education at the University of Hamburg, and one of the most influential figures in IEA from the 1960s onward. During much of this time, he was the IEA executive director and then chair of the whole IEA organization. Another leading figure in this group was John Keeves, director of the Australian Center for Educational Research (ACER), who like Postlethwaite had been one of the earliest leaders of IEA.

Trying to mediate between these two groups was the second SIMS international center at the Department of Education in Wellington, New Zealand, under the leadership of Roy Phillipps, who in the 1970s had succeeded Postlethwaite as executive director of IEA at its Stockholm headquarters. Like Travers, Phillipps reached out to MSU for support in ways that greatly affected the future of international research at MSU. For example, in 1978 I was invited by Phillipps to go to New Zealand for two months to work on planning for the study. Then, after returning to East Lansing, I organized an additional international planning meeting at MSU in the snowy and frigid month of January 1979. Those were the years when IEA was continually in trouble for lack of funds. Having individual universities organize and partially fund meetings was one way to help SIMS make ends meet.

The Illinois-based group and this additional work in New Zealand had a profound effect on the future of international research at MSU. It was Bill Schmidt's acceptance of my invitation to go to New Zealand in 1979 that set him on the road to his subsequent success in international research and advocacy of reform in mathematics and science education. Although there were changes in membership over time, the kitchen cabinet that took shape to advise Travers in SIMS evolved formally and informally over time to become an MSU-based team working with Bill Schmidt. It flourished on into the twenty-first century and IEA's first teacher education study. As time went on, Richard Houang, Lee Cogan, and David Wiley were key additions to the group working in support of Schmidt. The names of many members of this group can now be seen on numerous publications based on IEA data and coauthored with Schmidt. This team was one of the key elements in the college's growing research strengths.

Beginning in 1983, toward the end of SIMS, a new era in comparative education research was taking shape, leading to large-scale studies with much higher levels of funding. This was a trend in which MSU was strongly involved and one that was consistent with MSU's goals to do international research in multiple countries, emphasizing implications for research and practice in the United States as well as in other countries.

It was the publication in 1983 of the U.S. report *Nation at Risk*[5] that most dramatically improved the prospects of funding for IEA research. This report by a National Commission on Excellence in Education has been recognized ever since as one of the key events inaugurating a new era of educational reform in the United States. When the report was finished, Secretary of Education Terrell Bell came to MSU to release it and at the same time to give an award to the MSU Institute for Research on Teaching. Obviously, his visit was a coup for the college. But of more lasting importance was the fact that the report drew so much of its evidence for problems in American education from the earlier IEA studies. It made the argument that the United States was at risk because, in comparison with other industrialized countries, its educational system was not producing good enough achievement in mathematics, science, and other subjects. As a result, the U.S. government, through the National Science Foundation and the U.S. Department of Education, began to take a keen interest in future IEA studies and was willing to spend much more on these studies than in the past. From then on, it was clear in Washington and elsewhere that political support and pressure for the continuation of international assessment studies had greatly increased.

This increasing interest in cross-national studies of educational achievement led ultimately to the landmark IEA Third International Mathematics and Science Study (TIMSS) of 1995. Initial interest in testing two subjects together at two points in time came from the United States. The origin of the U.S. call for TIMSS can be traced to agreements reached at an Education Summit held at Charlottesville, Virginia, for the U.S. president and fifty state governors in September 1989. Governor Bill Clinton of Arkansas, then chair of the Governors Association, and President George H. W. Bush both gave their support to the unprecedented formulation of national goals for education.[6] When the exact wording of these goals was agreed upon in the following year, one goal was that the United States would become first in mathematics and science by the year 2000. However preposterous this goal may seem, given the slow pace with which change ordinarily takes place in educational systems, it was still taken seriously enough to warrant measuring progress toward its attainment with an international assessment of mathematics and science at two points in time before the year 2000. As a result, the IEA General Assembly meeting in Beijing in 1990 endorsed the proposals of its Standing Committee, which, in turn, were rooted in the desire of President Bush's administration for a joint study of mathematics and science and a repeat study later that decade. Given this commitment, funding was never a problem for TIMSS 1995, which developed into the largest and perhaps the most complex educational research project ever attempted up to that time.[7]

The Beijing agreements and what followed cleared the way for MSU to become a key center for TIMSS. MSU under Schmidt's leadership assumed three important responsibilities for this huge and complex study. It became the center for an unprecedented, in-depth curriculum analysis, based on content analyses of over eleven hundred textbooks and curriculum guides for more than forty countries.[8] The results of this analysis were widely reported and discussed, including, for example, at a conference sponsored by the Council of Chief State School Officers and reported in a June 22, 1994, *Education Week* article.[9]

In addition, MSU got a grant from NSF to do research that would contribute to the design and instrumentation of TIMSS. This was the Survey of Mathematics and Science Opportunity (SMSO), based on over one hundred classroom observations carried out in France, Japan, Norway, Spain, Switzerland, and the United States, not only providing input into instrument development for TIMSS, but also resulting in a book reporting on this data.[10] Finally, at the national level Schmidt became the NRC to take charge (along with National Center for Education Statistics) of TIMSS data collection in the United States and the production of U.S. national reports on the study.

The importance of TIMSS in its original 1995 and repeat 1999 versions would be hard to overestimate. In the spring 2007 issue of *Education Next*, an article on the thirteen "most influential education studies of the past decade" ranked TIMSS second. As soon as the first results of TIMSS 1995 were released, the study attracted enormous attention. Results were reported in more than seven hundred news articles (including front-page coverage in the *New York Times* and *Washington Post*) and fifty-plus TV spots (including ABC, NBC, CNN, MSNBC, and Fox News). TIMSS was featured regularly throughout much of the 1990s in *Education Week*, the newspaper of record for K–12 education in the United States (e.g., the issue of April 26, 1995).[11]

In terms of capacity building, TIMSS 1995 required putting together one of the strongest coalitions in IEA history. A significant step for maintaining continued widespread support for international assessment in the United States was the establishment of the Board on International Comparative Studies of Education (BICSE) at the National Research Council, an arm of the U.S. National Academy of Sciences.

As TIMSS was becoming more visible and politically important to the governments involved, the study developed shortcomings that were in urgent need of fixing. Chester Finn, assistant secretary for educational research and innovation in the Reagan administration, Dorothy Gilford, a former head of the National Center for Educational Statistics (NCES), and Emerson Elliott, a later head of NCES, took a number of initiatives to solve these problems at the national and international levels. The establishment of BICSE was one of these initiatives. It was a welcome innovation, especially for several of us who had long been active in IEA studies in the United States. We had been unhappy for years about the way IEA was organized in the United States, with just one university (Teachers College, Columbia) as the national center. One university could not really speak for the United States as a whole and, more importantly, could not mobilize the U.S. educational research establishment to take an interest and be involved in IEA studies and secondary analyses.[12]

To remedy this situation, Finn, the head education research official in the federal government, announced in a speech to the IEA General Assembly in 1987 that his office had "plans to establish, in a joint effort with the National Science Foundation and the National Academy of Sciences, a consortium of scholars to review IEA (and other international) proposals that seek U.S. participation." Among the responsibilities proposed for this consortium was to designate the U.S. IEA national center and General Assembly member.[13]

As a result of steps like this one, taken by Finn, Gilbert, and Elliott, BICSE was first convened in 1988. I was invited to join in 1990 and served two terms until 1996. Later, Lynn Paine was also appointed to BICSE and became one of its leaders, ending up as vice chair.

One of BICSE's earliest acts was to designate the Council of Chief State School Officers (CCSSO) as the IEA national center and Gordon Ambach, CCSSO executive director, as the GA member. CCSSO was the United States' version of a council of state ministers of education; it was not in any way a research organization. Nevertheless, this move was a brilliant one. CCSSO had not only a great deal of legitimacy to represent the United States, since each state's "minister of education" was represented, but it also gave IEA unprecedented access to the U.S. Department of Education, to Congress, and to the various state departments of education, governors, legislatures, and so on.

In this way BICSE became an important actor in IEA internationally as well as nationally. Its core mandate was to advise the federal government on whether the United States should participate in and fund international studies in education such as those proposed by IEA. In TIMSS as in the past, U.S. funding of IEA's international costs was critical, since there were no obvious alternatives. BICSE came together three times a year in meetings that were always attended by representatives of NSF and NCES, who were jointly responsible for paying a majority of the international costs of IEA as well as the U.S. national costs.

Not surprisingly, by May 1991, TIMSS was the biggest topic on the BICSE agenda. Schmidt was one of several researchers representing TIMSS at the meeting that month. Bill and Senta Raizen spoke to the board about MSU's SMSO project. For the next decade BICSE became one of the most important ways in which research on internationalization at MSU was linked to national discussions of existing and possible studies.

Having a prestigious board like BICSE was also important because in the United States this was a period of not only powerful support for IEA studies, but vociferous criticism as well. Unfortunately, under the new Bush administration that began in 2001, the U.S. Department of Education decided it no longer needed the advice of BICSE and stopped funding the board. But by that time BICSE had left its mark not only in its reviews and appointments but also in publishing a number of significant publications relating to international research in education in general and international assessment in particular.[14]

A Smaller Side Channel for MSU: The Second Civics Study within a Changing IEA Paradigm

Although by 1990, IEA had a track record in subjects like mathematics, science, and reading as well as plans for improved management and quality control, it still faced many obstacles. Another of the subject matters proposed for a second study—civic education—continued to pose challenges in both management and substantive terms. Responsible for a number of underfunded studies, IEA in the 1990s was increasingly a two-tiered organization. One tier was amply funded to improve what had been done earlier and to impose stricter quality control measures. This was the case with TIMSS and subsequently the reading literacy study PIRLS (Progress in International Reading Literacy Study), to which the U.S. government continued to make a generous financial commitment sufficient to do repeat studies in a predictable, high quality, and timely way. During this time Boston College, under the leadership of Ina Mullis and Mick Martin, became the continuing international study center for these studies and along with the IEA Secretariat the most influential part of the organization.

The second IEA tier was composed of studies that had little chance of reaching the funding levels enjoyed by TIMSS, PIRLS, or the Organization for Economic Cooperation and Development's PISA (Program for International Student Assessment), but which were freer of organizational constraints than the repeat studies and could therefore strike out in new territory beyond the emerging Boston College–IEA modus operandi. The IEA second civics study was in this tier.

Having worked on the first IEA civics study in the early 1970s, I was one of the first persons asked by Judith Torney-Purta, head of both the first and second studies, to join her on the leadership team for the second study. Although I was the only MSU person extensively involved in this study, even this limited involvement was useful in keeping MSU visible in IEA in a way that went beyond TIMSS.

The substantive challenges of the second civics study were many. Not only were there skeptics of both the validity of the test used to measure cognitive outcomes in civics and the reliance on attitude scales in the first civic education study; the landscape in which civic education was embedded had profoundly changed. These changes in landscape began to take shape in the period of student rebellions in the 1960s, which shook the foundations of civic education. The field continued to evolve in response to breakthroughs in attitudes about gender and politics, substantial changes in the political climate and regimes of participating countries, as well as international hostilities and economic crises, all contributing to greater and greater globalization and culminating in the breakup of the Soviet Union and its client states. The result was an era in which the ideologies of markets and multiparty democracies were at least temporarily dominant across the world.

In the end, the second civic education study overcame these challenges successfully, with more than two dozen countries participating (eleven postcommunist countries, twelve other European countries, two Latin American countries, Australia, Hong Kong SAR, and the United States). Approximately ninety thousand fourteen-year-old students from twenty-eight countries responded to the test in 1999, as well as a questionnaire.[15] As a result, by the time the second civics study ended, comparative research on civic education had established itself as a major and continuing area of interest to policymakers, researchers, and educators alike.[16] And as one of the major authors for the study, I had been able to add to the list of publications associated with MSU that met the criteria set forth at the beginning of this chapter for multicountry research of domestic as well as international importance.

Opening a Second Priority Channel: BRIDGES Research in Developing Countries, 1985–92

Although it did not predate SIMS, BRIDGES was the first multinational channel of international research to open up with MSU leadership in the design and execution of studies in the new era of integration-infusion at MSU. BRIDGES turned out to be a very lucky break for MSU. When I first received the request for proposals (RFP) issued by USAID, I called around the country to see who might be planning to compete to do this research on primary education in multiple, undesignated countries. Harvard and Stanford seemed to be the only ones prepared to mount a viable proposal for this very ambitious project. Noel McGinn, who was heading up the project at Harvard, agreed that we might join his team. This seemed a splendid opportunity for the college, especially since we might avoid responsibility for what was unrealistic in the RFP—even somewhat utopian—in calling for research-based computer modeling as a basis for educational policymaking. Harvard took that on, so MSU did not have to worry about it. We hoped to concentrate on research, and in fact that was what happened.

BRIDGES was not only an extraordinary opportunity to do research with funding from USAID, which normally had funded very little research in education. It was also the project that brought faculty members Steve Raudenbush and Chris Wheeler into MSU international research. Their earlier duties at MSU had in no way predestined them for international work. In addition, Teresa Tatto, Richard Navarro, and Mun Tsang, all of whom had been prepared by their doctoral programs to work on international development, had a chance to do research in countries outside their previous spheres of involvement. Above all, research on the quality of primary education in developing countries fit very well with college-wide strengths in research on teaching and learning in primary schools and in the effectiveness of such schools as organizations. Although Harvard was the prime research institution for the entire multicountry BRIDGES project, MSU took the lead in Thailand and Burundi and was a major partner in the Sri Lanka work. In addition, Mun Tsang did a good deal of work in BRIDGES Pakistan.

At the beginning we were reluctant to work in Burundi because of its troubled history of conflict between Tutsis and Hutus. At the time the government was controlled by Tutsis who numbered only 15 percent or so of the population. Should we become involved in such a country? We were encouraged to consider it by David Wiley, director of the MSU African Studies Center. But before a decision was made, the leaders of our consortium decided on an exploratory visit to Burundi. Noel Mc-Ginn and I were designated to go, along with Tom Eisemon, a gifted McGill professor who had done related research in East Africa. The fact that this was my very first trip to Africa and that I was the only person on team who could speak the French required to communicate with Burundian officials and educators provoked some anxiety on my part. But in the end, after much negotiation, we reached agreement on working in Burundi with a project that proved very challenging but successful in the end. For me it was the beginning of a love affair with Africa and Africans in almost all the countries in which I was fortunate enough to work.

In Sri Lanka, Teresa Tatto through BRIDGES had become the leader of a sophisticated study of the cost-effectiveness of three teacher education programs. In my view, this is still the best quantitative study of teacher education in a developing country.[17] The three programs included a residential preservice program in colleges of education; a residential, campus-based in-service program at teachers colleges; and a distance education program. The complex quasi-longitudinal study gathered data from subjects at the beginning, the end, and after the conclusion of training. It analyzed multiple outcomes, including what teachers knew at the end of training, what they did in the classroom after training, and how well their pupils did. It was able to provide empirical measures of teacher knowledge, skills, and attitudes at three points in time. The measures of what the teachers did in their classrooms were based not on self-report but on ratings by trained observers. Care was taken to collect data on the characteristics of the program as well as characteristics of the trainees and graduates of the program. Program effects were calculated while controlling for potentially confounding variables such as school type, pupil, and teacher backgrounds. The research included measures of cost so that cost-effectiveness indices could be computed. The results indicated that the distance education program was the most cost-effective of the three programs in improving the knowledge, skills, and attitudes of trainees. (It should be noted, however, that the distance education program included face-to-face components and that it was more effective in learning to teach language than in learning to teach mathematics.)

The entire BRIDGES project ended with considerable evidence of MSU success, including a third-party evaluation that gave MSU's efforts a very favorable review. The project was prominently cited in the literature on basic education in developing countries at the time, including, for example, a major synthesis of research on primary education in Third World countries (*Improving Primary*

Education in Developing Countries by Marlene Lockheed and Adrian Verspoor, 1991). A subsequent 1993 book (*Effective Schools in Developing Countries*, edited by Lockheed and Levin) included a chapter on BRIDGES Burundi work dealing with school effectiveness.[18]

But it was the MSU BRIDGES Thailand work that received the most recognition. It was the only BRIDGES work featured at the historic, global 1990 Jomtien conference "Education for All." Presented at the conference was a videotape prepared by Chris Wheeler, working with the Academy of Educational Development. This video was also viewed at the White House by First Lady Barbara Bush. In 1991 the National Education Commission in Thailand (the educational policy arm of the Office of the Prime Minister) honored the entire Thailand BRIDGES project as an Outstanding Policy Project in Education. Then in 1992, Steve Raudenbush, San Jin Kang (a Korean who had received his PhD from MSU), and a Thai colleague received the CIES award for the best *Comparative Education Review* article of the year for their BRIDGES research on preprimary education in Thailand.[19] Using advanced statistical methods, this article reported on the positive effects of access to and quality of preprimary education on later student achievement in mathematics and Thai language.

The Beginnings of a Third Main Channel: International Teacher Education Research, 1984–2003

Given the importance of teacher education and research on teaching and teacher education in the college, MSU's interest in doing international research on teacher education was to be expected. And indeed this interest was expressed very early in the era of integration and infusion since international teacher education research offered an ideal way to combine the domestic and international priorities and strengths of the college. But no one at the time would have predicted how long it would take—nearly thirty years—for this intent to reach fruition. While some of the early efforts were pioneering, others were abortive, indicating that the desired combination of vision and opportunism can take a very long time to work.

Shortly before the position of assistant dean for international studies in education was created to promote the integration-infusion approach, I wrote a memo in February 1984 arguing for comparative research on teaching as part of the agenda for the college's flagship research unit, the Institute for Research on Teaching, founded in 1976. Among the points made in this memo was a suggestion to focus on a comparative study of teachers' tacit knowledge: "One possible result of a new generation of cross-national studies could be a better understanding of tacit knowledge in teaching. Previous research indicates that much of what teachers know about what they do is implicit or, if not outside conscious awareness, at least taken for granted. Research that asks how and why this tacit knowledge varies across countries would shed light on the importance of tacit knowledge for any one country." To make a start, this proposal called for the IRT to increase contacts with researchers and institutes in other countries, and also to review literature from outside the United States.

Since the federal government then moved to create a National Center for Research on Teacher Education through a competition open to all contenders, this seemed to be an ideal opportunity to propose comparative research in teacher education. In 1985, as part of the preparation of a proposal for this competition, serious planning began for an international component. On June 14, 1985, Andy Porter, one of the leaders in this proposal writing, and I circulated a draft proposal section for this component. This early version of our plan proposed a network and newsletter for existing international networks working on teacher education, with an annual meeting with one representative from each regional network, as well as an exchange of doctoral students.

At about the same time we sent out twenty-eight inquiries to persons in other countries who were known to us as important in research on teaching, teacher education, and related endeavors to ask if they were interested in our proposal; the response was strongly positive. Twenty-one respondents showed interest in participating; four declined; and four did not respond.[20]

MSU won this competition for a National Center for Research on Teacher Education (NCRTE), but the federal government balked at funding the international component even after MSU had agreed to a cut in that part of its budget. The international project remained a part of the center but without enough funding to do more than planning. The following year, it was pretty much the same story.

Nevertheless, 1987 was a year of intense planning in the search for further funding. Harry Judge, who had been working closely with MSU on teacher education reform, picked up the ball and got money from the Spencer Foundation for a conference at Oxford in September 1987 to continue discussion of possible international research on teacher education. One implication of this shift of leadership for MSU became apparent when Judge did not include anyone from MSU in the two slots for Americans on his steering committee, preferring instead Lee Shulman, the former

MSU professor who had gone to Stanford, and Patricia Graham, then dean of the Harvard Graduate School of Education. Nevertheless, MSU continued to actively discuss and contribute to the planning for this conference under the leadership of Lynn Paine.[21]

It was at this time that Judge first unveiled his vision for what he called *triadic* studies. By this he meant a study of three countries in which a researcher from country A would study and report on country B, with researchers from countries B and C taking responsibility for countries C and A, respectively. In a March 25 letter he suggests that one such triad could be composed of the UK, France, and the United States, with Harry focusing on France, a French colleague focusing on the United States, while the U.S. researcher would take responsibility for the UK.

Back at MSU, the International Teacher Education Project Group, headed by Lynn Paine, held a series of meetings to discuss their own ideas for research. This led to a proposal for a study of "definitions of success in teacher education" that would include China, Israel, the United States, and Germany. Although by the time the September 1987 conference was held at Oxford, twenty proposals from various countries and researchers had been submitted for consideration, the MSU proposal was the only one discussed in plenary session. Hence, it received close scrutiny, and various critical questions were raised. Work on this proposal continued after the conference. In the first half of 1988 Lynn scheduled eight additional meetings to discuss and agree on revisions. At the end of this period the plan was to submit a proposal to Spencer Foundation.[22]

But what ultimately happened instead was that the proposal for a triadic study got firmed up with the UK, France, and the United States as participating countries, as Harry had proposed and with him as the principal investigator. He obtained funding from the Spencer Foundation for a three-year study, starting in 1990. MSU's Lynn Paine and Michael Sedlak agreed to do the research and write up that part of the study that dealt with the UK.[23]

Meanwhile in 1989–90, preparation of a proposal responding to a federal competition for a second-generation National Center for Research on Teacher Learning took MSU in still another direction as far as international teacher education research was concerned. It was about that time that mentoring and induction (i.e., the process by which beginning teachers adapt to and learn about their roles) began to receive substantial research attention and become the target of major interventions. Thus, the NCRTE proposal took a timely initiative in including research on mentoring as a major component. With the encouragement of Sharon

Feiman-Nemser, who was the leader of this component, mentoring was seen as a promising area of comparison with other countries. In October 1990, when Lynn Paine wrote a memo on the plans for such a study, she argued for the inclusion of sites in China and England to complement what would be learned from a set of domestic cases.

While plans were being made for these two international teacher education research studies in 1989–90, the international teacher education study group continued unabatedly with one of its most intellectually rich and stimulating series of discussions. It was undeniably a pivotal year.

MSU's Pioneering Cross-National Mentoring and Induction Research, 1990–2003

When MSU's second-generation National Center for Research on Teacher Learning was launched, Lynn Paine joined principal investigator Sharon Feiman-Nemser in a mentoring study of how novice teachers learn to teach in the company of experienced teachers who are reformers in their schools and classrooms.[24] Although the mentoring of novice teachers had come into vogue as means of improving teaching, initially most of the attention in the United States was given to how to organize a mentoring and induction program for beginning teachers, not on what the mentor actually needs to do to improve novices' ability to teach.[25]

Data for this study were collected not only in the United States but, as Lynn Paine had proposed, in contrasting programs in the UK and China. These data consisted of logs, observations, and interviews.[26] They revealed striking differences between the sites in China and those in England and the United States.[27] Chinese participants in the project, when observing videos of American mentors working with their mentees, were surprised to find that the mentors did not seem to be doing or saying anything of note to show more competence at teaching than their mentee. As described by Lynn Paine, the Chinese observers were "puzzled that so much time was spent on emotional support and so little direct engagement in working on the actual challenges/content of teaching." The whole idea of what constitutes "dialogue" between mentor and novice in such a case was challenged by Chinese colleagues, who maintained that dialogue cannot be assessed from just one session since it is rooted in a continuing relationship and arises from interactions over time in more than one session.[28]

Americans in the study were equally amazed when they observed videos of a Chinese mentor known as one of the star teachers who are influential in Chinese practice. The mentor watched the mentee teach a first-grade lesson in beginning subtraction, using an image of a bird cage from which she extracted birds to show visually the mathematical operation of taking away and asking how many are left. Although the Chinese mentor after watching this lesson complimented the student on some aspects of the lesson, she was not at all satisfied. So then, to the special surprise of the U.S. researchers, she proceeded to teach the very same lesson to the mentee alone. In short, mentoring in China meant critiquing the mentee's teaching and demonstrating how to teach better, in contrast to the typical U.S. practice, in which the mentor concentrated on moral support and advice on adjusting to the school environment.

This mentoring research then led to other projects focusing on induction of new teachers. Lynn was one of the leaders along with Senta Raizen, David Pimm, Ted Britton, and Suzanne Wilson in a five-nation study of teacher induction. The resulting book by Britton, Paine, Pimm, and Raizen[29] consists of case studies in countries that all had well-established national programs of induction. The countries were France, Japan, China (Shanghai region), New Zealand, and Switzerland (three cantons). In each of the five countries the focus was on studying teachers' opportunities to learn to teach mathematics in lower secondary school. Nevertheless, the programs studied varied dramatically in goals, purposes, structures, logic, and scope. As might be expected, they were generally designed to address what beginning teachers lacked, and what they were perceived to be lacking varied from country to country. In preservice programs that required a great deal of field experience in elementary or secondary schools as well as instruction in pedagogy or didactics, these components tended not to be emphasized in the induction that followed completion of such programs. But other preservice programs provided very little field experience, concentrating instead on subject-matter learning, not on how it should be taught. As a result, induction programs in such instances tried to compensate by emphasizing the pedagogical aspects that had been missing from the preservice programs.[30] For example, in France, where novice teachers already possessed extremely high levels of subject-matter knowledge, mathematics pedagogy was considered central to their induction learning. About one-third of their first year of teaching was devoted to professional development, including subject-matter-specific didactics as well as general pedagogy and other foundations of teacher knowledge.[31]

Likewise in Japan, where educators began developing special in-service programs for beginning teachers in the 1960s, the novices were considered well prepared in terms of content knowledge, but not in how to deal with students or with pressures from parents or society at large. More generally, since the prior education of these Japanese novices was considered too theoretical without needed practical experience, the subsequent induction programs were designed to redress this imbalance.

In the Shanghai area of China, induction was very different from the other countries studied. It took a systematic approach to organizing various activities and services to introduce novices to a special language of teaching as well as to distinctive ways of thinking and norms of practice. In fact, this meant that induction in Shanghai was the most comprehensive, extensive, and systematic of the programs studied, as well as the one with the most nearly unique features.

Finally, induction in Switzerland had the broadest mandate of all. It concentrated on developing the whole person, with extensive opportunities for counseling, cooperation, and reflective practice. Induction in the three cantons studied was also distinctive in giving novice teachers a strong voice in deciding what they would learn and do during induction. Induction in the Swiss settings included "formal and informal practice groups, individual and group counseling, classroom observations and follow-on discussions, review of personal and professional status and progress, specially designed courses and help booklets."[32]

Overall, this five-nation study gave various answers to the question, *Should induction programs focus directly on teaching the novice to teach better?* To some, the answer to this question might seem obvious, but earlier research on induction and mentoring by Feiman-Nemser, Paine, and colleagues suggested that emphasis in the United States was on providing emotional support for the stresses of beginning teachers and on helping each teacher find his or her own approach to teaching; there was virtually no direct teaching of how to teach. In China, it was the opposite; the mentors of novice teachers were more likely to assume the role of master teacher and coach, providing more direct guidance to the novice on what he or she needed to know and do in order to teach well.[33]

While some activities were found in virtually all studies of induction, this cross-national review of contrasting programs turned up some that were highly distinctive. For example, according to Britton et al., one of the unique features of the Shanghai system was a competition centering on "talk lessons":

The event [that one successful competitor] participated in, typical of these competitions, had three elements: a "talk" lesson in which teachers have ten minutes to talk through how and why they would teach a topic they have chosen; a multimedia section, with five minutes for contestants to use and describe how they would use technology to help pupil thinking; finally, a five minute section demonstrating "blackboard skills," something this teacher (as well as many others we interviewed) stressed as very important.[34]

Each talk lesson was then evaluated by a jury in terms of reasons for choosing the lesson, how the topic is organized, appropriateness of the approach, and effectiveness of the language used and the teacher's demeanor.

This channel of international research on teacher education has also helped us understand how much countries differ in the extent to which teaching is a private, individualistic practice, as opposed to a collective, collegial one. The literature suggests that collegiality is a resource that can be drawn upon to support and reinforce the learning of novice teachers.[35] Thus, in developing induction policy and in planning induction programs and practice, it is important to ask how much collegiality is present, how much is possible, whether it will develop naturally or artificially,[36] and what can be accomplished as a result. For example, under existing conditions, can teachers in a school be expected to work together to coach and mentor novice teachers? Are they willing, and how much time do they actually have to do this? Is teaching an open and public activity, as in China and Japan, where experienced teachers and novices alike expect to be observed by peers, mentors, and other novices and where the criticisms and suggestions of other teachers are freely offered and nondefensively received after such observations? In three other countries studied (France, Switzerland, and New Zealand), Britton et al. found significant restrictions on the extent to which teaching is public. But in contrast:

New teachers [in Shanghai], in being asked to teach a "public" lesson, are being asked something that any teacher would be expected to do. . . . That others get to see your practice is, thus, not a marker of novice status, a marker of still becoming—on the contrary, it is a mark of being a teacher. While the specifics are tailored to meet the needs and possibilities of the beginner, the assumption that all teaching is public—and can and should be shared and discussed—is widely held in schools. In fact, the "public" lesson is not solely for the benefit of the individual beginning teacher who is teaching it, but can support the learning of others as well—especially other young teachers.[37]

Nothing more need be said to indicate the importance of the MSU research on mentoring and induction in challenging the U.S. teaching profession to rethink existing practices and norms of teaching and to reach higher standards of performance, whether by emulating to some degree what has been documented in other countries or by finding alternative, equivalent ways of enhancing the learning of novice teachers. And indeed, the five-nation induction project has influenced subsequent efforts in the United States and elsewhere. At MSU, Lynn Paine and Ted Britton used the framework for comprehensive induction, developed in the five-country study, for a study of induction programs and learning opportunities at U.S. sites.[38]

Expanding the Teacher Education Research Channel through IEA, 2002–13

In spite of not being funded for all the research that had been proposed, by the year 2000 MSU had acquired a great deal of experience with international research in education. We had addressed various issues and topics.[39] The question was where to go next. To start to answer this question, in spring 2000 I convened a group of faculty members (namely Teresa Tatto, Bill Schmidt, Lynn Paine, Chris Wheeler, Bob Floden, and Gary Sykes) to discuss what priorities should be set for further international research in education at MSU. At the time, our role in TIMSS of the 1990s had almost come to an end, and the research of others like Lynn Paine, Teresa Tatto, and Chris Wheeler was at a crossroads. I was afraid that, sidetracked by other priorities and commitments, we might lose the exceptional capabilities we had built up for doing international research. The assembled group discussed this and, surprisingly, came quickly to a consensus. The time had come to do international research on teacher education—TIMSS and other studies had made clear the importance of well-qualified teachers, but there was no cross-national data to help answer the question of whether teacher education does or does not help teachers become effective. Our position at the time was summarized in a memo I sent to this informal MSU group in October 2000:

Tomorrow Tuesday, October 17 we will have another meeting to continue discussions of last spring on what directions the college should take in international research related to quality of teaching and teacher learning. The idea is to consider how to capitalize on our tremendous comparative advantage in this area based on our track record with TIMSS, teacher mentoring-induction research and various related projects in developing countries. Ideas run the gamut from initiating a new large-scale IEA cross-national study of teacher quality and development to smaller more focused studies to follow up on particular issues raised by our previous research.

At one of our meetings, Teresa and Bill agreed to head up writing a proposal to get NSF support for an international study of teacher education. This was the beginning of the preliminary study we first called Pre-TEDS (later renamed MT21). The proposal, first drafted by Teresa in November 2000, was submitted to NSF as a preliminary proposal in April 2001 and as a full proposal in June of that year. Although submitted independently of IEA, the proposal suggested that the proposed project might subsequently seek to become an IEA project. As is often the case, since the first proposal was reviewed with some favor but not funded, we submitted a second full proposal to NSF in November 2001, one year after Teresa drafted the first version. It took NSF so long to review that second proposal that by summer 2002, I assumed it was dead.

At the same time, unbeknownst to MSU, IEA had been preparing on its own to launch a teacher education study. By 2002 IEA was a stronger organization than it had ever been before. Under the leadership of Hans Wagemaker, the organization had a coherent strategy for its research that was much more sustainable than in the past. This strategy was built around the success of the repeat studies in science-mathematics (TIMSS) and reading literacy (PIRLS). These studies embodied a capacity to do projects on time with higher quality standards.[40] In turn, the participating countries paid participation fees that gave the organization much more viability and even some financial reserves. The Data Processing Center and secretariat were becoming staffed at a size and level of relevant experience that would have been unimaginable at earlier times.

It was in spring 2002 that the IEA secretariat announced a competition for an institution to take the lead in an IEA teacher education study. At MSU, we decided immediately to compete, and so apparently did the Australian Council for Educational Research. Lawrence Ingvarson, an ACER researcher who had been a visiting scholar at MSU, called Gary Sykes at MSU to see if we were interested in participating under ACER leadership. We said no, we would submit on our own. In reviewing the submissions, IEA surprisingly decided that it wanted MSU and

ACER to work together to design and coordinate the study. Initially, there were two main tasks to be accomplished: prepare a preliminary proposal to submit to NSF in September 2002 and a more extensive proposal for discussion by the IEA General Assembly at its Morocco meeting in October of that year.

In the early days of MSU-ACER collaboration in 2002, we learned to our astonishment that NSF had decided to fund the other, earlier MSU proposal I had considered dead. Since at the time there was no external funding for IEA TEDS, this grant was a lifesaver. Until we got another NSF grant for this study in 2005, we had to rely for three years on a combination of P-TEDS funding and internal MSU resources just to keep going. Without P-TEDS, we could not have made enough progress to justify the subsequent, larger NSF grant. Moreover, P-TEDS work in six countries (Korea, Taiwan, Bulgaria, Germany, Mexico, and the United States) was vital to the design of the larger TEDS study.

But P-TEDS also raised further concerns about relationships among MSU, ACER, and IEA, and even within the MSU team. It was the source of strong tensions to follow. To try to resolve these tensions, we had formed a Joint Management Committee (JMC) for TEDS-M. When the JMC met in Melbourne in February 2003, it was decided that the unexpected first MSU grant would become an integral part of the larger study, now called TEDS (hence the acronym P-TEDS, meaning Pre-TEDS). This agreement was intended to ensure that the larger study would benefit more fully from the work of P-TEDS. This decision reduced the tensions a little, but it was the pragmatic need to make decisions about the design and execution of the study that overcame many disagreements, since all members of the team were committed to bringing the study to a successful conclusion.

Even with P-TEDS funding, the future of the larger TEDS study remained in doubt until we could get an additional grant large enough to cover much of the international costs. NSF, the only funding agency that was likely to cover those expenses, was very hesitant about investing such a large amount in an unprecedented study that it would have to justify to their stakeholders. It took a lot of time to meet the NSF's conditions, including finding a prominent mathematics educator willing to be a co-principal investigator (CO-PI) with Teresa Tatto and me. NSF made clear that one of the PIs had to be a mathematician or mathematics educator, and neither Teresa nor I met that stipulation. Nowhere in the study were the obstacles identified by Bourdieu clearer: in the *field* for this study, the hierarchy of mathematician over mathematics educator over others was not to be challenged. However, getting one of MSU's well-known mathematics educators to cross boundaries and make such a commitment of time and reputation to a study outside his or her primary area of work (*field*) was not easy. We had to be patient and were ultimately rewarded when Sharon Senk, a mathematics education professor appointed in the College of Natural Science, agreed to fill this role. She was respected for her other work, especially for codirecting with Zalman Usiskan the development of secondary school materials for the University of Chicago School Mathematics Project.

With that and other NSF-required revisions done, it was during a snowstorm two days before Christmas 2004 that the final proposal went in. Teresa and I trudged through a lot of new-fallen snow to the MSU Contracts and Grants Office to make sure the proposal got to NSF before Christmas. But to little avail—again NSF was in no hurry. After waiting for the final questions from NSF until July 2005, we did not get the grant until September 2005. One of the final obstacles was NSF's insistence that we have funding for U.S. participation as well as funding for international costs. This demand was very reasonable; we expected it, but unfortunately we had no such funding. Finally, after much communication back and forth with Teresa and others, NSF compromised and decided to begin the grant, provided that we agreed to come up with the U.S. national funding within a year. In my view, the only way we could get this funding was to rely on Bill Schmidt's reputation and demonstrated ability to obtain large grants. Bill agreed to try. And by the next year, using what had already been accomplished in P-TEDS (as well as his other accomplishments) as part of our case, Bill had raised several million dollars from foundations that did not generally fund such projects (Boeing, Gates, Carnegie, and General Electric).

The NSF grant for international costs of TEDS-M was for only three years (the most time it was allowed to provide us). The TEDS timeline showed that more time would be required. To provide for later years, Teresa obtained supplemental grants, as well as saving for no-cost extensions. Nevertheless, after grant funds ran low, MSU faculty had to contribute time for which the university could not be reimbursed.

When the P-TEDS and TEDS NSF grants are added to what Schmidt raised from foundations for U.S. TEDS, the total MSU funding for this whole effort reached a multimillion-dollar level rarely achieved by projects in education that are exclusively for research. In contrast, virtually no funds from participation fees paid by participating countries to the IEA secretariat in Amsterdam ($32,000 per year per country) were used for MSU. These were needed by ACER, the IEA Data Processing Center (DPC), and the secretariat, which had no other source of funding. Teresa was left to raise additional funds herself to fill MSU gaps. In the end, our sole compensation at MSU as we ran out of grant money was our satisfaction in having ourselves raised the grants on which we had drawn.

Although the intent was for the First IEA Teacher Education Study (TEDS-M) to operate in the businesslike manner of TIMSS and PIRLS, circumstances and institutional histories conspired to prevent this from happening consistently. Organizational interests, funding opportunities, and researchers' points of view, all under the strain of an unprecedented study, were far too different to allow for the more highly integrated, systematic approach developed for TIMSS, and PIRLS at Boston College. The MSU-ACER partnership arranged by Hans Wagemaker was what in American parlance is called a "shotgun" marriage, an alliance that was not the free choice of either partner. As in many such marriages, this one was marked from the beginning with disagreements, especially since this marriage of two very different institutions was to be consummated by seven leaders (plus other influential collaborators).[41]

For example, in addition to ACER (more or less, the "ETS of Australia"), TEDS-M also required tight collaboration with the IEA Data Processing Center in Hamburg, Germany, with its staff of over one hundred people, several of whom were assigned to TEDS-M in order to carry out sampling, provide special software to each country to collect and enter its data, and develop administrative manuals for the study. The TEDS-M team at MSU was also in close touch with the IEA secretariat in Amsterdam on all aspects of the study and especially in verifying the translation of instruments and in implementation of IEA's quality control procedures. In addition, in each country there was a national research center with staff to carry out the study under the leadership of a prominent NRC.[42]

In the early stages, there was much tension over who, among such a complex leadership team, was really in charge. At the center was a great lack of understanding between MSU and ACER. Ultimately, Hans and the NSF project officer attempted to resolve this problem by confirming Teresa Tatto as the principal decision-maker. But that was not sufficient; although the seven leaders constituted the JMC that met and dealt with the tensions to some extent, the JMC never became a body able to resolve all disagreements, as was initially intended.[43]

One critical design challenge of this study was how far to depart from the existing Boston College–IEA paradigm. This paradigm, with its emphasis on comparing the intended, implemented, and attained curricula of participating countries, was certainly relevant to the higher-education context of TEDS-M, but how to put this framework into practice within a completely new context, that of postsecondary education, was not clear. Within postsecondary systems, as compared with the primary and secondary systems, there was more autonomy for institutions to establish different programs as well as to cooperate or not cooperate with the study. Within higher-education institutions, students (having become adults) had much more autonomy than students in elementary and secondary school, the higher-education instructors likewise. These challenges led to heated arguments within the TEDS-M team over, for example, how to deal with consecutive programs in which future teachers learn mathematics in a first university degree and pedagogy in a second, whether it was justified to study teacher education without collecting data on what new teachers were learning on the job, whether it was sufficient to limit outcome data to student teachers' knowledge of subject matter and pedagogy, how to get a fix on opportunities to learn (including those not documented in syllabi and other curriculum materials), and what curriculum information to collect.

Recruitment of countries for this major new study was another daunting challenge. It was not like TIMSS, where many countries had had experience with an earlier version of the same study. Moreover, the IEA organization was built on member institutions that typically were mainly or exclusively concerned with elementary and secondary education, and hence lacked the knowledge of, interest in, and influence over higher education that TEDS-M required. Seventeen countries ultimately participated in the study: Botswana, Canada (but only four provinces), Chile, Germany, Georgia, Malaysia, Norway, Oman, Philippines, Poland, Russia, Singapore, Spain, German-speaking Switzerland, Taiwan, Thailand, and the United States. This was a disappointment because initial expectations were for thirty or more countries. And seventeen was too few to meet IEA's projected financial break-even point (based on participation fees and the expenses anticipated at the international level).

We first unveiled our plan for TEDS-M at the IEA General Assembly (GA) meeting in Morocco in 2002. This proposal ran into a rocky reception. Some of the most important GA members criticized the plan severely and questioned whether it was feasible. Ultimately, the Europeans had so many objections and unanswered questions that Teresa Tatto had to promise to go to a follow-up meeting that European researchers in IEA were to convene in Brussels. This, in fact, took place, and Teresa was able to address the concerns sufficiently to get support for continuing to plan this new study and resolve issues not raised in previous IEA studies.

The plan was to continue the search for funds while developing what IEA had come to call a *conceptual framework document*—a lengthy, published discussion of the design and rationale that would answer questions like those raised in the Morocco meetings.[44] For the purpose of putting this document together, a series of expert panels took place in Amsterdam, East Lansing, and Hamburg. For the first meeting in Amsterdam in June 2003, the TEDS-M leadership team invited experts in the pure and educational aspects of mathematics and science, as well as in teacher education, research methodology, and measurement.

All the invited scholars were viewed as potential collaborators in further work on TEDS-M. It was in organizing this meeting that we discovered Sigrid Blömeke, who became an indispensable source of expertise and support for the study. She was nominated to attend the Amsterdam meetings by the IEA General Assembly member from Germany. It turned out that she was not only productive and competent in research on teacher education but passionate about it. She stood out for her knowledgeable contributions to the discussions in Amsterdam and went on to become the NRC for TEDS-M in Germany and then spent two years at MSU as a visiting researcher, working mainly with Bill Schmidt's team (2007–9).[45]

Although the number of countries was smaller than hoped for, Sigrid's case exemplifies the fact that, within the seventeen participating countries, an extraordinarily capable group of NRCs emerged. Bill Schmidt was another case in point. For him to become the NRC for the United States was a serendipitous arrangement for MSU since otherwise it would have been very difficult to find a suitable role for Bill. In spite of his extraordinary competence and productivity as well as interest in the study, he did not have the support from other parts of IEA needed for him to be one of the principal investigators (PIs) at the international level. Nevertheless, he was an essential member of the MSU team who could and would make great contributions to the project. So when Bill himself decided he wanted to be the U.S. NRC, that proved to be a great solution to a very ticklish issue.

In 2003 we returned to the IEA General Assembly meetings for a second year. They were held in Cyprus. In this way we were introduced to the yearly cycle of rigorous review for all of IEA's current studies, which we then experienced every year until 2010 in Botswana. The routine always went like this: First, the directors of all the current IEA studies led off the week of meetings—always on Friday—by discussing methodological design and analysis issues with the IEA technical executive group (TEG). This review was scheduled twice a year, once at the GA meeting and once at the American Educational Research Association, which researchers from outside the United States attended as well.

The response of the TEG to the TEDS-M Cyprus report was positive, but this was only the beginning. The next day we made another presentation to the IEA Standing Committee, which worked with the IEA executive director, Hans Wagemaker, to oversee IEA management throughout the year. This session typically served as a dress rehearsal for our project's main presentation to the entire IEA General Assembly, which was always scheduled to meet on Monday, Tuesday, and Wednesday of the following week. Since we spent our spare time at the meeting discussing how to improve our report and address the concerns that were being raised, by the time TEDS-M came up on the plenary schedule, our presentation had become quite polished. Even so, in Cyprus we still ran into strong criticism from a few Europeans who said the study was putting too much emphasis on subject-matter knowledge in the preparation of teachers and not enough on pedagogy and other important aspects of teaching. Still, in the end, TEDS-M got off lightly at this GA, especially when compared not only to Morocco and our later experience, but also to another IEA project team which had an especially rough time at the Cyprus meeting.

Once we had recruited as many countries as we could for TEDS-M, most of the subsequent work focused on the survey phase of the study, in which data were collected from representative samples of teacher education students in the last year of their programs and also from their instructors and their institutions. The students were tested on their knowledge of mathematics content and mathematics pedagogy. Most of the execution phase of the survey was done collaboratively by the IEA Data Processing Center in Hamburg, MSU, and the national centers.

Five years after Cyprus and many other international meetings for the project, the NRCs of TEDS-M came together for their fourth meeting in Bergen, Norway, in the fall of 2008. After all those years of preparation and trial data collection, the final data collection was finished, and almost all of the countries had submitted data to the IEA data-processing center in Hamburg for initial processing, checking, and cleaning. This Bergen meeting therefore served to demonstrate that, whatever happened from then on, TEDS-M was already an extraordinary, unprecedented, and, in the eyes of many, unexpected success. This was the conclusion stated most forcefully at the end of the meeting both by IEA executive director Hans Wagemaker and by Professor Liv Grønmo, the Norwegian TEDS-M NRC. They both recalled that, when we began the study, skeptics said it could not be done. As Grønmo put it, skeptics had the idea that we were building an airplane that was never going to fly. These skeptics had claimed that, in contrast to TIMSS and other such studies of elementary and secondary education, the institutions, faculty members, and students of higher education would never cooperate in a large-scale international survey in which all were asked to fill out fairly lengthy questionnaires, provide syllabi, and in the case of the students voluntarily submit to a test of their knowledge of mathematics content and mathematics pedagogy. Moreover, the difficulty of getting cooperation was exacerbated because the participants were not volunteers. They were instead selected as part of a national probability sample (or census in the case of the smaller countries). But inasmuch as those selected could not be forced to participate, skeptics charged, the study would not be able to meet the very demanding IEA technical standards for response rates, which were far higher than most surveys of higher education are able to achieve, even ones that have no need to test the student participants.

Using the airplane metaphor to great advantage, Grønmo asserted that by the time of the Bergen meeting, the plane was flying quite successfully. All that remained was to finish the flight by bringing the plane safely back down to earth. One key indicator of TEDS-M success was that the achieved response rates and coverage of national target populations of students were arguably unmatched in the history of voluntary national probability surveys of higher education. IEA had demonstrated that it could do cross-national assessment in higher education, overcoming various challenges that exceeded what it had experienced in elementary and secondary education.

Nevertheless, after the Bergen meeting, further setbacks were in store for TEDS-M. The study fell behind in the reporting phase. Instead of being released to the public in 2010, as originally planned, the four main international report volumes did not finally come out until 2012–13.[46] In the meantime, the TEDS-M national centers had been authorized to issue national reports before the international reports—contrary to IEA's normal procedures. Once these were authorized, Germany, Switzerland, Poland, Taiwan, and the United States quickly released their reports.[47]

This final delay was hardly surprising, given the dissension within the management team at MSU, ACER, and IEA, as well as ten years (2002 to 2012) of the immense management challenges associated with this study. The project had to cope with seventeen participating countries, in which data were collected from national samples on the routes, institutions, programs, practices, and outcomes of teacher education. Approximately twenty-two thousand future teachers from 750 programs in about five hundred institutions were surveyed and tested on their knowledge of mathematics content and mathematics pedagogy. Close to five thousand teaching staff (mathematicians, mathematics educators, and other education instructors) were also surveyed.

The highly sophisticated methodology adopted by IEA for TEDS-M, requiring use of some of the most advanced psychometric and survey methods, made the work still more challenging. In particular, the process for developing the TEDS-M instruments was likewise elaborate and intensive. The instruments for assessing teacher knowledge of mathematics content and mathematics pedagogy were developed gradually over the course of five years or so in consultation with mathematicians and mathematics educators throughout the world. Taking P-TEDS as well as TEDS into account, many of the test items had been piloted five times in multiple countries before being put in the final version.

This story does not end with TEDS-M. Already before TEDS-M was finished, Teresa was on to the planning of another pioneering, follow-on study. Once again I was amazed at how much work she would tackle at the same time. This time, while still working on TEDS-M, she was in charge of preparation of a preliminary proposal for a study of teachers with five or fewer years of teaching experience and what they were learning from their induction years about the teaching of mathematics. Originally in TEDS-M, we had hoped to do the preservice and induction study at the same time in order to address the common complaint of practicing teachers who say that everything they learned about teaching they learned on the job and not at a college or university. But that study soon proved impossible. Now without TEDS-M being totally finished, Teresa was designing another pilot study, recruiting a team of collaborators, identifying countries, and writing a proposal. It all left me breathless, but in the end, as soon as TEDS-M was over, Teresa had funding to carry out this second pilot study, known as FirstMath. As of this writing, new instruments have been designed, a new probability sampling plan drawn up to deal with the great difficulty of finding, at an acceptable cost, teachers teaching mathematics with five years or less of experience, and finally, collection of the data undertaken from twelve countries. These data include a TEDS-M-like test of what teachers know about mathematics content and mathematics pedagogy, but modified to be appropriate for practicing teachers. This all indicates that an important new research channel in the map of integration-infusion at MSU is already under way.

Conclusion

TEDS-M was a major institutional effort, requiring capabilities not normally found within a school of education. It was proof that the integration-infusion approach had borne fruit in the capability to conduct research of such major importance both internationally and domestically. The outcome was initially in doubt, but by 2012 MSU, with the extraordinary support and collaboration of the multiplicity of individuals and agencies involved, had passed the test. This foundation of IEA research and capacity, together with MSU's experience in research on teacher education, had made it possible for MSU to take the lead in solving seemingly intractable problems and finish the first IEA study of teacher education, the first IEA study in higher education, and in fact the first international assessment of learning outcomes in any field of higher education using representative national samples.

CHAPTER 6

Building New Channels for International Development Work

International development projects were among the first non-domestic ventures to play a major role in the College of Education at MSU, as illustrated by the faculty members who worked full-time and on-site in the creation of the University of Nigeria, Nsukka during the years 1960–67. But by the time a new approach to international work was adopted in 1984, the college's work on international development had diminished to no more than an emphasis on nonformal education. Thus, one of the important questions to be resolved was how much of a place to save for international development within the new spectrum of college activities. The answer we gave to this question was some, but not too much. Although continuing this stream of international work was becoming more and more difficult, it was judged too important to let drop.

Much of the work we subsequently were able to do took place in Southeast Asia, where MSU's reputation in education and international development was rescued by Chris Wheeler and his fieldwork with ministries, universities, NGOs, schools, and rural villages as well as his on-campus leadership at MSU in related areas. Although MSU had been very active in Southeast Asia in the 1950s, 1960s and early 1970s, with project work in education and a large number of Thai students in our college, this had been followed by a hiatus and period of decline.

CHRIS WHEELER

Starting in 1987, Chris Wheeler reversed a decline in MSU's activity in both Thailand and Vietnam. He set the bar high for a new era of college work in education and development, leaving his mark on research, teaching, and outreach. His international accomplishments ranged from innovation in international development to leadership in university linkages, study abroad, and mentoring of international students. In leading multidisciplinary teams of faculty from diverse MSU colleges, he put into practice what the university long preached about the virtues of cross-college collaboration. His work was featured in notable publications (e.g., a full-page article in *Education Week*, the newsweekly of record for U.S. K–12 education, September 5, 2001, titled "Thai Schools Find Enlightenment with Forestry Project"). In both Southeast Asian countries, his achievements were also recognized by prestigious awards from Thai and Vietnamese sources.

Starting with a PhD in political science from Columbia, experience as a liberal arts professor at Beloit College, and work as an advocate for people with disabilities at the federal Office of Civil Rights, Chris Wheeler at MSU was able to transform himself once again and become a professor of education. Unstinting and unwavering in his commitments, he first earned his educational research credentials in a telling case study of the National Council for Accreditation of Teacher Education (NCATE) and his teacher education credentials by working week after week and year after year with teachers to create an MSU inner-city professional development school in Flint, Michigan. But ultimately he channeled most of his energy, intelligence, and savvy into two of his passions.

One was his continued focus on teaching undergraduates as part of his search for greater equity in American education. Coordinator of one of MSU's largest single courses in education, TE 250, he mentored many teaching assistants, helping them start down the road toward being, like him, master teachers in higher education. He and the assistants in turn demonstrated their capabilities by leading students in the course to be more insightful and sensitive in matters of justice in education. This domestic work was a perfect complement to his international work, putting the integration-infusion approach into practice. In fact, TE 250 was one of the first domestically oriented courses that, through Chris's leadership, underwent systematic internationalization with, among other things, professional development for instructors in the course.

Chris's other passion in the pursuit of justice led him far outside the university to the villages of Thailand and Vietnam, where, as the leader of interdisciplinary teams from different MSU colleges and together with Thai and Vietnamese colleagues, he developed new forms of collaboration between schools and their communities to improve teaching, learning, school-community relations, and community development more generally. This work started in Thailand, where the intensive part of it lasted more than ten years, followed by the subsequent Vietnam work, which took another ten plus years to complete.

Before Chris started these efforts, he had never worked in Southeast Asia. Nor, as emphasized above, did he have the background typical of an education professor. But he did have international experience. After earning a master's degree in African studies from Columbia University, he went on to a doctoral program in comparative politics and specialized in the study of interest groups in Sweden. A revision of his dissertation was later published by the University of Illinois Press.* Subsequently, as a professor of political science at Beloit College in Wisconsin, he did more work in Sweden, and became so proficient in Swedish that he could lecture in the language. I first met him in 1972–74, when I, too, was working in Sweden.

Wheeler began his Southeast Asia work in 1987. Not long after he joined our USAID BRIDGES research team, where his expertise in qualitative case studies and general ability to conduct research were major assets, he was selected as the country coordinator for the project's research on primary school quality in Thailand. In this position he was soon able to revitalize MSU's relationship with the National Education Commission in the Office of the Prime Minister, which MSU had helped set up years earlier, but whose collaboration with MSU had lapsed for some time. Over the next four years (1987–91), with funding from USAID in collaboration with U.S. and Thai colleagues, his team designed and carried out research on the quality of elementary schooling in Thailand. This work was selected by the Office of the Prime Minister as the Outstanding Policy Project/Study in Education in 1991.†

At about the same time Chris organized and got funding from the United States Information Service for a linkage to create a policy center at Thailand's most prestigious university, Chulalongkorn. This led to a series of exchanges between policy studies professors at Chula and MSU, exchanges fastidiously planned and coordinated by Chris.

After these initial successes, MSU was invited to work on the reversal of deforestation in rural Thailand. From its inception in 1992 until completion of the initial phases toward the end of the decade, Chris served as MSU director for the Social Forestry, Education, and Participation Project in Thailand, a project that linked rural primary and lower secondary schools in northern Thailand to their communities in novel ways.[‡]

The success of this Thailand work on education and deforestation opened the door for efforts in Vietnam. In 1998, Chris and his team were invited to Can Tho University in the Mekong Delta to start new work combining school-community collaboration with environmental education and action. After much negotiation, the work took the form of two complementary projects. Each was funded by different grants that Chris was able to obtain. One was a Shell Foundation Sustainable Communities Grant and the other a U.S. Department of State linkage between Can Tho University and MSU.[§] The Shell grant supported multiple projects intended to raise average income among households in the Mekong Delta.

To prepare schools for a more ambitious role in community development, the linkage grant with Can Tho University concentrated on improvement of teaching methods, research capacity, and linkages to elementary and secondary schools to prepare them to contribute to community development. In particular, the linkage project trained prospective teachers in more active learning strategies and the use of community resources in teaching.

In short, Chris's work in Thailand and Vietnam brought together different facets of development and education that ordinarily are not integrated, such as the transition to student-centered learning, the improvement of classroom teaching, new forms of professional development for teachers, changes in school-community relations, protection of the environment, new income-generating activities for rural families, and integrated community development more generally. For the work of integration and infusion, these interrelated accomplishments brought to our college a new appreciation of the potential importance of education in rural low-income areas of developing countries, an important area of work that before Chris had not been well represented in the college since the 1960s, but which instead had compensating support from other parts of MSU that valued College of Education strength in international development.

NOTES

* Wheeler, 1975.
† AR ISP 1991–92.
‡ AR ISP 1991–92, 1992–93, 1993–94, 1994–95, 1995–96, 1996–97.
§ AR ISP 2001–2.

Taking a College-Wide Perspective

Some of the reasons for continuing to emphasize international development were admittedly self-serving from the college point of view. International development projects brought in substantial funding and maintained visibility for the college in this very important sector. But other more substantive reasons were also important. These projects served as professional development for faculty who had technical expertise required by a project but no international experience in the region served or perhaps no developing country experience at all.

But even more important and underlying all these practical reasons is the belief that the development of education systems in postcolonial and low-income countries is one of the most, if not the most, important educational efforts of our era, completing the worldwide spread of mass education that started over two hundred years ago. Part of what it takes for an American university aiming to be less ethnocentric in educational scholarship and teaching is, I would argue, expert knowledge concerning this monumental change. Helping in some small measure to reach the finish line in this last difficult stage of education for all is likewise an important part of what it means for a school of education to be internationalized and to have international credibility.

Along the same vein, the 1984 College of Education task force report by Hanson[1] made clear that attending to international development in education was an ethical imperative. The report made four arguments for internationalization of the College of Education. One of them was an ethical argument, introduced as follows:

> International concern is a moral obligation for educators. Just as we can argue that well-to-do suburbanites have a moral obligation to be concerned with the education of inner city children, we can also argue that as U.S. citizens we have an obligation to be concerned with the education of all the world's children, not just those who, by accident of birth in the U.S., have a call on a disproportionate share of the world's resources.[2]

College policy did not favor a token effort to meet this need simply by arranging consultancies for pay by individual faculty members who agree to do work in developing countries. Such an approach to international development, although attractive to some faculty members, would always be seen as marginal to the college at large. Instead, acquiring grants or contracts through the university was judged more beneficial in terms of meeting the overall university goals for internationalizing its programs and capabilities.

As stated above, the USAID BRIDGES project was a perfect fit with college priorities because it focused on international development through research, and BRIDGES research was of significance to the college more generally. But USAID did not typically focus on research, and, therefore, it was necessary to compete for other development assistance projects, some of which might offer opportunities for research, although many would not. Thus instead of being completely opportunistic, we needed to look for projects that would fit well within college capabilities and priorities.

In short, the international development channel was big in the past, dominating other channels at MSU, but by the early 1980s had nearly dried up as a major priority in the College of Education. At the time it was two dynamic and exceptionally capable doctoral students (first Joan Claffey and then Mary Joy Pigozzi) who carried on and kept the college in this sphere of activity by directing the Nonformal Education Information Center (NFEIC), which had been established in 1975 with a good deal more funding from USAID and much more faculty involvement than nearly ten years later, when the integration-infusion approach was first adopted.

The Lame-Duck Nonformal Education Information Center

At the beginning of the integration-infusion era, the college's role in developing countries was thus limited to the NFEIC, a clearinghouse and dissemination center for fugitive literature on nonformal education in developing countries. In the 1984 report of the task force that led to adoption of the integration-infusion approach, the NFEIC was characterized as follows:

> The NFEIC, funded from 1975 until this year by the Agency for International Development with additional external assistance for specific research and training functions, has served program planners, practitioners, and researchers concerned with the generation and use of knowledge about non-formal education and development through a worldwide network that has grown to number more than 5,000 participants in 145 countries. Its services have been offered through individualized research service, workshops, training opportunities, and technical

assistance designed to strengthen information centers and networks abroad and an extensive body of publications.[3]

By 1984–85, in spite of having served a worldwide clientele in an area that just a few years before had been one of USAID's top priorities, the center was on its last legs because of difficulties in finding continued funding. Moreover, even at its peak, the center had proved problematic in its lack of appeal to the college at large. Much of the interest in nonformal education was centered outside the College of Education in Agriculture, Women's Studies, and the like. While a good number of faculty members in education had been involved earlier when funding and donor interest were strong, in 1984–85 there was less faculty interest and certainly no large amounts of funded faculty time committed to the center. In fact, there was an intellectual gulf between the center, on the one hand, and most of the college faculty, on the other, due to the fact that the center was built on a discourse of criticism of formal basic education in developing countries and the advocacy of nonformal education as an alternative. Separated from all but a few faculty by this gap of interests and perspectives, the center was in a poor position to support and enhance the new policy of integration and infusion. In fact, its history had been downright inconsistent with this policy.

Nevertheless, the center was kept going at the time by a dynamic, enterprising, and forceful doctoral student in education, Mary Joy Pigozzi, who in turn supervised a student staff to maintain the library of fugitive NFE literature, answer inquiries, publish newsletters, and put out other more specialized publications. But, without more funding, this work could not continue. As the financial situation of the center became more desperate, Associate Dean Andy Porter took up this challenge (this was before I became an assistant dean responsible for the center). An opportunity arose when Peter McPherson, administrator in charge of USAID and MSU alumnus, was awarded an honorary degree in June 1984.[4] As part of his visit, he came to Erickson Hall to look the center over. In a follow-up letter, Dean Lanier and Porter reminded McPherson that the college itself had funded the center over the previous year, but could not continue to do that. External funding of at least $100,000 per year was required and requested.

Nevertheless, on July 30, 1984, a key senior staff member at USAID, Nyle Brady, called Ralph Smuckler, dean of international studies and programs at MSU, to say he and McPherson had decided USAID would not provide more money. About a month later McPherson himself called Porter with the same message.

In another blow to the center, Mary Pigozzi left at end of August 1984 for the Institute for International Research in Washington, D.C., beginning a remarkable career in international development that would take her on to the Midwest Universities Consortium for International Activities, UNICEF headquarters in New York, UNESCO headquarters in Paris, the Academy for Educational Development in Washington, and finally the Educate a Child Foundation in Doha, Qatar, under the patronage of Her Highness Sheikha Moza bint Nasser, where Pigozzi remains as of this writing.

Since more money was not immediately forthcoming, the question was what to do with the center. Should it be abolished? Instead of doing away with the center, I argued for changing its mission to allow collection of documentation on formal basic education as well as nonformal, all under a new name—Office for International Networks in Education and Development, so that the office would be more tightly and logically associated with faculty in the college whose interests were in formal education.

There was, however, some resistance to this change from the Adult and Continuing Education faculty. An October 18, 1984, letter from Joe Levine pointed out that "there has not previously been any compelling need to lobby or otherwise promote this [NFE] area since we had faculty working together in nonformal education, courses available for graduate study, the Nonformal Education Information Center, the summer Institute for Studies in Nonformal Education and a growing group of graduate students committed to the further study of nonformal education. Today it seems that all but the last point are being threatened due to a series of events over the past few years." Nevertheless, nothing was done in response to this letter because the lack of funding and the feeling among college leaders that NFE was no longer a priority, even in Washington. After an interregnum of some months, Alemu Beeftu, a young Ethiopian about to complete his PhD in adult and continuing education in the college, took over as director. He had achieved this success not so many years after running away from his remote rural home in Ethiopia at age ten because he wanted to get an education that was otherwise not available to him.[5]

In spite of these changes, the new center was never successful in obtaining further funding for the documentation library and dissemination. Still, it did serve a useful purpose of expanding the home base of the Office of International Studies in Education, in which the NFE center was embedded. It provided a large former classroom to serve as a place for international students and other faculty and students with international interests to work and congregate. It also gave important new projects like BRIDGES adequate space. And it continued to make the collection accessible until it was too outdated and ultimately rendered obsolete by the revolution in electronic documentation.

Fighting the Marginalization of Universities in International Development Work in Education

The desire to continue to be involved in international development was made clear in the task force report and in other ways. But getting such projects became harder and harder. MSU got its start in earlier decades when the capabilities of competitors were more limited and funding more abundant relative to offerors. At least since the 1980s universities have been severely disadvantaged in the competition for development assistance funding, especially in USAID, given the profit and nonprofit firms that had come to dominate this market, such as the Academy for Education Development (AED), the Educational Development Center (EDC), Research Triangle Institute, and Creative Associates. Organizations in other industrialized countries (e.g., France, Britain, Canada, Norway, Sweden, Finland, Germany, and Japan) were also becoming more important in funding and managing development projects. Given these emerging capabilities, the principal multilateral funding agencies like the World Bank could hardly justify continuing to allocate their funds too much within the United States. There were also more and more vocal critics who criticized international development projects as badly conceived, poorly executed, generally ineffective, even harmful, perpetuating a dependent state of postcolonialism. Thus, some of the most active universities either withdrew entirely or greatly reduced their international development activity in education (e.g., Florida State, Harvard, Stanford). At MSU, although these critical views were represented in our faculty, we continued to search for appropriate projects, but with mixed success.

The competing firms had the networks and the flexibility to tailor their approach to whatever USAID called for. Universities, on the other hand, could not readily send faculty for international work of any substantial length on short notice. Faculty members had prior commitments for much of the academic year, and even if not, they were free to decide for themselves whether to accept the challenges of international development work, weighing the appeal not only of the work but of the country in which it took place. Given these factors, it was ordinarily most feasible for MSU to have a subcontract or subagreement with one of the dominant firms rather than to be prime. This made it possible to negotiate a good fit with college capabilities and not be responsible for everything that an RFP or RFA (request for application) might call for.

The Importance of International Development Work in Thailand and Vietnam

It was not until the early 1990s that Chris Wheeler and colleagues (most notably Jim Gallagher, another College of Education professor) began to turn international development work in the college around in a way that was innovative and state of the art.[6] After finishing his BRIDGES research, Wheeler continued to concentrate on Thailand, then turned in more recent years to Vietnam, putting together a long record of achievement that often went against conventional wisdom. Working with government officials, other leaders, and project staff in Thailand and Vietnam as well as at MSU, he turned visionary concepts into effective, funded projects.

It was in the spring of 1991 that a group of senior Thai education officials visited a number of universities in the United States seeking a partner to help improve the curriculum and instruction of environmental education in Thai primary and lower secondary schools. MSU faculty gave the visitors ideas for changing teaching practice away from rote memorization toward the understanding of concepts with application to real-world problems. The suggested approach called for schoolchildren and adult community members to work together to resolve environmental issues at the local level. Favoring this approach, the Thai Ministry of Education asked MSU to collaborate in developing a pilot program.[7]

Starting in 1992, this pilot program became the Thailand Environmental Education Project with six rural primary and two lower secondary schools in northern Thailand, focusing on deforestation issues. Funding was provided primarily by the Ford Foundation, with additional support from Mobil, MSU, and USAID. Fifth- through eighth-grade students in the target schools studied local forest-related problems in their villages, interviewing community members and collecting physical data. Students then presented their findings to community members and worked with villagers on small-scale social forestry projects to address the problems they had identified. Examples of projects they undertook included community patrols to prevent forest ground cover burning, new school-community forestry committees that decided how local forests were to be used, and creation of community woodlots.

As a result, the communities became laboratories for learning concepts in the school curriculum. Teaching and learning changed from just "chalk and talk" to become more interactive and participatory. The resulting action-based curricula served to teach important concepts of science, social science, language, and culture in a practical way. In the process, students became more motivated, active learners, while schools and communities learned how to work together to address critical local problems of soil and water conservation, scarcity of fuel-wood sources, and forest regeneration in a highly deforested region.

Project staff carefully documented these changes in teaching, learning, and school-community relations, using a variety of research strategies. Trained fieldworkers observed teachers regularly to document these changes. They also conducted surveys and observed students out in the communities and conducted focus group interviews with teachers and villagers. The project team published these results and completed a videotape that was distributed internationally to explain the project.[8]

The results of this pilot were impressive. Some 70 percent of the teachers in the pilot schools changed their teaching away from "chalk and talk" methods to more learner-centered instruction. Student engagement in learning increased. Test results showed students performed as well as or better than students in the same schools in previous years or in nonproject schools. Especially important was the improvement in process skills, traditionally not measured on tests but crucial to later effective adult life. These included the ability to define a problem, to work in groups to collect and analyze information, to stand in front of the community and present ideas, and to evaluate project results. Moreover, as students applied what they had learned to their communities' problems, the role of schools began to undergo a transformation. Schools started to make a contribution to community development by working with villagers to initiate and evaluate projects to address local needs. School-community relations improved, local knowledge became an important part of teaching and learning, and schools provided important technical information to villagers.

On September 5, 2001, an article in *Education Week* by Jeff Archer brought this project to life in describing a typical experience of students in their study of deforestation:

In a straw hat and rubber boots, 6th grade teacher Vichai Khunnaseangkhum leads his students on a trek up a wooded hill near their school here in northern Thailand. With the help of three local farmers, he points out edible mushrooms and trees that produce dye. The students learn how an empty cocoon can become a thimble to protect fingers while slicing bamboo. Even the biting red ants they try to avoid serve a purpose—their eggs are used in cooking.

Then the forest thins out as the party comes to a patch where, until recently, villagers had cut and burned the trees to make charcoal to sell. New growth is coming back, but a quick scan of the area makes clear the impact of the cutting: fewer edible plants and mushrooms, fewer insects, fewer of anything that could be put to use. It's a lesson no textbook could make more vivid, which is why the teacher has brought the youngsters here.

In a February 17, 1995, email, Chris Wheeler told an even more extraordinary story about a visit to project schools by Bangkok officials and how the pathbreaking nature of the project was brought home to them:

The crowning experience [of my trip] was the visit by Bangkok "Big Wigs" during the last week of our visit. Director-Generals of the departments involved in this project, including the person who determines the K–12 curriculum for all of Thailand, spent two full days visiting all our schools. Let me tell you about the afternoon of the second day.

Picture a small, rural primary school with five sixth grade students coming up to a table to make a presentation about what they have been doing to fifteen high ranking officials from Bangkok and the province and other project schools in the province. Their teacher sat in the audience as they made their presentation.

Imagine our apprehension and the general sense of drama, as the first young girl rose to speak into the microphone, softly introducing her nervous co-students and briefly describing the new kind of teaching and learning they had been using.

Watch the first boy, barely half her height, take the microphone and pick up a pointer as he walked around the edge of the table on his way to a large flip chart. He announced that he was going to show how their way of learning had helped them understand patterns of tree and forest use in the past, and how such usage affected the community's economy and its social structure, including religious beliefs. He was going to conclude with a discussion of how government policies had contributed to the depletion of this important resource by outside businesses and local villagers who had cut down many of the trees. . . .

Now imagine [a third] student, a girl, flipping over the chart to another . . . example, and using her pointer to adroitly describe how the school was working with the village to address some of the problems related to deforestation. The "Big Wigs" could wait no longer. They started asking questions of each presenter. Which were answered completely and, at times, with humor. Then one Director General said, "Well you've had experience asking questions of villagers, do you have any questions for us?" My heart sank. Couldn't we just stop now, when things were going so well? I shouldn't have worried. The students put their heads together and came up with eight of the best questions I've ever heard. For example, they asked the woman responsible for all K–12 curriculum in Thailand to come to the front. After bowing politely, one girl asked, "You've had the chance to see how we learn different subjects by visiting our villages. Do you have a better way of learning?' And handed her the microphone! . . .

Well, the rest of the afternoon was a blur. We talked with other teachers about their projects, chatted with some principals about the kind of support they were providing teachers, and talked with students. But the magic of [the earlier] session lingered on for all those present. The Director of the Department of Curriculum and Instruction captured the afternoon well when she closed the session by saying:

"I've travelled to Japan. I've travelled to Canada. And I've travelled to the U.S., looking for teaching and learning where students are actively engaged in material relevant to their own lives. And I found that all I had to do was travel to Lamphun and Wiang Pa Paw provinces."

The success of this pilot phase in schools of northern Thailand led to a second stage in which UNICEF incorporated the community study component into an expansion of its "Child Friendly Project" with the ministry, starting with 60 and then adding 210 additional primary schools. In addition, the fifth-grade teachers in 14,000 other schools were trained to help students do the sort of community study piloted in MSU's earlier project.[9]

Over the next decade, Ministry of Education staff participating in this project succeeded in infusing this issue-focused community study approach into a range of other projects (e.g., malaria, HIV-AIDS, integrated pest management). By the turn of the century, primary and lower secondary schools in rural areas were therefore more likely to be engaged in community development activities as learning strategies than before.

As MSU work wound down on this Thailand project, Wheeler and colleagues took the lessons learned to Vietnam. Extensive planning for Vietnam work took place in 1997 and 1998 in close collaboration with Can Tho University. Founded in 1966, Can Tho University (CTU) is the leading public university in the Mekong Delta, a region with a population of 18 million (i.e., 22 percent of the country) and the country's most important center of agriculture. Until 2000, CTU was the only university in the region. In addition to units for such fields as agriculture, business, medicine, technology, and law, it included a faculty of education that trained secondary school teachers.

When the rector of CTU, Tran Phuoc Duong, came to MSU in 1997 to receive a distinguished alumni award, this event proved fortuitous in planning a joint MSU-CTU project. Another MSU alumnus on the CTU faculty, Phung thi Nguyet Hong, also played a key role in this planning and remained a principal collaborator throughout the project. These two alumni had received their PhDs over two decades earlier, before MSU's remaining links with Vietnam were broken off in the 1970s.

In integrating school reform in Vietnam with community development in marginalized rural villages, the goals were broader than just dealing with forestry issues as was the case in Thailand. This became clear in 1998 when Chris Wheeler, Jim Gallagher, Maureen McDonough (of the MSU Forestry Department), and Benjalug Namfa (an MSU PhD and our chief Thai collaborator) were invited to Vietnam to start a new project combining school-community collaboration with environmental education and action.[10] The community development component came to include aquaculture, animal husbandry, vegetable growing, and improved use of rice seeds, all financed though development household projects and supported by microcredit funds. The school component focused on promoting the learning of concepts through active teaching methods in the use of school gardens and school grounds, a process that required teachers to work together in a way that was influenced by the participatory mode of teachers' professional development known as Japanese lesson study.

This school and community work was made possible by three interrelated grants from the Shell Foundation, the U.S. State Department, and later the McKnight Foundation. In addition, the MSU provost provided $70,000 to support faculty participation from MSU departments—a very unusual cost-sharing contribution relative to the amount of external funding coming to MSU for the project. The first funding breakthrough took place after much negotiation when Wheeler was able to get funding from the Shell Foundation for Sustainable Communities for a project focused on reducing poverty (including child malnutrition) in very poor rural villages through use of strategies to promote environmentally sustainable practices. The goal was to increase household income in target hamlets by 10 percent more than the average increase for the Mekong Delta. In this project, households were supported in a variety of ways to diversify sources of family income, including projects in biogas, integrated pest management (IPM), organic vegetable gardens, aquaculture, animal husbandry, and integrated farming (e.g., rice-fish and pig-biogas-fish raising). Schools that served children in these villages were called upon to play key roles in expanding and improving the effectiveness of the community development strategies. A subsidiary goal in education was to transform teaching and learning in participating schools from rote memorization to emphasis on concepts and their application. Schools became the catalyst for the introduction and spread of small-scale projects in the areas mentioned above, with MSU and CTU experts from relevant departments acting as advisers. School demonstration projects with organic gardens and IPM rice-growing projects helped parents see the benefits of these activities. As a result, student knowledge and expertise became important resources for the families.[11]

On August 20, 2002, Jim Gallagher, a key member of Wheeler's team, reported enthusiastically to senior colleagues at MSU on one of his trips to a project site:

I am writing this from the bubble of a 747, looking out at the cloudy Alaskan scene. . . . [After a bit more of this scene setting, Jim goes back to describe the beginning of his visit about two weeks earlier.]

After breakfast we took a taxi to the An Binh Middle School which is located a few kilometers outside of Can Tho. There, Chris, Dr. Hong . . . and I each hopped on the back of a motorbike to make the rest of the journey to the site. . . .

Finally we came to a farmer's house which was the site of the class. Twenty grade seven students, four teachers and the agricultural agent were busy at work examining nearly mature rice plants, preparing posters that portrayed them and examples of the diseases that were noted on them. This activity lasted all morning, punctuated by reports from students about their observations and posters, presentations by the agricultural agent and others present, including short commentary by Dr. Hong, Chris and me. . . .

Sunday was equally exciting. We [again] departed at 7 am for Ho An Research

Station. . . . We spent over an hour visiting family organic gardens in the neighborhood which had been developed by the primary school children and their families as a result of the school-based project.

The gardens were impressive. Each is about 20 feet square with very well-manicured rows of vegetables about 2 feet wide on soil built up above the walkways. Pole beans and cucumbers formed an artistic boarder, climbing on the peripheral fences. The harvest was even more impressive. The teachers and children from Ho An primary school gathered our lunch from the garden. One vivid image of the productivity was a teacher holding an armful of long beans (green beans about a foot long) she had picked from the vines on the periphery of the garden. This amounted to about half a bushel of beans. Children and other teachers picked lettuce and other greens for our "hot pot" lunch consisting of noodles, vegetables and locally collected squid all from the garden and the research station. . . .

A garden 20 × 20 feet can feed a family of five on a continuous basis, year round with healthful, nutritious vegetables. This is important in this region of high poverty and poor child nutrition.

The later grant from the McKnight Foundation supported further work from 2008 to 2010. At this point the project was described in a diagram with three circles of activity.[12] The largest circle was for community development through use of microcredit for farmers. The farmers who were selected for credit worked on one or more of the following areas: aquaculture, animal husbandry, vegetable raising, use of more cost-effective rice seed, plus integration of a number of these areas. The second circle focused on schools and educational change. It emphasized the learning of concepts through active teaching methods, including use of school gardens and school grounds. Support from Can Tho University faculty for these practices had changed from working with teachers individually to a collective Japanese lesson study approach for teachers working together to improve their teaching.

The third circle consisted of summer projects involving teachers, students, and community members. The best example of this was an effort to prevent dengue fever, a community campaign launched to teach students and community volunteers how to safely store water and prevent access to mosquitoes and how to eliminate existing larvae. The goal was to reduce the incidence of dengue fever in the fourteen hamlets of Hoa An village. To achieve this, the project used three forms of intervention. One consisted of repeated contacts with all households in the community in order to investigate household conditions and provide guidance on how to prevent dengue fever. Another was to organize student dengue fever prevention clubs at five project schools. This intervention trained students on the causes and prevention of dengue fever and then assigned students to monitor their own homes and a home of a relative once a week to limit the mosquito breeding that causes the disease. Still another third intervention trained teachers to provide extra instruction about the fever and how to prevent it. As a result, the incidence of dengue fever in participating hamlets declined by 87 percent from 2006 to 2009. By the end of 2009, over 90 percent of the households in participating hamlets had been visited at least once by volunteers, monitors, or school club members.[13]

To prepare schools for these ambitious community development roles, the U.S. State Department funded a linkage grant between CTU and MSU. Through faculty exchanges, intensive workshops, and follow-up assistance, this linkage helped CTU faculty in the School of Education to use more interactive methods in training prospective secondary teachers, develop closer links to primary and secondary schools, and improve faculty research skills. In particular this included developing the capacity to use the Hoa An research station for hands-on science and social studies learning of CTU prospective teachers. A major goal for these new teachers graduating from CTU was to use more active teaching methods in their own classrooms.[14]

Wheeler also worked hard to develop further institutional relationships between MSU and Can Tho University outside their schools of education. In May 2003, for example, in a visit to MSU organized by Wheeler, the Can Tho rector met with forty MSU faculty and senior administrators across a range of disciplines. In return, Wheeler set up a reciprocal visit to Can Tho in December 2003 by a high-level MSU delegation (representing. e.g., units under the dean of international studies and programs, the Center for Microbial Ecology, the Department of Civil and Environmental Engineering, the Department of Forestry, and the Department of Geography). Working with Can Tho administrators and faculty, this delegation made plans for collaboration in the following areas: biotechnology, GIS/remote sensing and forestry, administrative capacity building, instructional technology, and English language competency.[15]

By the time Chris Wheeler ended his work in Southeast Asia, having retired from MSU in 2008, this work had served to demonstrate much the same level of capability in international development as TEDS-M had in research. It was another demonstration of what it meant to internationalize a school of education with achievements that could profoundly influence standards of performance for an international dimension throughout the college as well as in other universities with similar interests.

A New Approach to Teachers' Professional Development in Guinea

Another development assistance project that was highly rewarding to me personally in terms of professional accomplishments and satisfaction took place in Guinea in West Africa, funded by the government of Guinea from World Bank funds.[16] It came about because at the end of BRIDGES, I was asked to do some consulting with the World Bank. Ordinarily, I did very little consulting on my own even though MSU policy permitted four days of outside work for pay per month. My interest was not in short-term assignments but in long-term relationships with particular colleagues, institutions, and countries. To be effective in international development, one has to work for a long time to develop relationships and know enough about the country to avoid foreseeable mistakes and unwise decisions. Moreover, the college as a whole as well as the individual faculty members could benefit from this in-depth approach to learning about the educational systems.

But in this case I made an exception to my usual practice. The consulting in Guinea was an opportunity for me to learn more about the World Bank, which had come to play such an important role in developing educational systems. And in spite of my doubts about consulting, I hoped this opportunity would lead to longer-term work. Guinea was of special interest at the time because it was doing better than other similar countries in using its World Bank loans. So we took the chance of starting with individual consultancies for me and my former student Martial Dembélé. Before long there was more work to be done than could be handled in four days a month or less, and that gave us a reason to negotiate an institutional contract between MSU and the government of Guinea to do what was needed.

However, although an important project with many possibilities for crossing boundaries, the Guinean project turned out to have limited impact within MSU's integration-infusion approach because working on it required fluency in French, and I was the only faculty member at the time in our college to have the fluency required. Without this Guinea project, this important region would have been almost totally neglected by our college—an undesirable situation given the importance and priority of African studies across the board at MSU. In the absence of faculty with French language capabilities, we used a consultant team that varied between three and four experts of African origin, plus a Franco-Lebanese finance expert from Brazil.

The project we developed was a way to make good on MSU's overall commitment to international development and the education of all the world's children, as stated in the college's 1984 task force report, and to do this in a country where conditions were especially challenging in virtually every respect—poverty, education, health, transportation, living conditions, and so on. The project was also one that I hoped would help bring students to MSU from francophone countries in Africa, which, to repeat, was a region that our college had had almost nothing to do with. In addition, this project was an example of the importance of faculty competence in languages other than English. As such, it challenged the common assumption among Americans that one can do university work in English virtually anywhere in the world. It helped make the case that the integration-infusion approach calls for faculty competence in all the major world languages.

In spite of such difficulties, this Guinea project, as it developed in collaboration with Guinean educators, turned out to be the source of many lessons for education and development, which could be applied in other countries. It was attractive as a place for experimentation and study because, after disappointing experiences with top-down programs of in-service teacher education, the Ministry of Pre-university Education in Guinea started using World Bank funding in 1994 to experiment with a very different, more bottom-up approach, providing incentives for both professional development and school improvement. The goal was to enable teachers to become partners in improvement of the educational system by initiating and carrying out their own professional development projects. Rather than imposing changes from the top, this program sought to give teachers more professional autonomy. With the help of ministry personnel designated as facilitators, teams of teachers designed projects and competed for small grants to carry them out. The underlying intent was to begin a long-term process to make schools (rather than ministry headquarters) the locus of educational change and thereby redefine the roles of teachers, principals, staff development specialists, and other school administrators.

Each year this small grants competition began with a series of workshops for groups of teacher teams, led by a facilitator. After the facilitator explained how the program worked, the teachers decided what they wanted to achieve and prepared a budget for the supplementary resources they needed (e.g., textbooks, services of resource persons, school supplies for students, reference books for teachers).

Upon completion of a preliminary proposal with assistance from the facilitator, the proposal was submitted to a jury at the level of the prefecture, presided over by the prefectural director of education and composed of local educational leaders. The most promising proposals were then sent back to the teacher teams, along with written feedback from the prefectural jury, for revision with still more help from the facilitator. Finalist proposals were submitted to a regional jury, which made the final decision. This two-step process was intended to reduce the risk of favoritism and provide for wider sharing of school improvement ideas. Likewise, we worked with the Ministry of Education to make the process of transferring money from the central ministry in the capital, to the regional authorities, to the teachers themselves transparent enough to allow the beneficiaries to make a fuss if there was any money siphoned off along the way.

The selected teams were given project implementation support. This included a project launch workshop at the beginning of the school year, close-to-school assistance throughout the project cycle from the project facilitator, and often other resource persons as well, plus three visits by an evaluator.

All these procedures were generated from scratch during the project in collaboration not only with ministry officials at the central level but also teachers and administrators at the local level. The whole process was then piloted in one region before being expanded to all other regions. The pilot centered on the hilly Fouta-Djalon area around Labé and Mamou in the middle of the country. The first planning activities took place in 1994, including a three-week mission that I led to Guinea in May 1994, the hosting of three visitors from the Guinean Ministry of Education at MSU in August 1994, a short follow-up trip to Abidjan in November to meet with other team members, and an initial dissemination activity in Montreal in October 1994 to participate in a Seminar/Workshop on the Methodology of Action Research in Basic Education at the University of Quebec at Montreal.[17]

Then in May 1995, one of the most important activities to launch the project took place, a two-week seminar to train forty ministry regional staff members to work with teachers as facilitators. It was organized by Martial Dembélé and myself, working with Guinean colleagues. The May 1995 seminar took place in Labé, and the "in-class" portions of the seminar were held in the largest auditorium of the Teacher Training College of Labé. In spite of challenging working conditions (hot weather, absence of running water and electricity, dirty toilets), this facility proved to be an excellent location for such events throughout the program.[18]

The May 1995 seminar was designed as a sequence of practical exercises for participants, introduced and interspersed with explanations and discussions of the program, including its philosophy of bottom-up self-education. The first week was devoted primarily to the writing and evaluation of simulated grant proposals using a proposal-writing guide developed specifically for the program. During this first week, the future facilitators were in effect role-playing, taking the part of the practicing teachers they would later be called upon to assist while the national and international team was simulating and modeling the role of facilitators. Once these proposals were written, they were evaluated by simulated juries composed of the national and international seminar leaders, and feedback was given to the facilitators on the proposals they had written. In addition, the role of facilitator was discussed, drawing examples from the small-group work just completed and warning facilitators against being too dominant or dirigiste.

The second week consisted of a second cycle of proposal writing, beginning with a field experience in which each facilitator was assigned to a team of practicing teachers who were recruited for this simulation—thirty-six teams in all. The facilitators went out to the schools to work with these teachers for two and one-half days to explain the proposal-writing guide so that the teachers could then produce a rough simulated proposal. Although, given problems of transportation, this was very difficult to organize logistically, the field experience, still more than the first week, gave a sense for how the program was supposed to work, which would otherwise have been impossible to achieve.

This seminar was well received by the Guineans, leaders, and facilitators alike, in spite of the extremely long hours (with few short breaks) it took to bring it off—8:30 A.M. to between 5 and 6 in the evening for all participants (with no days off), followed by a stock-taking session for the leaders, which usually lasted until 7:30 P.M. or so when it was so dark we could no longer continue since there was no regular electricity in Labé at that time of year (we had a generator but only to run the audiovisual equipment).

The success of this seminar was due in part to the fact that it was a hybrid that brought together in an innovative and productive way diverse elements that were considered important by one or the other or both parties—Guineans with a lot of seminar experience in the country and the international consultants with a different set of experiences. For example, the Guineans were keen to have a lot of structure, specified in advance (even if difficult to put into practice exactly as planned), with precise written instructions for all small-group activities, end-of-the-day stock-taking by the leadership team, formal opening and closing ceremonies, and rapporteurs to give written daily and cumulative reports on every aspect of the seminar. The national team of leaders also put a lot of effort into prepared lectures, which allowed them to give very good explanations of the various aspects of the program, but made them uneasy when various changes were proposed to the seminar during the course of the two-week session. Participants in turn (like the students they had taught) were expected to take detailed, almost verbatim notes. Into these highly organized habits and framework, the international consultants proposed putting emphasis on practical exercises and simulation of program tasks, with the idea of demanding much more self-direction and frank expression of divergent opinions from *all* the seminar participants (not just the leaders) than had been expected in the past. The idea was for the participants to start living with uncertainty and divergent views and not seek to prematurely impose a single presumably correct answer to every question or problem.

As the program developed and expanded to other regions of the country, the level of interest in the program was extraordinary, as shown by the number of teams formed and proposals submitted. During 1998–99 (the fourth year of competition) 755 teams representing about a thousand schools and over five thousand primary school teachers were competing for 240 first-year grants. In total over four years, teacher teams wrote nearly two thousand preliminary proposals.[19] Each year regional dissemination conferences were held for teachers to report on what they had accomplished and learned. After the first regional dissemination seminar held in Labé in summer 1997, a report submitted by Schwille and Dembélé gave a sense of the ambiance of this meeting:

> As one entered the main auditorium in Labe's teacher-training college and voca-
> tional school, one was struck immediately by two rows of tables along the walls.
> As one got nearer, one realized that these tables (or stands) were used to exhibit
> the implementation of the first teacher projects funded in 1996–97 by the Small
> Grants Program. Each table bore the name of one of the 54 teams funded in 1996–97
> and was occupied by a teacher who had in advance prepared a poster showing
> the problem his team dealt with, the objectives of their project and its impact
> on teaching and learning. Thus, one could see on the tables, among other things,
> lesson plans written by teachers, geometric shapes designed with local materials
> by students, audio or video cassettes, student work, results of evaluation tests,
> graphic representation of the school success rate at end-of-primary school exam,
> observation or interview write ups, journal entries, etc.

By the year 2000, when the program had been extended nationwide to all regions, over half the primary school teachers in the country had participated in the writing of proposals. That year, eight regional dissemination conferences were held, one for each region, in which the representatives of teacher teams shared their results with nearly two hundred other participants from the region.[20]

That same year the first national dissemination seminar, modeled on the regional conferences, was held to discuss the results of this program. Fifty of the best-prepared teams of teachers at the regional conferences were invited to the national conference held at the University of Conakry. Two members represented each team. The teams all had their own stand to display artifacts of their project and also had a chance to report on their results in small-group breakout sessions. In addition, four of the very best performing teams were selected to give an overview of their whole project in plenary sessions. The fifty projects covered all the main subject matters of primary school (e.g., reading, French grammar, mathematics, history as well as some cross-curricular aspects of schooling). As we experienced all aspects of the conference, we wondered whether there were any other examples in sub-Saharan Africa where a national conference had been organized to focus in similar ways on the presentations and accomplishments of practicing primary school teachers.

To explain why a seemingly modest and bureaucratic program launched in the West African country of Guinea with World Bank funds attracted such extraordinary efforts on the part of its participants, one of the national leaders explained that it was a matter of their "dignité en jeu," their self-respect being at stake.[21] And indeed so it seemed, since the international consultants attached to the project and I had not experienced in other countries (however well or little developed economically) a comparable project with such a large proportion of participants who were willing to go beyond the call of duty, working hard at times when funds were blocked, often nights and weekends, and lacking what might be considered essential supplies and services (e.g., electricity, transportation, and adequate lodging when away from home).

With such effort and support, the large and complicated Guinea project continued very successfully over the ten years MSU was involved (1993–2002), and was regarded by many as an exemplary project at the World Bank[22] (although toward the end, one influential Bank official turned sour on the project after he visited a few classrooms that did not satisfy him). For me this project was in many ways the most satisfying and rewarding such experience, personally and professionally, that

I had ever worked on. I made twenty-one trips to Guinea from 1993 to 2002, most of them three or more weeks in length. One of the biggest lessons I learned from this was to see how much effort and competence our Guinean colleagues (a total group of about two hundred facilitators, one hundred evaluators, eight regional coordinators, and a few officials at the national ministry) were willing to put into leading the project and how much they were able to do in the face of so many challenges in a country where, inside and outside the Ministry of Education, life was extremely difficult. It was the sort of lesson we felt others in our college should have in learning from work on international development.

But, alas, the goal of longer-term institutional relationships was not to be achieved. Together with our Guinean colleagues, we had developed an elaborate plan for a new round of World Bank loans, which built on what the project had done and incorporated many additional features for school-based management.[23] The plan was very favorably received at the World Bank and helped Guinea get an unusually large loan for the next phase of educational improvement. However, in the end, the Guinean government did not want to continue using World Bank funds to cover the MSU assistance that we judged necessary to make the more ambitious plans work, nor was it willing to make cuts in their plans to reduce the implementation workloads. So in a bitter ending to an outstanding experience, we decided that it was no longer financially possible for MSU to continue in the role that we thought necessary.

Throughout this project, as already mentioned, the expatriates on the project learned a great deal about international development that was relevant to the integration-infusion approach at MSU, although we never succeeded in getting colleagues at MSU to take much interest in it. Lacking that, we were left with the hope that the various journal articles and book chapters about it would have some continuing value to the field.[24]

The Benefits and Frustrations of Continued Work on USAID Channels (Ethiopia, Egypt, Pakistan)

Throughout most of the period covered by this book, we continued our efforts to work through USAID channels of international development and met with continued frustration. We had three large projects in Ethiopia, Egypt, and Pakistan that were terminated prematurely. All were well suited to MSU because of their focus on teacher education. MSU in 2001–2 joined a consortium led by George Washington University (GWU) for participation in staff development for twenty teacher education colleges in Ethiopia. Our role was to work on summer institutes to be organized at the University of Addis Ababa. MSU funding was initially budgeted at $688,373 for five years.[25] From our perspective the project went well in its early stages. In collaboration with several other universities, we were meeting the requirements for improving teacher education in the country. But our main partner, the University of Addis Ababa, got into one of the university-ministry disputes that have been common in sub-Saharan countries. This dispute ultimately led the government to block the program and terminate it. GWU also had limited experience in managing USAID projects and ran into some difficulties in that regard as well.

Since we had a much larger role in USAID-funded projects in Egypt and Pakistan, these projects deserve more consideration as far as lessons to be drawn from the experience. We got these projects because we were one of a very few universities included in the winning proposals for two USAID leader-with-associate awards— EQUIP-1, which focused on school-level interventions with the American Institutes for Research (AIR) as leader, and EQUIP-2 for policy-level interventions with the AED as leader.[26] Leader-with-associate awards were a relatively new mechanism in which consortia competed to win the right to get large USAID projects without further competition. But in this case, the mechanism took a strange turn and ended up more like a cartel. Essentially, three of the most dominant firms in the USAID education business—AIR, AED, and EDC—had been able to get together and divide up the EQUIP business among them. Each not only took the lead in one of the three EQUIP proposals but also became a member of the other two. The additional members of these consortia were also well known in the development world, making the three proposals virtually unbeatable. Subsequently a great deal of USAID funding was put through this noncompetitive EQUIP arrangement. But MSU ended up with relatively little business—not surprisingly, given the market dominance of the leaders and other members of each consortium. Our lead partners felt little need of universities, whose costs were high and whose faculty members tended to find much that they considered wrong with what the consortia were asked to do.

However, Egypt and Pakistan started out as major exceptions. In both cases the AED as the leader of EQUIP-2 came to us, asking us to participate and explaining that it was expected to include a university in the work. Since both these projects were in teacher education, our strongest suit, they were attractive, and we agreed to join the team responsible for carrying out the project.

The EQUIP Egyptian work had been planned as a gigantic project with projected funding for MSU alone at $8 million plus.[27] Both EQUIP-1 under AIR and EQUIP-2 under AED were asked by USAID to take responsibility for part of this Egyptian work. Most of the work was in primary and lower secondary education under the purview of the Egyptian Ministry of Basic Education. Asked to take responsibility for the Faculties of Education Reform (FOER) component, MSU became the only part of this huge project to work with higher education and the Ministry of Higher Education. MSU was also separate in having to put together a field office in Egypt that would be organizationally separate and in a different location from the AED and AIR offices for EQUIP work in basic education.

The first big challenge we faced was the agency's expectation for choosing this office's director. Initially, it was a challenge that seemed impossible to meet. We were asked to come up with a senior American professor, "a graybeard" (*sic*), well qualified and well known for his or her work. This professor would be expected to commit to spending two years in Egypt. At first I said it would be impossible to find such a person, in part because USAID work in Egypt had long had a reputation for being difficult, frustrating, and unsuccessful because, according to the Camp David accords, huge sums of U.S. money had to be spent on education in Egypt whether or not the work was likely to succeed. Egyptian colleagues could be confident that they would get the money even if they were uncooperative and opposed to the work that was to be done. Spending two years on this work was unlikely to be attractive to a successful senior professor at an American university, not to mention the difficulties of simply freeing up such a professor for two years.

But I agreed to try to find someone, and amazingly enough, we did. When my associate Anne Schneller called around asking for recommended persons, she talked to Professor Mark Ginsburg, director of the International Institute for Studies in Education at the University of Pittsburgh. I had known Mark since the 1980s as a prominent scholar and leader in comparative education. In response to our inquiry, he had no promising leads to suggest, but when Anne reported back to me on this conversation, she noted that he had said in a curious way that maybe he should take the job himself. At first we thought he was joking, but Anne said there was something serious about the way he said it. So we called back, and to our astonishment and relief, Mark agreed to be listed in our proposal. Thus, when the work came through, Mark took leave from the University of Pittsburgh and moved to Egypt to head the MSU office. We found him to be an exemplary colleague who did an excellent job under difficult circumstances, proving congenial, patient, and devoted to the work as well as technically competent and well informed. Under Mark's leadership, a small professional staff of Egyptian university professors on leave from their universities was assembled to staff our office. This team was very competent. Particularly prominent was Nadia Touba, a professor from Alexandria who had a strong reputation for her efforts to improve policy on teaching and teacher education in Egypt. She was particularly committed to developing nation-wide standards for teaching. Politically well connected, she once said that if the ministry did not move faster in putting the standards into practice, she was going to go to parliament herself and lobby to get the standards mandated.

In East Lansing, we also found staff members of first-rate competence. Gretchen Sanford (later Neisler) was hired to manage the project at MSU. Highly organized, very perceptive, and with a talent for problem solving, she quickly became one of my favorite colleagues. Betsy Bricker was our second hire as administrative assistant. She came to us with extensive experience on international projects in the College of Agriculture. On the Egypt project, she quickly demonstrated that she could follow USAID's byzantine regulations and produce the budgets and financial accounting required more quickly than anyone I had worked with before in a similar situation.

The project was called upon to mobilize seven university faculties of education with a strategy to improve their capacity to prepare new teachers. The seven universities we were given to work with ran the length of Egypt from Alexandria to Aswan—specifically Alexandria, Aswan, Beni-Suef, Cairo, Fayoum, Minia, and Qena. At each university, we had one liaison professor assigned half-time to provide local leadership. Again we were in luck. This team turned out to be terrific. We were confident that good work could be done.

The plan was to foster leadership development for deans, vice deans, and department chairs; engage the faculties in the establishment and implementation of performance standards for teachers; and improve curricula, assessment, student teaching, and faculty performance—all with an emphasis on working toward more learner-centered instruction and reducing the overly didactic nature of what the faculties had been doing. This work included establishing and maintaining collaborative relationships with primary, preparatory, and secondary schools as sites for teacher education. But the project did not last long enough to make more than a start on this plan.

It was not long before long the project got into trouble with ministry authorities. It turned out that some of what we were required to do had never been cleared by

USAID in advance with the Egyptian authorities. We found that the World Bank had a program that overlapped with ours, and no one was conscious of this duplication until we had made a good start on the work. Moreover, the Ministry of Higher Education wanted to control the project more than USAID regulations allowed, in terms of making detailed decisions about budget and so forth. This dispute percolated along without resolution until a new minister of higher education was appointed. Early on, he had a meeting with the director of the USAID resident mission in Egypt. They got into a big argument over the ministry's attempt to micromanage the project. In retaliation, the USAID director decided to terminate all USAID higher-education projects within a week, including ours! Actually there were only two such projects. Fortunately, although the director of the other project was put on a plane out of Egypt by the end of the week, Mark and our other MSU staff could be reassigned to the part of the EQUIP project that was under the Ministry of Basic Education. However, the project never functioned well after that, and MSU's work came to an end before long. In the meantime, MSU participants in the project had learned a good deal about Egypt and its educational system, and our wonderful Egyptian colleagues seemed to have benefited from the project. Our work during this period, 2004–6, had earned the $2 plus million that MSU received in payment before termination.[28]

It might be said that we did not learn our lesson in Egypt, because just a couple of years later we got into another USAID EQUIP-2 project in Pakistan that took a similar nosedive. Again the consortium leader, the AED, needed a university with strength in teacher education because this project, too, was charged with reforming teacher education. The project was known as Pre-Service Teacher Education Program in Pakistan, or Pre-STEP. MSU was one of three main partners selected to do the work. The others were two nonprofit firms based in Washington, DC: the AED and the Education Development Center, or EDC. Funding for MSU (including its subcontracts) was projected initially in 2008 at $6.9 million.[29]

When the AED first called in 2008 about this project, I was very cautious in responding to the invitation, not knowing whether I could get MSU faculty to go along or whether Dean Ames would let colleagues from our college set foot in a country that had such a reputation for political unrest and violence. I said I needed to consult with our dean and others, which I did, and surprisingly they agreed that we could join the project. But since no one from the AED called back, after a few days I called them. They had already scratched MSU from the list because they thought we were not interested. "Not so," I said. I had just not wanted to mislead them into thinking we would join the effort before I had made sure that within MSU we had enough agreement to participate. As it turned out, the project was easier to staff than I had imagined. We got a good number of excellent faculty members to go to Pakistan. And Reitu Mabokela, one of our most effective higher-education professors, took charge as the PI (primary investigator). It was our first opportunity to give her the major management role that she clearly deserved and which had been on my mind after conversations in which she kept asking for "new challenges." In addition, we hired a person previously unknown to us, but highly experienced as a USAID development specialist, as the on-site MSU leader.

MSU faculty and staff were soon at work to support the Pakistan Higher Education Commission initiative to create a standard curriculum for a four-year baccalaureate of education degree at Pakistani universities. Mabokela and her team collaborated with fifteen universities from Pakistan's four provinces in this effort to improve their training and certification programs for students becoming qualified to teach at the secondary school level. In addition, our College of Education welcomed six doctoral students from Pakistan as an initial contingent of a much larger number who were supposed to be funded by the project. The students turned out to be able and easy to integrate into the college. In fact, funding for such students was one of the most important incentives for us to participate in this project. At this point, therefore, like Egypt, the project seemed to be going well. Like Egypt, we found good colleagues at participating universities to work with us.

But differences developed between MSU and the chief of party for the overall AED project. Part of this argument was over how much MSU faculty would be involved in the on-the-ground work. We had long taken the position that we had no interest in projects in which we could make money by hiring professionals from outside MSU on fixed-term assignments, but where our own faculty were not themselves learning by working on the ground with ministries of education or schools. Although some American universities were open to such a deal, to us it was opportunism run amok since in such cases there would be little benefit to MSU in terms of learning opportunities and capacity building for faculty.

As it turned out, the AED eventually moved in the direction we opposed and decided to make changes in what we were asked to do, reducing our role and influence on the project. In our view, their request constituted an unauthorized change in our scope of work and could be accepted only if there were a written amendment to the contract agreed upon by both parties. The AED disagreed, claiming that the changes were consistent with the existing scope of work. When we stood our ground, the AED terminated the MSU contract, but not before we had received and spent a substantial amount of what had been promised.

In both cases, these two projects had developed in ways which we thought beneficial—excellent local colleagues, progress in collaboration, and moving forward in areas of mutual interest. But both eventually proved abortive through circumstances over which we had little control. Nevertheless, we learned a lot from both projects, made some contributions to the understanding of teacher education in both countries, and prepared ourselves to work in these and similar environments in the future.

Serendipitous Work in Algeria and Lebanon

MSU faculty member Joe Codde's work in Algeria and the Middle East was one of our best examples of how faculty commitment and making a track record in a new location can develop out of serendipitous, chance situations and not from conscious advance choices based on rational calculations. This was a good case of opportunism bringing vision to pass. It started when Joe was at a conference and sitting at a hotel swimming pool where he engaged a stranger in conversation. The stranger was interested to find out what Joe had been doing in the educational technology area, helping teachers learn to use technology in their teaching. This led the stranger to suggest that Joe might be interested in doing some work in Algeria. Joe said he was, and this developed into a grassroots educational project in Algerian schools, beginning in 2006, in which Joe's team worked to help teachers use technology and also to enable classes of Algerian students to connect online with counterpart classes in the United States.

The main problem in this project was the unsettled security situation in Algeria at the end of the civil war between the military and Islamist groups. The schools participating in Joe's project were at times too dangerous to visit. This led Joe to take special precautions and become the College of Education faculty member best prepared to deal with such situations, and one who was willing to share his understanding and to work with others when MSU was faced with security issues. In my experience, faculty members when confronted with risky situations tended be of two sorts, both undesirable, or at least not optimal. There were those who would not hear of going anywhere near a volatile situation. The other group was composed of those who minimized risks and who therefore might not take sufficient precautions. We needed people in the middle, ready to consider any promising work, while at the same time making sure that the risk level is kept as low as possible. Joe was definitely in this middle ground, a person willing to go anywhere if he was convinced that sufficient security precautions had been taken. I hoped that, with Joe's example, those in both of the two camps would learn how to apply such a prudent approach to their own cases. One problem that made this especially difficult was the fact that, when MSU was a subcontractor to another organization that was prime on the project, the other organization was often responsible for the protection of all staff in the field, including the subcontractors. In the case of Algeria, the prime contractor's security office was definitely in the second camp of those who minimized risks, and therefore Joe had to be vigilant not to let them to take him where, in our view, it was too dangerous to go.

The Algeria project was such a success that it led to other opportunities. Codde, who had never done international development work before, even in calm areas, was sought after, especially in the Muslim world. It was in Lebanon that he did the most subsequent work. The Lebanon project was partnership between MSU and the Lebanese American University–Beirut. It created and tested a program to teach Lebanese practicing elementary and secondary school teachers how to use and how to teach with computers in their classrooms. It was modeled after a similar MSU program. The teachers were primarily women and represented all the major religions in the country.

This work in Algeria and Lebanon was a source of pride for me because it took place in two especially challenging countries in which American universities had not often been able to do good education projects.

Teacher Education in Indonesia and Malaysia

Over the years we also did a substantial amount of international development work in teacher education in Indonesia and Malaysia. Although this work was all completed successfully, unfortunately it did not lead to any continuing institutional partnerships. MSU teacher education professor Tom Bird was the main leader for this work in both countries.

In Malaysia we spent several years in the early 1990s trying to develop relationships. We had had a lot contacts through Malaysian students at MSU and visiting scholars. One student, Rajendran Nagappan, a Malaysian of Indian descent who had come to us from the Ministry of Education, was particularly active in helping us to recruit more students and do more work in the country. In September 1993 I made a trip myself to Malaysia at the invitation of the Division of Teacher Education in the Ministry of Education, which was responsible for operating the thirty teacher-training colleges in the country. During the visit I was charged with being lecturer and discussion leader for six one-day seminars, four at different TTCs in the Kuala Lumpur area and two in different Ministry of Education divisions. But my main goal was to move forward on a better linkage between the Ministry of Education and our college and to iron out details for bringing selected ministry personnel to MSU for further training. After this trip, one such person was admitted to the MSU teacher education doctoral program, while another six were scheduled in fall 1994 for staff development at MSU.[30] As a result, six visiting scholars, all lecturers or administrators in teacher-training colleges, participated in a specially designed noncredit program of study for four weeks in September and October 1994. I organized this in collaboration with Teresa Tatto, Anne Schneller, a Malaysian graduate student, and our secretary, Chery Moran. The program focused on planning, delivery, and evaluation of teacher education programs. The first week dealt with design and implementation issues, including conceptualization and the role of research, together with study of the implementation of MSU's new five-year program. The second week focused on evaluation issues in teacher education. Then, during the third and fourth weeks, the participants started to work on individual projects that they could continue after returning to Malaysia. Twenty MSU faculty and advanced doctoral students were involved in leading sessions or facilitating this work (in addition to the organizers). Two years later, in September and October 1996, five teacher educators from Malaysia came for another study visit, concentrating on "helping novices learn to teach through experienced support teachers."[31] But in spite of all this activity, we made little progress in finding a larger longer-term project, for example, one that might have been funded by World Bank loans to Malaysia, and one in which we could have worked with Malaysian colleagues on a continued, longer-term basis.

In Indonesia, the relationship was a little less ad hoc and more organized on a continuing project basis. MSU was selected by the Ministry of Education to participate in a World Bank project for secondary school teacher development. It linked MSU with two Indonesian teacher education institutions, in Padang in West Sumatra and Gorontalo in North Sulawesi. In fall 1997 MSU faculty members Tom Bird from the College of Education and Jerry Cafagna from the College of Arts and

Letters organized a study visit to MSU for eight Indonesian teacher educators for six weeks.[32] Then in January and February 1999 the college hosted two lecturers from Sulawesi to observe in the MSU teacher education program and to meet with MSU instructors and collaborating K–12 teachers. In March of that year Tom Bird offered five-day workshops for teachers colleges at Padang and Gorontalo with an enrollment of twenty lecturers and twenty schoolteachers in each workshop. These workshops were designed to engage the participants in collaborative action research.[33]

Conclusion

Our international development work during the period covered by this book was a mixed success, with some dazzling achievements, on the one hand, and projects that ran into major problems, on the other. Nevertheless, progress had been made on several fronts. That is, the college demonstrated its commitment to advancing the education of all the world's children, its ability to do good work under challenging conditions in resource-scarce and conflict-ridden countries, and a record of value to educational research in general from the scholarship and publication accomplished in these projects. All this was important to making good on the infusion-integration approach.

The Fragility of International Partnerships Needed to Feed Channels of Internationalization

At MSU in recent years, President Lou Anna Simon and others have called for long-term strategic institutional partnerships with universities in other countries. Such partnerships are viewed as key to better opportunities for collaborative research, student exchange, joint degree programs, and so forth. But while the logic of such partnerships is compelling, in practice they are hard to establish and even more difficult to sustain in the long run. They require extraordinary and long-term commitments on the part of individual professors with strong support from university units and their directors/administrators. They also demand very substantial and continued funding. We have had during the period covered by this book various partnerships that were promising at the start but fell by the wayside, plus others that exist currently but do not meet all the criteria for a long-term institutional strategic partnership as envisioned by President Simon. Examination of both the more and the less successful efforts can provide lessons for doing better in the future. Faculty member Punya Mishra is a central figure among the successful examples.

PUNYA MISHRA

Pilani is a tiny village in India, on the edge of a desert and around six spine-crunching, nerve-rattling bus-hours away from Delhi (the capital). Pilani's singular claim to fame is an engineering college and it is there that I (along with 2000 others) lived for four years, as an undergraduate student in engineering. I don't remember much of what I learnt in my classes there (apart from a sinking realization that I did not want to be an engineer). But if there is one thing I have wonderful memories of . . . it is of Tea! . . .

Tea was the axis around which our world revolved. We skipped class to have chai. We ran back from class to have chai. We came for chai in the afternoon and back again at night. Yes we had a lot of tea . . . and not much technology.

I was reminded of chai and what it meant to us as I hear some of the latest rhetoric about online learning. People make a strong case for virtual learning (anytime, just in time, bedtime, tea time what have you). But is it just me or do others also feel a sense of loss as they think of these virtual courses.

These few lines from Punya Mishra's website are enough to teach us something not only about his biography but also about his sensibilities, his disarming lack of pretentiousness, and his knack for looking at everything in his own distinctive way. If you go to his website, you will find much more bubbling up from Punya's well of creativity.

The website contains his vita, which, while framed in more conventional terms, is still far from typical. Punya received his undergraduate degree in electrical engineering (from Birla Institute of Technology and Science, Pilani), his two master's degrees in visual communication (from Industrial Design Center, IIT Mumbai), and mass communications (from Miami University, Oxford, Ohio), and finally a PhD in educational psychology (from the University of Illinois at Urbana-Champaign). Shortly thereafter he was appointed assistant professor of educational technology at MSU. Although it is a rapidly developing field with the promise of revolutionizing education, the term "educational technology" has never done justice to the field that absorbs Punya's many talents and achievements. As a professor he does technology in ways that give him slack to be creative in challenging taken-for-granted assumptions and the sacred cows that have grown up even in this relatively new field.

According to his website, his research has focused on "the theoretical, cognitive and social aspects related to the design and use of computer based learning environments."

In plain language, this has meant that he is as interested in people as he is in machines, leading him to work on what in the local jargon is called "technology integration in teacher education and teacher professional development both in face-to-face and online settings." He has become especially well known for developing a framework (with Matthew Koehler) that he has used for analyzing what teachers know about technology integration. His recent interests, self-described, have focused on teacher creativity and on creative ways of thinking that cut across disciplines, placing emphasis on the role that new digital technologies can play in this process. Punya puts all these talents to work in his love of teaching, for which he has won many awards and accolades. And as if this were not enough, he is also a visual artist, photographer, and poet. It is not surprising that in 2011 the readers and editors of *Technology and Learning* journal named Punya as one of the *ten most influential people in educational technology*.

In short, Punya is celebrated for his U.S.-based achievements, comfortable in his persona as an inimitable, forward-thinking, and never completely orthodox faculty leader at MSU. And as far as internationalization is concerned, India, his home country, is never completely out of the picture. Punya brings the same discerning, critical eye to happenings and the evolution of India that he has brought to the United States. Sharing these insights at MSU, he has made his own unique contributions to our integration and infusion approach. To see India through his camera has helped us understand the state of education and technology in a country that still seems so foreign to so many Americans. Just wandering the streets of Indian towns and cities, he was able to assemble a montage of street advertising and tell a story of unparalleled social change.

Thus, it's not surprising that an especially promising current international partnership of the College of Education owes its existence to Punya—a partnership allowing MSU to work with Azim Premji University and the Azim Premji Foundation in the creation of a new university school of education in Bangalore. It came about because some years ago Punya met top executives of the foundation at a conference in India and was impressed with what they were doing. He found that not only was the foundation in the field influencing the education of several million disadvantaged Indian children, but it was also one of the few foundations that, in developing its program, took research evidence seriously. So after a few years of on-and-off discussion, it was welcome news when the foundation executives came back to East Lansing and told us that MSU was one of two North American universities they wanted to work with because they judged that we shared the same values, including especially a strong commitment to social justice. As a result, a contract was signed for MSU to work with administrators and faculty at APU in developing the programs, curricula, and related capabilities of this new institution, giving MSU faculty with no experience in India (and even little international experience at all) as well as some of our more experienced internationalists the opportunity to start collaborating online and in person with the new faculty at APU. It would never have happened without Punya's ability to attract the attention of some of the most promising Indians on the educational scene and convince them that MSU has not only much to offer, but shares many of their passions and commitments.

Taking a College-Wide Perspective

When we started working on the integration-infusion approach in 1984, the most salient MSU institutional partnership was with the University of Zimbabwe, spearheaded by the African Studies Center and its director, David Wiley. The College of Education was under considerable pressure to do its part in this relationship, and so the history of our partnerships starts there.

The University of Zimbabwe and Other Early Efforts

Our experience from then on shows, if any demonstration is necessary, that unforeseeable political and economic conditions can put an end to any such partnerships, even if all else is going well. For example, the college's commitments to the University of Nigeria at Nsukka fell victim to the Biafran war, and the college's commitments to the University of Zimbabwe no longer proved viable when that country fell into economic and political chaos under the dictatorship of Mugabe. Mugabe, to our lasting embarrassment, had been given an honorary degree by our university during the honeymoon period after independence when the University of Zimbabwe was touted as MSU's most important institutional relationship in the world.

As long as it was working, much good was accomplished through this linkage. For example, not too long after I became assistant dean, Anne Schneller in our office suggested that it would be good for our college to gather together all the faculty members from the University of Zimbabwe who at the time were in North America to study for PhDs in education. Accepting this idea, we organized a conference, "Education in the New Zimbabwe," and asked the participating Zimbabwean graduate students each to present a paper on Zimbabwe in their area of specialization. With editorial help from Anne Schneller, these papers were then published in a book.[1]

In addition, during this period, we formed a special relationship with Cowden Chikombah, then dean of the faculty of education at the University of Zimbabwe. He wanted to spend his sabbatical at MSU, and therefore, with encouragement from our dean, Judy Lanier, we applied for a Fulbright Scholar in Residence award for him. These awards were hard to get, but we got one and were able to host Chikombah for his sabbatical in 1985.

In the same period during the late 1980s, faculty across MSU were going to Zimbabwe to work with colleagues there. My spouse Sharon and I went in the summer of 1988 as external examiners for a teacher education program at the university. This took place after secondary education had been greatly expanded in the newly independent country. The program was therefore a special one to meet urgent needs for teachers. It took individuals with a first university subject matter degree and put them in classrooms and a special university program to qualify them as teachers at the same time. They spent their vacation time at the university in teacher education classes, and also had assignments to complete between these "vacations." My assignment was to validate the assessments given by university staff who had visited their classrooms. In theory, I was empowered to change the grades they had received for classroom performance on the basis of my one observation. I refused to do that, saying it would not be valid to make such a judgment based on a single observation. Instead I submitted my reflections on what I had learned from these observations and discussions with participants about the program. We visited classrooms all around the country, accompanied by Levi Nyagura, a research mathematician who had become chair of the Curriculum Studies Department in the Faculty of Education. He was a brilliant person who always had insightful comments to give the teachers we observed, no matter what their specialty. Later, however, I was surprised and disillusioned when he became the chief academic administrator at the university and a Mugabe loyalist who stayed in that position when others left or were forced out as the government became more repressive.

In 1990, a Fulbright Group Projects Abroad grant enabled Joyce Cain and John Metzler to lead a delegation of U.S. teacher educators for a six-week visit to the

University of Zimbabwe and associated teacher colleges. The participants from the United States represented diverse institutions of higher education; eight of the twelve participants were African Americans. Then in fall 1994 Susan Peters spent her sabbatical at the University of Zimbabwe, with a full agenda: working on a book on special education in Zimbabwe; teaching short courses and tutoring master's students; attending a National Congress on Disability and helping draw up a five-year action plan for disability rights. Five years later she returned to spend most of summer 1999 in Zimbabwe to finish the book (with Robert Chimedza, a University of Zimbabwe faculty member with an MSU PhD and specialization in education of the hearing impaired). It was titled *Special Education in an African Context: Different Voices.* Susan continued along with Anne Schneller and John Metzler to be the mainstay of this University of Zimbabwe relationship as long as it could be maintained in any viable form.[2]

The Heyday of South African Linkages

Thanks to David Wiley, former director of the MSU African Studies Center, and other Africanists at MSU, MSU became one of the early centers of U.S. opposition to apartheid in South Africa. This group pushed the university toward disinvestment, MSU being the first U.S. university to do so. Given this history, as soon as South Africans were allowed to do graduate study in the United States and U.S. universities were able to work with South Africa in the postapartheid era, contacts with MSU blossomed. In our college, leadership in fostering these links was taken by Anne Schneller, John Metzler, David Plank, and others. Moses Turner, after he stepped down as MSU vice president for student affairs in 1992 to return to our higher-education faculty, also took a particular interest in South Africa. He made several visits to South Africa, representing the American Council on Education to help the University of Durban Westville develop student support services. Then in 1995–96, together with Kay Moore, his department chair and noted higher education professor, Turner took part in an international conference in Salzburg, Austria, to review the National Commission Report on South African Higher Education. Then Sandy Bryson, Susan Melnick, Kay Moore, and Moses Turner visited several South African universities to discuss possibilities for offering programs in teacher education and higher education.[3] In 1998, Turner chaired another conference, "Academic Partnerships with South Africans for Mutual Capacity Building." It was cosponsored by MSU, the Committee of Technikon Principals, the Historically Disadvantaged Institutions Forum, and the South African Universities' Vice Chancellors' Association.[4]

During the same period David Plank cochaired MSU's university-wide Action Group on South Africa and also was consultant on educational finance in several South African provinces. Susan Peters visited South Africa to give talks and engage in discussions on education and disability. John Metzler and Anne Schneller went to three universities and the Ministry of Education to prepare for their MSU study abroad program. And Chris Wheeler gave a seminar, based on his Thailand work, to high-ranking Ministry of Education officials from a number of African countries meeting in Johannesburg.[5]

During the 1990s, the strongest MSU institutional linkage in South Africa was with the University of Durban–Westville, historically an institution for people of Indian descent, but one that had moved quickly to embrace the admission of blacks and those formerly classified as "colored" students. One of the most memorable MSU efforts at UDW occurred a few years later when Jim Gallagher and Loyiso Jita (one of our most outstanding South African alumni, then still a student) conducted a three-week seminar on ethnographic research methods for science educators in September 1998. Participants were drawn from universities and teacher-training colleges throughout KwaZulu-Natal province. The workshop included observations and videotaping of classes in schools in the Durban area; interviews with students, teachers, and parents; plus analysis of these data and writing of proposals and reports.[6]

Even though a high point was reached in 1999 when a South African scholar, Reitumetse Mabokela (PhD from the University of Illinois), joined our faculty and was rapidly promoted on the basis of her exceptional accomplishments, in general the extensive South African relationships we had at that point never led to the sort of long-term, strategic relationship with just one or perhaps two universities envisioned by President Simon and others. To the contrary, in South Africa, as in other countries with multiple important centers of higher education, MSU faculty with vested interests and connections in different institutions tended to be resistant to changes that would give what they considered undue emphasis to one institution. In South Africa, where we developed close relations with faculty and administrators at quite a number of universities (e.g., Pretoria, Durban-Westville, Nelson Mandela, Stellenbosch), a consensus in our college on which one to favor over others never developed.

The one near exception is Nelson Mandela University in Port Elizabeth, where an important linkage continues under the leadership of Ann Austin. Ann is another example of how a faculty member can begin international work as an individual, develop this interest and make progress toward a major institutional relationship. When she first joined our faculty, she was already a well-known and highly regarded scholar of higher education. But she had not done international work and was looking for a chance to do it. The opportunity came when she got a Fulbright to spend calendar year 1988 at Nelson Mandela, working on curriculum design, new approaches to teaching and learning, and more generally, the transformation of postapartheid higher education in South Africa.[7] Spending that year with great success and personal satisfaction led her to seek and cultivate continued collaboration with the same university. Since then Ann has returned to Nelson Mandela year after year to work with the central administration on issues of strategic planning, faculty development, and the like. Then in what was institutionally a quantum jump forward for MSU, she started taking a small group of her doctoral students with her to share in this collaboration with South African administrators and faculty members.[8] This is a model that would be good to replicate as much as possible, but, alas, so far it remains one of its kind in our college. It is localized within the Higher, Adult and Lifelong Education (HALE) program and faculty group, and Ann Austin is still the one person who has made it happen.

The Paradoxical Dependence of Institutional Relationships on One Person in the Case of Thailand and Vietnam

South Africa reflects the fragility and often temporary nature of such partnerships. In that case as in other countries, the faculty members involved can leave without being replaced. Opportunities change in terms of a match of MSU faculty interests and the agendas of the host universities. Thus, on the whole, the MSU College of Education has generally not been able to form institutional partnerships that have lasted ten or more years at an intensive level. In the shorter run, however, we have had some great successes as well as partial ones. A key to the institutional relationships that were most successful in the short run has been paradoxically the wholehearted and passionate commitment of a single faculty member like Ann Austin or Chris Wheeler to create and sustain mutually beneficial relations. In the College of Education within the period in question, Chris is the best example of how these relationships can depend on a single person. The college's work in Thailand and then in Vietnam over the last twenty-five years can all be traced to Chris's leadership. He started to work on BRIDGES in Thailand without any previous experience in the region, but once involved, he turned out to be instrumental in developing a funded linkage agreement in 1989 with Chulalongkorn University, the most prestigious Thai university. This led other faculty to get involved as well. In 1990–91, for example, the second year of this USIA linkage grant with Chulalongkorn University, Chris Wheeler, Bill Schmidt, Mary Kennedy, and Lauran Young all made extended visits there.[9] In return, three Chula faculty were in residence at MSU during the spring term. After this Chula linkage, Chris moved on to a series of environmental education efforts in the North that involved other Thai universities. Then, with these demonstrated accomplishments in Thailand, he moved to establish ties with Can Tho University in Vietnam, an even more successful linkage that drew in other faculty members not only from our college but from other MSU colleges as well. As a result, Can Tho has been regarded as one of MSU's most important relationships.

Azim Premji University, a Potential Breakthrough

In principle, a huge country like India should be a place with large numbers of promising institutional linkages in higher education, but until recently our faculty had done relatively little work there.[10] That changed when Azim Premji University in Bangalore gave us the opportunity for the sort of long-term institutional relationship we had long sought. Billionaire businessperson and philanthropist Azim Premji, twice one of *Time* magazine's one hundred most influential persons in the world,[11] established and funded this new university and gave unprecedentedly large gifts to his foundation. This took place within the last decade, when he first increased the assets of the foundation by $2 billion and only two years later by another $2.56 billion. These gifts came from the fortune he made by transforming Wipro, a vegetable oil company he inherited, into one of the world's most successful software companies, headquartered in Bangalore. Wipro is noted not only for making money in the very competitive world software industry but also for its integrity in operating without paying bribes, which is unusual in India. In recognition of his lifelong accomplishments as well as the MSU-APU partnership, Azim Premji received an honorary degree in and gave the main address at the MSU commencement ceremony for undergraduates in 2014.

To be able to work with this foundation in the creation of a new university of education in Bangalore and have it fund our partnership is, as one of our doctoral students put it, a once-in-a-lifetime opportunity for participating faculty and students. In February 2013 Sharon and I went to Bangalore, the thriving ICT capital of India, to see the university for ourselves. We spent three weeks doing our own work while meeting with faculty and giving seminars. During the second of our three weeks, we were joined by four other MSU colleagues: Punya Mishra, Leigh Wolf, Ann Austin, and Kris Renn. Punya and Leigh did a short course on the psychology of motivation for the Azim Premji students, while Ann continued her ongoing discussions on matters related to faculty development. Ann also organized with APU colleagues a colloquium on excellence in teaching. Sharon took responsibility for one of the sessions in this colloquium, where she argued for the importance of seeing work with teacher education students in their field experiences as an important form of teaching that deserves as much reflection and specialized expertise as any other type of teaching. For my part, I did a workshop to discuss some of the areas that faculty were said to be wrestling with: how to move forward on their personal research agendas, how to do research writing in a way that would be effective and yet fit with their personal style, how to find time to do research, how to think about collaborating within research teams, and how to work with Premji Foundation staff and practicing educators facing the challenges of education in disadvantaged settings in India.

In preparation for what I would be doing, I looked into who the recently recruited Azim Premji faculty were and how they thought about their work. Some were senior faculty with much higher-education experience and strongly felt views on all aspects of a university, while others were people with recently completed PhDs in India, the United States, and other countries. There was even an especially strong subgroup of persons without university faculty experience, even without PhDs, but who had remarkable records in various NGOs and other agencies doing education and development work. Some came to the university from the Azim Premji Foundation, where they had worked with the field on more pragmatic programs and interventions. But while there was great diversity of backgrounds, specialties, and interests, each of the faculty members had in various ways shown commitment to the university's goal of promoting social justice and equity in India in all that they do. Thus, in my view, the biggest achievement so far at APU is the recruitment of a superb group of faculty in terms of their experience and commitment to addressing issues of social justice. Here are a few examples from the APU website, consciously selected without too much cherry-picking.

- Anu Joy has a PhD in Science Education from the National Institute of Advanced Studies, Bangalore. Her research is in the area of Cognitive Ethnography of Science learning. She holds an MSc in Physics and works with children on science learning projects. She is involved in developing research based curricula and pedagogies for meaningful learning of science in schools. Prior to her PhD, she worked as a Researcher in the area of Nuclear Magnetic Resonance Spectroscopy at NMR Research Center of IISc, Bangalore for two and a half years.
- Anupama has an MSc in Mathematics and has also done her MEd She has eleven years of experience in teaching Mathematics for higher classes in the Aditya Birla School, Kumarapatnam, Karnataka; three years of experience as a teacher trainer in The Teacher Foundation, Bangalore. She has worked on teacher development and teacher support, by conducting workshops, observing classes and giving needed support in teaching for the teachers.
- Trained in urban and rural community development from the Tata Institute of Social Sciences, Benson Issac has been working in the development sector for over 12 years. During this period he has been associated with child rights issues, anti-communalism initiatives, has worked for Greenpeace as a climate change campaigner and also worked as a faculty member in social work at St. Joseph's College. . . . He has done extensive work in sensitizing and mobilizing youth around social change, trained youth in alternative livelihoods and contributed to developing the body of knowledge around youth studies.
- Bharath Sundaram's current research interests include resilience of social-ecological systems, global change and livelihoods, and the long-term monitoring of social-ecological systems. Bharath's doctoral research centered on a non-native, invasive plant called Lantanacamara in a peopled forest landscape in Karnataka India. In addition to having significantly negative effects on native biodiversity, Lantana also affected tribal livelihoods, and presents an ideal context to explore issues like sustaining livelihoods linked with forests, co-management of forests affected by invasive species, and adaptive management.

- Chandan Gowda worked as Associate Professor of Sociology at the Centre for the Study of Social Exclusion, National Law School of India, Bangalore, after earning his PhD degree at the Department of Sociology, University of Michigan, Ann Arbor, in 2007. He obtained an MA degree in sociology from the University of Hyderabad in 1996 and a PhD Certificate in Cultural Studies from the University of Pittsburgh in 1998. He is presently completing a book on the cultural politics of development in old Mysore state. Besides academic publications, he has written for newspapers and published translations of Kannada fiction and non-fiction in English. His interests include social theory, caste, Indian normative traditions, ethnography of law, Kannada literature and the media, especially Kannada cinema.

Wouldn't any American university be fortunate to have some of these faculty? Their diverse strengths explain, in part, why MSU faculty members who have visited APU are enthusiastic about this new institution. For such a new university, the progress that has been made in such a short time is hard to believe. Part of the reason is excellence in leadership. Anurag Behar and Dileep Ranjekar were CO-CEOs of the Azim Premji Foundation who led the effort to establish the new university and reached out to MSU and made multiple visits before they were convinced that a partnership was in order. Anurag is now the vice-chancellor of the university. He spent much of his career as a leader in the high-tech world of Wipro and has the look of Mr. Silicon Valley in the jeans and sweater he ordinarily wears for work and travel. Don't be fooled! An APU visionary, he is in reality an Indian through and through, totally devoted to the future of his country. To the realization of his vision he brings intellect, charisma, charm, and an unyielding belief in what education can do for social justice.

Since the university was established, still another leader has played a key role in the MSU-APU partnership, S. (Giri) Giridhar, who now bears a heavy responsibility for keeping the university running. Interpersonal connections between these three and Punya have proved critical in making the partnership what it has become.

What it has become, as viewed from the vantage point of the visit that Sharon and I made in 2013, plus follow-on events like the honorary degree for Azim Premji, has given me even still more confidence in the future of this new institution. From my often expressed point of view, APU enjoys an important competitive advantage over other schools of education throughout the world. This advantage stems from the fact that organizationally APU is under the same umbrella as the field operation of the Azim Premji Foundation, which works with so many disadvantaged schools in a number of Indian states and has field units at the district and state levels. Thus, the university is in a position to collaborate within this now well-established infrastructure in new ways without all the obstacles often faced by schools of education that want to do innovative work on the ground with elementary and secondary schools in other parts of the world.

Moreover, proof that the Azim Premji partnership is ideally suited to the integration-infusion approach has come, at the time of this writing, in the form of an initiative of Wipro Limited, Premji's worldwide information technology company. Wipro, a company of Indian origin, has a policy of social responsibility that leads it to make grants in the countries where it works, the United States being one. In 2014, it collaborated with MSU to launch the Urban STEM and Leadership Fellowship program with a $2.8 million grant. The aim of the yearlong fellowship is to enable math and science teachers in urban K–12 schools of Chicago to create innovative and transformative instructional experiences for their students. Thus, for perhaps the first time at MSU, a company from outside the United States has made a major investment in U.S. domestic education, completing the interactive cycle of mutual benefits called for by the integration-infusion approach.[12]

Collaboration with Irish Universities on Issues of Disability

As this book was being written, the college's most successful institutional partnership was developing in ways that we had never been able to match in earlier efforts. It is actually not in education per se, but in rehabilitation counseling, which at MSU is part of the College of Education. According to *U.S. News and World Report*, the college's graduate programs in rehab counseling have ranked as number one or two in the country.

This partnership is a welcome example of how the integration-infusion approach can add up to more than the sum of its parts. It started out, not as an institutional linkage effort, but instead as the result of working with one extraordinary international student and one innovative study abroad program, followed by an international conference that became the catalyst for firming up the partnership. The international student in question was Sister Martha Hegarty, an Irish Roman Catholic nun who came to MSU in 1987 to do a master's degree in rehabilitation counseling. This nun has devoted her life to people with intellectual disabilities, becoming a pioneering leader and leading advocate in the field. She belonged to the Daughters of Charity, who have worked in Ireland for over one hundred years to improve conditions for persons with intellectual disabilities. Ultimately, she became the director of RESPECT, an organization formed by the Daughters of Charity to provide services to this population.[13]

Sister Martha did not spend as much time at MSU as she had hoped. She was forced to return to Ireland to take charge when a building for persons the sisters served was condemned as a fire hazard. The order had to find other housing immediately for the short term and develop new housing for the long term. Still, Sister Martha was at MSU long enough to develop a special relationship with Professor Mike Leahy, director of the MSU Office of Rehabilitation and Disability Studies and one of the most prominent scholars in his field, author of more than 150 refereed journal articles, books, book chapters, and research monographs.

It was Mike who had the idea and organized the study abroad program that became the second key step toward the unprecedented partnership that exists today. The study abroad program began in 2007. Titled Disability in a Diverse Society, it was intended, on the one hand, to expand study abroad opportunities for students with disabilities and, and on the other, to examine disability issues from an international perspective. It combined coursework and service learning during the trip to give students a transformative experience. Ireland was an appropriate location for this because it has a "universal design" policy that frames disability as a natural aspect of life.[14]

This study abroad program led to discussions of organizing an international conference on implications of technology for persons with intellectual disabilities. This conference, cosponsored by MSU and Daughters of Charity, resulted in the formation of a collaborative research partnership. This partnership, known as the Daughters of Charity Technology and Research in Intellectual Disabilities (DOCTRID) is now supported by all universities in the Irish Republic as well as in Northern Ireland. MSU has been a main partner from the beginning. DOCTRID enjoys the support of a very wealthy Irish financier, Dermot Desmond. It has also received an $11.3 million grant from the European Union to fund forty postdocs. At least five of these postdocs have been allocated to MSU. In addition, in support of this partnership, MSU has a Hegarty Fellowship program that funds several additional research fellows.[15]

Carolyn Shivers, one of the DOCTRID postdocs who has been featured in the college magazine, *The New Educator*,[16] received her doctorate from Vanderbilt in developmental psychology. She was quoted in the magazine as saying, "This was my dream post-doc." Her aim in the postdoc has been to develop a program in which siblings undertake interventions to teach social skills to brothers or sisters with autism.

In short, DOCTRID is an unparalleled network devoted to serving persons with autism or other intellectual disabilities. The focus is on the use of assistive technologies to make their lives better.

Conclusion

Although experience has shown that institutional partnerships are fragile and difficult to sustain, there have been successes, and the current efforts with Azim Premji University and with Irish universities are more promising than earlier efforts at MSU. The key here, as in other areas, seems to be patience in waiting for opportunistic chances to connect with and build on other channels of internationalization in ways that can be qualitatively different and better than what has been done before.

Lynn Paine with colleague Joe Tobin from the University of Georgia, author of *Preschool in Three Cultures*, a book she and others have used for internationalization at MSU (with permission of Dwi Yuliantoro, photographer).

Teresa Tatto, principal investigator for the landmark TEDS-M study, with Mark Reckase, distinguished psychometrician on that study who worked closely with Teresa (with permission of Dwi Yuliantoro).

President Clinton visiting the Michigan legislature, shown with MSU research leader Bill Schmidt (*right*) and Michael Cohen, leader of the educational reform organization Achieve (*left*) (with permission of William Schmidt).

Two Vietnamese boys studying plants in one of the school gardens that were of such importance to the work of Chris Wheeler and colleagues in the Mekong Delta (with permission of Chris Wheeler).

Chris Wheeler (*in bare feet*) and Vietnamese teachers discussing the concepts underlying integrated pest management (IPM) (with permission of Chris Wheeler).

Azim Premji was twice named one of the one hundred most influential persons in the world by *TIME* magazine. Here (with Jack Schwille and Punya Mishra) he is shown at MSU after receiving an honorary degree for his record as entrepreneur, philanthropist, and educational leader (with permission of Punya Mishra).

Jack Schwille, Martial Dembélé, and a local school superintendent crossing the Niger River in Guinea on a ferry on the way to a project meeting (with permission of Jack Schwille).

Professor Mike Leahy and Sister Martha Hegarty (*left*) with participants in MSU study abroad program in Ireland focusing on issues of disability. Leahy and Sister Martha, beginning when she was an international student at MSU, have gone on to create an unprecedented MSU institutional relationship with all the universities in the Republic of Ireland, plus Northern Ireland (with permission of Michael Leahy).

Sally McClintock, founder of LATTICE, at a party in her honor when she gave up her position in charge of the project. The man to her left is the brother of Qasim Al-Shannag, one of the students profiled in this book (with permission of Kurnia Yahya).

Motasem Sayaheen holds the book of Jordanian short stories for young readers that he had reprinted at his own expense in order to make the book available to LATTICE members and Lansing area schools (with permission of Dwi Yuliantoro).

Steve Backman, whose previous international experience led to his selection as the first doctoral student to lead a college study abroad program, is shown here during the time he spent doing dissertation research in Lesotho (with permission of Steve Backman).

MSU student teacher in front of South African class during the college's Preinternship Teaching Study Abroad Program (with permission of Margaret Holtschlag).

Dean Carole Ames (*left*) with Dean Patricia Wasley of University of Washington (Seattle) on one of the initial visits that paved the way for doctoral study visits and other ventures in China (from MSU College of Education Photo Library).

Lynn Paine and Margo Glew (*both back row center*) at school in China with MSU teacher preparation students, members of the Global Educators Cohort Program (from MSU College of Education Photo Library).

Lynn Paine, Yong Zhao, Jack Schwille, and doctoral student Aaron Bodle in 2010 all-college planning meeting to discuss the future of college work on China. Bodle was, of all the MSU doctoral students, one of the most ardent advocates of internationalizing U.S. education. Dean Carole Ames, also at the meeting, is not in this picture (with permission of Dwi Yuliantoro).

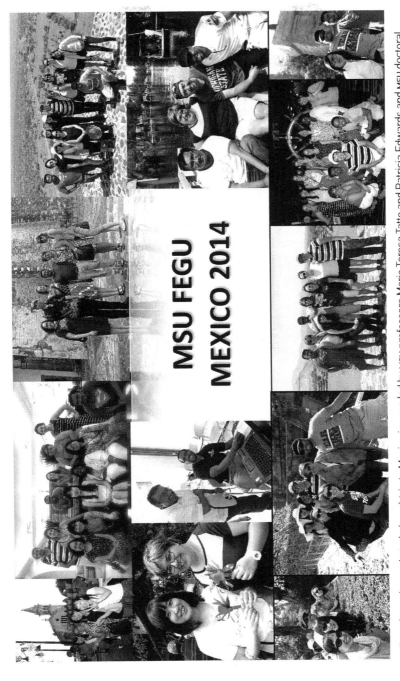

Collage from doctoral study (FEGU) trip to Mexico in 2013 led by MSU professors Maria Teresa Tatto and Patricia Edwards and MSU doctoral student from Mexico Abraham Ceballos (with permission of Iwan Syahril).

Yong Zhao speaks at Conference on Internationalizing Michigan K–12 Education while colleagues Barbara Markle, conference organizer, and Mike Flanagan, superintendent of public instruction for the State of Michigan, look on (from MSU College of Education Photo Library).

Leaders of the Wipro-funded MSU teacher development project in Chicago: Leigh Graves Wolf, MSU; Sonya Gunnings-Moton, MSU; Anurag Behar; and Punya Mishra, MSU. Anurag Behar is a former executive at Wipro, the company that grew to be a global software giant under the leadership of Azim Premji. Currently, Behar is vice-chancellor of Azim Premji University, which has become a major partner of the MSU College of Education (with permission of Punya Mishra).

Irfan Muzaffar, exceptional teacher educator noted, among other things, for his op-ed contributions to newspapers in his home country of Pakistan, is here being hooded by Professor Helen Featherstone in PhD graduation ritual (from College of Education Photo Library).

Norseha Unim (Malaysia), Kamila Rosolova (Czech Republic), and Dwi Yuliantoro (Indonesia) at potluck in the college for internationally oriented graduate students (with permission of Dwi Yuliantoro).

Anne Schneller at a reception in her honor after she received Distinguished Academic Specialist Award, and Kurnia Yahya, a doctoral student from Malaysia much appreciated for her enthusiasm and her numerous contributions to the integration-infusion approach (with permission of Kurnia Yahya).

Faculty for 2003 summer session at GSEO center in Valbonne, France. *Front row*: Patricia Edwards, Bruce Burke, and Michelle Johnston; *second row*: Bob Floden, Maenette Benham, Steve Koziol, and David Pimm. All were tenured MSU faculty except Johnston, a PhD alumnus with adjunct assignments at MSU. At this time Burke was director of GSEO, to be succeeded later by Susan Melnick (*below, left*). Norris (Sandy) Bryson, longtime program manager of GSEO is shown below, right (with permission of Susan Burke and MSU College of Education Photo Library).

Anne Schneller working with South African students during Preinternship Teaching Study Abroad Program she codirected (with permission of Margaret Holtschlag).

MSU conference coordinator Inese Berzina-Pitcher (*right*) and volunteers Robert Coffey (*left*) and Kaliamma Ponnan (*center*) behind staff registration desk at CIES in Chicago 2010 (with permission of Dwi Yuliantoro).

Preparing the Ground for Channels of International Content and World Languages in K–12 and Teacher Education

From the 1980s on, schools of education in the United States have faced demands to do more to prepare teachers to deal with international matters in K–12 and to help K–12 schools internationalize in other ways.[1] But this movement for internationalization of teacher preparation, professional development, and school practice initially had little effect on education schools, and the criticism continued unabated. MSU was no exception in this regard, even though internationalization for K–12 teachers and schools was advocated in the 1984 task force report. In fact, the executive summary of this report made a daunting recommendation in that regard:

> The College should introduce international content into the education of professional educators through developing exemplary programs of teacher education with an international orientation; through identifying, using, and supporting courses throughout the University which have an international focus; through reconceptualizing its own international courses to provide content appropriate to overseas students and educators and designed to assist them in applying their U.S. education to their home situations; through searching out opportunities for field study and dissertation research overseas; and through endeavoring to introduce

competence in international matters into school curricula, teacher certification, and teacher training accreditation.[2]

This was the most difficult part of the 1984 report to act upon, and for a long period of time we were not able to accomplish much, even though external pressures continued to push us to do more. It was hard to get faculty members to take this shortcoming seriously. The internationalists in the college were preoccupied with other international work, while other faculty and their K–12 collaborators typically lacked the experience, knowledge, and motivation needed to be effective in meeting the challenge of this type of internationalization. Nevertheless, starting in the 1990s a number of breakthroughs took place—all opportunistic in some respects although visionary in others—carving out new channels of internationalization potentially affecting many teachers and students in K–12.

The first major success in this area was LATTICE (Linking All Types of Teachers to International, Cross-Cultural Education), which was started by Sally McClintock, a well-known and highly respected area K–12 educator from outside the college.

Taking a College-Wide Perspective

The earliest programmatic effort to respond to the demand for internationalization of schools of education took place in the 1980s when a proposal for internationalizing teacher education at MSU was submitted to the U.S. Department of Education under Title VI, Undergraduate International Studies. To our delight, the proposal was funded—one of the very few funded proposals in this competition from a school of education, perhaps the only one up to that time. This project was for internationalization of specific MSU teacher education courses and for strengthening of foreign language opportunities for teacher education students. But in the end, the results were not good, and the project was a disappointment. This small project did not generate enough of a faculty commitment to make much of a difference. Mainly it taught us how difficult internationalization could be outside fields like history and geography, where it had been inherent to the development of these disciplines. Elsewhere, efforts to internationalize were not perceived as opportunities to increase the capital of faculty without international qualifications.

SALLY McCLINTOCK

Our first breakthrough in K–12 internationalization came when Sally McClintock, having just retired as a principal in East Lansing, came to the College of Education with an idea for a new initiative in international education. She had been making her way around the university and so far everyone had said her idea was excellent, but no one wanted to be the first to help her put it into practice. The idea was to form a professional development group of MSU international students and Lansing area teachers. Sally wanted to do this because she had been able to spend two years on sabbatical with her MSU faculty spouse in Poland and China, and felt it had a huge impact on her as an educator. Realizing that international experiences could bring more global perspectives into U.S. classrooms, she concluded that if all teachers could not have sabbatical experiences, the next best thing was for teachers to develop long-term relationships and engage in meaningful conversations with persons from other countries. This would give them a vicarious experience with a similar impact. Based on the promising nature of this idea and Sally's credibility as an educational leader in the Lansing area, I knew right away that this project was going to work. I told Sally I would help. And now twenty years later, LATTICE is still going strong, even though its founder is no longer with us. The project has survived in spite of not having had substantial external funding and therefore remaining completely financially dependent on local resources from the school districts and university.

Sally's original ideas continue to be at the core of LATTICE. As a senior school district administrator who belonged to LATTICE told us: "LATTICE is a personal experience that changes the way you look at people and the world."* Actually LATTICE has proved to be a much greater success than we expected at the beginning. Not that our expectations were small.

The reason Sally's concept seemed bound to work was, in large part, because she was totally committed to it, willing to spend extraordinary amounts of uncompensated time on it, drawing on her social capital and credibility in Lansing area schools stemming from her earlier career as a successful K–12 teacher and administrator. If anyone could create a new space for internationalization, she could. She was a perfectionist who devoted so much time to LATTICE that her perfectionistic ideals were almost entirely realized in practice. No detail escaped her notice. At planning meetings, she steered the group to consider all aspects of upcoming monthly meetings in detail. She made clear the expectations of LATTICE to participants—they had to commit to regular attendance and stay to the end of each meeting. She reminded members that doctors' appointments and the like could be scheduled at another time. For the most part members observed these constraints, and those who failed too often could expect a diplomatic reminder.

During the monthly meetings, Sally was good at making sure the timing of the agenda, often laboriously worked out in the planning meeting, was followed as well. One of Sally's firm convictions that became dogma for the group was that time had to be allowed for small-group discussion, which would allow the international students and teachers to bring their own perspectives to whatever was being discussed—usually the topic was introduced in a talk by university experts who typically had an irresistible urge to talk longer than Sally and the planning committee had envisioned or wanted. Her technique when speakers went on too long was to sidle up close to the speaker when time was about up and just stand quietly until the speaker got the message and stopped. Rarely was a more explicit message necessary.

Although these discussions were the main entrée served at LATTICE, Sally made sure the other rituals were observed and respected: celebrations of births and marriages, usually with a small gift to mark the occasion; sending of cards to members to express congratulations, condolences, and so on; the continuation of a name ritual in which members (especially new members and guests) got a chance to explain their name, write it in national script, tell what it meant and why it was chosen and who chose it. The food break at LATTICE also went beyond the ordinary custom of members bringing refreshments to the ritual of bringing food of special significance to the person who brought it, either because of family history, holidays, or just personal favorites—the offerors had to stand behind the table and explain what they had brought.

After leading LATTICE successfully for ten years, Sally decided it was time to give up this role, though she continued to be active as a member of the project and always kept in touch with many of its former international members. Conscious that many projects that are the creations of and dependent on their founder fail to make the transition successfully to new leadership, Sally worked carefully within the group to avoid this trap. Among other things, a number of retreats were held to strengthen the organization and be more explicit about its aspirations, best practices, and needs for support.

Although Sally fell ill suddenly in 2011 and died a few months later, her influence on LATTICE and as a consequence on the college at large continues, and is often mentioned by those who knew her best. She was celebrated for having taught for many years and then becoming a very successful and respected elementary school principal. But it was LATTICE that ultimately sealed her reputation for being, as her obituary said, "a force against narrow-mindedness, ignorance, and prejudice, and a force for peace and understanding." But, although LATTICE became a highly regarded project that got awards, it could not by itself be sufficient as a way for the college to work for internationalization in elementary and secondary education. Given the pressing need for more international understanding in teacher education and K–12 schools, more was called for. For another breakthrough we had to await the arrival of faculty member Yong Zhao and the beginnings of his collaboration with Barbara Markle, director of K–12 outreach in the college.

NOTE

* Reported in support letter from Dean Ames attached to nomination of LATTICE for MSU Diversity Award, January 27, 2005.

YONG ZHAO and BARBARA MARKLE

This breakthrough got rolling when Barbara teamed up with Yong Zhao to get Michigan K–12 educators to learn about China. Putting together his strong relationships in China with hers in Michigan, they organized a study tour to China in 2005 for the executive directors of all sixteen Michigan education associations (school boards, superintendents, principals, teacher unions etc.). It was a tour de force, an extraordinary success, after which participants asserted it had changed their view of the world. In fact, the impact of this study tour influenced several members of the State of Michigan Board of Education to join a subsequent study tour the next year. Together, those who had benefited from this first study tour concluded that many more educators needed experiences of this type. And more study tours there were, all organized under Barbara's direction with advice and advisory participation from Yong.

The two leaders who came together and turned the college around in this way had backgrounds as different as could be imagined. Yong Zhao came to MSU as a new PhD with a U.S. doctorate in educational technology. Although he was originally from China, his graduate studies had not given him any notable strength in comparative and international education. Barbara Markle was assistant dean and director of K–12 outreach in the college. Born and educated in Michigan, she had become a high school teacher, counselor, secondary school principal, and central office administrator in Michigan's second largest school district before she moved on to the state's Department of Education. She was the first woman appointed to be deputy superintendent of public instruction, with leadership responsibility for Michigan's education reform initiatives. Hence, when she later joined our college, she built on this experience and concentrated on relationships and collaboration with state government and K–12 districts, always with a strong emphasis on advancing reform. She had no mandate initially to work on international education.

Yong Zhao, too, was hired to continue his innovative approaches to educational technology, not to advance international education or work in other countries. He started at MSU as an assistant professor of educational technology in 1996, directly after completing his PhD at the University of Illinois, Champaign-Urbana. As an assistant professor he demonstrated that he could get large grants while publishing a great deal in reputable academic journals. He was the founding director of MSU's Center for Teaching and Technology, which was instrumental in helping college faculty and graduate assistants learn to use more advanced technology in their teaching.

Although Yong Zhao's degree was not in comparative and international education, it took little more than a decade after coming to MSU for him to become known around the world for his vision, his leadership, and his achievements in international education. He became an internationally noted scholar and author. His works focused on the implications of globalization and technology on education. He designed special schools to cultivate global competence, developed computer games for language learning, and founded research and development units to explore innovative education models. During these years at MSU he published over one hundred articles and twenty books, including *Catching Up or Leading the Way: American Education in the Age of Globalization* and *World Class Learners: Educating Creative and Entrepreneurial Students*.* He was a recipient of the Early Career Award from the American Educational Research Association and was named one of the ten most influential people in educational technology by *Tech & Learning* magazine in 2012.[†] By 2005 he had become the youngest University Distinguished Professor in MSU history.

In addition to these scholarly achievements and his creative projects, Yong built and maintained his reputation as one of the university's most in-demand speakers.

Because of his commitment to reaching as many people as possible in realizing his vision of global education, he made himself available to go almost anywhere—from rural Michigan to the cosmopolitan centers of Latin America to speak to audiences of the most diverse sort. Drawing on his down-to-earth sense of humor, lack of pretentiousness, and general goodwill, he showed that he could relate effectively to any of the stakeholders of American education as well as to their counterparts worldwide.

In short order, then, Yong Zhao had become a very hot item in the academic marketplace. This was his key to getting increasingly and heavily involved in international work. Since he was heavily recruited by other universities, he had leverage to get Dean Carole Ames to agree to most of the creative and innovative ideas he came up with. Previously, she had not wanted him to do any international work on grounds that this would interfere with our rapidly developing capability and ability to get grants in educational technology. But soon, with his quickly earned clout, his work moved on to include not only contributions in education to his home country, but also encouraging Americans to learn Chinese and to have the chance to experience Yong's home country itself. All this expressed Yong's growing passion for and work on the idea that U.S. colleges and universities (as well as counterparts in other countries) should do more to prepare young people for global citizenship.

Although Yong Zhao rapidly became well known in countries around the world, his MSU international leadership was initially concentrated in the linkages he created between MSU and institutions in China. For example, in 2004 only eight years after he earned his PhD, he was chosen to organize a major Asia Pacific Economic Cooperation (APEC) nineteen-country education summit in Beijing. This experience helped him obtain a large grant from the Sunwah Foundation of Hong Kong, which led in turn to the U.S.-China Center for Research on Educational Excellence at MSU and other important China initiatives, of which the best known at present is the MSU Confucius Institute, with its emphasis on online learning.[‡]

Yong's leadership was also responsible for creating bilingual immersion schools for preschoolers and students in early primary school in both Michigan and China (these schools are now known as schools that provide Education for Global Citizenship, or EGC).[§] In these schools, students spend half of every school day in Chinese-speaking and the other half in English-speaking environments. Initially Yong was instrumental in establishing one such school in Beijing under sponsorship of Sunwah Foundation. Another was created in the city of Lansing, Michigan, at a public school—Post Oak

Elementary School. It is Yong's firm belief that this sort of program is a key to global citizenship. In his view children, by being immersed in two such different language and cultural environments, acquire the cultural adaptivity and flexibility that will enable them to adapt more readily to other cultures later on.

Yong's astonishing career started in China, where he was born in a rural village in Sichuan province, where neither his family nor other villagers had previously experienced formal schooling. Nevertheless, Yong excelled in school, moving rapidly up the ladder of primary, secondary, and higher education at the undergraduate level, ultimately coming to the United States for his master's and PhD degrees.

Barbara Markle, for her part, first came to Erickson Hall not for the College of Education itself, but for the Michigan Partnership for New Education, an independent organization funded in the Judith Lanier era to sponsor state-level reforms in schooling and teacher education. When the Partnership moved away from the college, Barbara stayed. As the school reform movement grew throughout the late 1990s, a need arose for a way connect researchers with school practitioners with a focus on improving teaching and learning. As a result, the college established an office of K–12 outreach, headed by Barbara, for that purpose. But she still had no international responsibilities. Instead she devoted herself to a wide variety of projects to improve Michigan schools, and even today such projects constitute the largest part of her work. She won many grants to develop and implement programs for teachers, school administrators, and policymakers, bringing educational research to bear in schools and settings where educational policy is made. For example, she was in charge of organizing educational policy forums for state legislators. Overall, her work focused on teacher and administrative leadership with a goal of bringing about the redesign of American high schools.

But in fact Markle has been committed to internationalization of U.S. K–12 schooling for a long time. For example, while still a practicing educator in the Utica, Michigan, she led a group of high school students on a visit to the Soviet Union—at the time a challenging initiation in managing international education if ever there was one.

In short, Yong Zhao and Barbara Markle were able to work creatively together to help K–12 schools incorporate global perspectives into their curriculum and teaching as well as to facilitate internationalization within the college itself. Yong's interests remained diverse, but he was increasingly focused on a single vision, which was to advance the cause of international understanding and help young people throughout the world become the sort of global citizens who can meet the growing challenges of globalization. He has very strong ethical commitments to hold this all together, including, in particular, a belief that we must value and meet the needs of all children wherever they are (not just in our own country). His were the passions, beliefs, and actions that we hoped for in the 1984 task force report. Ultimately, in a big disappointment for us, he left MSU in 2010, accepting an offer from the University of Oregon that gave him more discretionary opportunities for internationalization and for getting the funding that these opportunities require. He currently serves as the Presidential Chair for Global Education in the College of Education, University of Oregon, where he is also Weinman Professor of Technology and professor in the Department of Educational Measurement, Policy, and Leadership.[||] But in spite of this move, his impact on the MSU College of Education continues to be felt.

Although Yong Zhao is gone, this has not stopped Barbara Markle from continuing the work they started together as well as new initiatives of her own. For example, through her position as assistant dean she has established a partnership with the United Kingdom's Specialist Schools and Academies Trust (now called SSAT). Within this partnership, Barbara has led many United Kingdom study tours designed to give the participants familiarity with the English educational system as well as knowledge of effective strategies for school turnaround. These strategies have transformed underperforming, high-poverty schools into high-performing schools in low-income areas of the United Kingdom and London, in particular. Thus, these study tours have given participants a deeper understanding of coherent strategies that could be used in Michigan's underperforming urban schools.

In addition, Barbara's office supports a group of master's degree students from China each year for a nine-month educational and cultural experience at MSU. Included is a traditional Thanksgiving dinner that Barbara hosts for the students at her home. In short, Barbara Markle continues to be a force for internationalization within the college and in the K–12 sector, providing strong leadership through periodic Michigan internationalization conferences, exchanges with China, and international collaboration on school reform.

NOTES

* Zhao, 2009, 2012 (although the latter book did not come out until after he left MSU).

† Zhaolearning.com

‡ www.experiencechinese.com.

§ http://experiencechinese.com/index.php/programs/immersion.

‖ http://education.uoregon.edu/users/yongzhao.

Slow Progress in Internationalization of College Courses

Progress remained slow even though MSU's transition from a quarter system to a semester system in the 1990s created unprecedented openings for courses with more international content. This change passed by only one vote when submitted by the provost to the university faculty for approval. But once passed, it was momentous. It required changing every course in the university to reflect the longer period of study. It was likewise a great opportunity to introduce new courses and programs. In the College of Education, this opportunity was used to put in place a completely new five-year teacher education program with a one-year internship. It was the culmination of reform efforts led over the previous decade by Dean Judith Lanier.

These opportunities during the semester transition to make changes to existing courses and propose new courses produced a flurry of interest in internationalization of the curriculum. But in the case of the College of Education, this opportunity produced a lot of talk, but relatively little action, together with some major disappointments. One proposal was developed by an internationally oriented group of faculty under the leadership of Mun Tsang, an economist of education. They put together a proposal for a special all-college master's degree tailored to the needs of international students and internationally oriented American students.[3] This was in response to a situation in which the master's programs offered at that time were not well adapted to the needs of international students and their educational systems. The MSU programs were targeted instead on professional development needs of practicing teachers and administrators in U.S. schools, whereas the international clientele for master's degrees tended to be instead persons destined for careers in teachers colleges or ministries of education. However, this proposal died under the prevailing pressure at the time for less proliferation of master's degree programs in the college. In another initiative, an ad hoc committee representing each of the four college departments was formed to foster internationalization of the new semester courses. Some of these courses have continued successfully to the present day, but an interdepartmental graduate specialization, pulling together these courses, plus others outside the college, died without being put into effect.

It was also at that time that a transcollegiate course looking at the nature of childhood from a cross-national, multidisciplinary perspective was proposed. Transcollegiate courses (TCCs) were a category of courses that had become part of the new integrative studies (i.e., general education) requirements for all undergraduates at MSU. Under the new requirements, each undergraduate was to take one TCC as the final step in fulfilling the university's general education requirements. The rule was that each TCC had to be interdisciplinary and developed collaboratively by more than one college to address at least one of a number of themes. The list of themes included *international studies*. These courses could not be counted toward majors; the intention was to bring students together across colleges in courses to finish off their general education. It was a large order. To be implemented successfully, enough of these courses had to be offered to accommodate an entire yearly cohort of undergraduates—some seven thousand students at MSU!

Unlike other colleges across campus, Education took this new requirement seriously. The new requirement was not only consistent with the integration-infusion approach, but offered the college a way to gain additional student credit hours without overloading existing college courses. Therefore, we went quickly from a course that existed only on paper to one of the first two such courses in the whole university to be authorized and put into practice.[4]

Thus it was that in spring 1994 a TCC course titled Growing Up and Coming of Age in Three Societies was piloted by education faculty member Maenette Benham and graduate assistants Marty Germain, Scott Johnston, and Naihua Zhang. It focused on childhood and adolescence in China, Japan, and the United States. Each of the teaching assistants brought to the course extensive experience and study of either China or Japan. The course included content from the humanities and the social sciences delivered in pedagogically innovative ways. For example, in the pilot, students produced a course newspaper and a museum piece emphasizing visual and decorative arts, were trained to be student leaders in discussion groups, and observed and analyzed various cultural events, such as a tea ceremony and tai chi. Then, in 1994–95, TCC 305 was taught for the second and third time in two quite different versions. In the fall, under Maenette Benham, the course was organized holistically around countries, focusing on China, Japan, and the experiences of Chinese Americans and Japanese Americans in the United States. Benham herself was a Native Hawaiian and had grown up in Hawaii. Lynn Paine the following spring took another approach; her course was organized not by country but around four key points in the life cycle: birth, entrance to day care or school, adolescence, and transition to adulthood.[5]

Since this was one of the first courses developed to satisfy a university-wide requirement, it was expected that it would grow rapidly into a large course taught by multiple faculty and a substantial number of teaching assistants. But this never came to pass. The other colleges remained resistant to this requirement, sitting on their hands and doing virtually nothing to develop the additional courses needed to accommodate anywhere near the seven thousand students who would need to take them. For a while the College of Education, for its part, stuck with TCC 305. On May 6, 1996, my annual report to Dean Ames noted that TCC 305, though marginal for lack of students, was to continue.[6] We kept it alive, pending further decisions about the TCC requirement at the university level. Maenette Benham and Lynn Paine remained committed to the course, and we could have recruited others if we had needed them. Maenette taught the course with twenty-six students in spring 1996.

Finally, the central administration, instead of enforcing this mandate, gave up and did away with the requirement. TCC 305 was converted into an education course, but after being taught a few times, disappeared from the schedule for lack of students wanting a course that no longer met any requirements. However, the course did continue in a new environment; it was well suited for use in study abroad programs that dealt with education in particular countries.

For further evidence of how strong resistance to internationalization could be, as Bourdieu might have predicted, one has only to examine the history of the proseminar required of all entering doctoral students in the teacher education department. For years, this course was taught by faculty who, though outstanding, lacked a strong background in and commitment to internationalization. Instead, the first term of the course was devoted to the history of American education as a means of understanding the multiple purposes of public education and in particular the idea that public education was one of the pillars of democracy in the United States, albeit an unsteady one. But the course always included a substantial number of international students—up to one-third or more of thirty or so students. I pointed out, whenever I had the opportunity, that the U.S. history as taught in this course was only one small part of the spread of mass education, which had started earlier in Europe than in the United States and then eventually took the form of an international consensus on the goal of "education for all." In principle, the course could have been readily redesigned around this movement, which constitutes one of the most important social changes of the last two hundred years. But it was not. And when the Department of Teacher Education distributed reading lists to help doctoral students prepare for comprehensive examinations, there were virtually no works with a focus outside the United States. When faculty were invited to review this list, I recommended books with such a focus, but they were not added.

After some years when the proseminar was focused almost entirely on the United States, there was hope for a change when Lynn Paine and Brian Delany were invited to teach it. And indeed they attempted to internationalize it, not with fragments of international content, but instead by building in a contrast between China and the United States throughout the course. But when they moved on to other teaching assignments, resistance to these changes came back, and this far-reaching attempt at internationalization was dropped.[7]

Internationalized Courses That Did Take Hold

Courses in comparative education had existed in the college before the semester transition. They were survivors of the comparative and international education degree programs abolished in the early 1980s. In fact, my first opportunity to teach comparative education came in 1979 when I was asked to take over a course taught for years by Karl Gross, a foundations professor who had retired. The course he taught was titled Education in the Western World. As developed by Gross, it was a conventional comparative education course, with one exception. That was a field trip to London, Ontario, to learn about education in that province and how it differed from the States. When I did this trip in fall 1979 and then again the next time I taught the course, it was a good experience not only for the students but for me as well.

By the time I taught this course for the second time in fall 1980, I organized it around four themes to bring coherence and some depth: (1) comparative school organization, (2) comparative socialization, (3) social stratification in education and attempts at democratization, and (4) education and national minorities. In short, the course was traditional in highlighting issues in comparative sociology of education without the emphasis on educational practice that emerged in the integration-infusion approach the college adopted later.

After the semester transition, in addition to the specialized courses throughout the college that were candidates for infused international content, we offered a number of courses with an international focus that presumably could have been taught in any university offering comparative education. Three of these courses were offered by the Department of Teacher Education, which had an especially strong multidisciplinary foundations faculty. One (TE 923, Comparative Perspectives on Teaching, Curriculum, and Teacher Education) was a doctoral course on the list from which PhD students in the department had to choose. This course was most often taught by Lynn Paine. More recently Lynn also taught a follow-on course, Advanced Topics in Comparative Education.

In addition, there were two master's level offerings that could also be taken by PhD students. One was TE 815, Comparative Analysis of Educational Practice, and the other TE 816, Education in Transition, in which faculty could offer a variety of topics as long as there was an emphasis on educational and social change. Both of the latter courses I taught, and when I taught TE 816, I always focused on the relation between education and democracy, a theme that allowed for discussion of various meanings of democracy, the state of specified understandings of democracy in the world, the study of democracy in schools, and empirical study of what students were learning about democracy and related matters in school (as in the IEA civic education studies).

In the Department of Educational Administration, EAD 813, Education, Development, and Social Change, was first developed and taught by Mun Tsang and David Plank, and then more recently by Amita Chudgar. Toward the end of the period of this book, there was further progress in the area addressed by that course when the College of Education began cooperating with the MSU Department of Economics in offering a specialization in economics of education, thus providing opportunities for more depth and more students with strengths in international development.

In the courses I taught (TE 815 and 816) I tried to use topics with research and readings that would be of interest to practicing K–12 teachers as well as aspiring PhD researchers. These courses were also a foot in the door in trying to convince colleagues and students that all graduate students in education could benefit from such courses, and, fortunately, in their evaluations a number of students themselves made this suggestion. In spring semester 2008, when TE 815 focused on secondary schools, which were a hot topic at the time, I made a particular effort to make the course material a matter of college-wide discourse. The course was organized around the theme "The world's secondary schools: how much do they differ and why?" in order to examine and critique the video documentary *Two Million Minutes*, which was produced in part to influence the presidential election campaign and was getting a lot of attention in the press. Several sessions in the course were opened to the public, as explained in this email sent June 3, 2008, to all college faculty as well as to our listserv of internationally oriented students:

> The next public session in my TE 815 course on "The world's secondary schools: how much do they differ and why?" will be held tomorrow, June 4, 4:15–5:45, in 222 Erickson Hall. This session will focus on French secondary schools and follows up on last week's class on Germany led by Sigrid Blömeke.

Tomorrow our fellow faculty member Kyle Greenwalt will share data and insights from his dissertation study in which he collected interview data from students in a French lycee or upper secondary school. His study deals with the relationship between nationalism, schooling and collective memory. After grounding his study in a wealth of earlier research and theoretical thought, he analyzes the narratives from his interviews. His purpose is to analyze student experiences that "shed some light on the processes by which French national identity is reproduced." . . .

In general, France offers a remarkable contrast with Germany which we discussed last week. Germany retains differentiated secondary schools starting in grade 5 whereas in the half century following World War II France, like most other European countries, moved from such a differentiated system to a more comprehensive lower secondary school. TIMSS data analyzed by Bill Schmidt and colleagues has provided evidence that the French school at this level is now more egalitarian and less tracked not only than Germany but also than the U.S. Please join us in this discussion.

Other special sessions were held along similar lines, including one session focused on Chinese students and their secondary school experience, and one on Korean students.

Sally McClintock and the LATTICE Breakthrough in K–12 Internationalization

Sally McClintock's idea became our first real breakthrough in K–12 internationalization—an excellent example of an opportunity for opportunistically realizing part of our vision.[8] A report of March 26, 1995, described the proposed project as a pilot project to demonstrate and evaluate how a study group composed of about half K–12 American teachers and half international students would give the teachers an international perspective that would influence their classroom practice. It was an effort to bring together for the first time two promising developments: (1) the power of teacher study groups to transform teacher thinking and practice as demonstrated by research in our National Center for Research on Teacher Learning (NCRTL); and (2) the use of international students as resource persons to enrich K–12 teaching practice. The 1994–95 academic year was spent planning the pilot program for the following year, using an All-University Outreach Grant.

The basic assumption of the project was that getting to know international students on a continuing, in-depth basis in a study group would change the American teachers' thinking in ways that short-term workshops were not able to do. We knew from educational research that teacher study groups could be particularly effective as a professional development strategy. Some years after the project was launched, two student members of LATTICE, Elena Papanastasiou from Cyprus and Paul Conway from Ireland, did an empirical study starting to assess this approach to professional development. It documented some of the benefits as reported by teachers and was published in the journal *Studies in Educational Evaluation*.[9]

LATTICE never had the advantage of substantial external funding. Instead, the university and school districts provided the necessary financial and in-kind support. The group met once a month during school hours for four hours (with the districts hiring substitutes for the teachers). During the monthly meeting, participants engaged in cross-cultural study and discussion of cultural identity, language and culture, childhood, school, families, and work, all as set in larger cultural and historical contexts. The diversity of LATTICE was illustrated—just to take one example—by the twenty-two countries represented at a regular meeting in September 2003: Brazil, China, Cuba, Czech Republic, India, Iran, Israel, Japan, Jordan, Korea, Malawi, Malaysia, Myanmar, Nepal, Palestine, Singapore, South Africa, Taiwan, Ukraine, United States, Uzbekistan, and Vietnam.

A particular advantage of all teacher study groups is that the participants are seen as the principal resource. These are not top-down professional development activities, nor are they driven by external experts. LATTICE's most important resource consisted of the experiences and cultural heritage of international students from many countries and the ability of American teachers to draw upon their own diverse experiences and to connect with international students in ways that could influence their own approaches. To put this conception into practice, all sessions were planned in a collaborative, nonhierarchical way by a team of about ten or so persons. It included international graduate students, local K–12 teachers, and MSU faculty or staff.

Sally McClintock liked to say that LATTICE was not a short term-fix based on one-shot or occasional interventions, a series of "make and take" workshops, primarily curriculum development, or more of the sort of professional development that teachers had found lacking in the past.[10] Instead the significance of LATTICE was expected to emerge from personal perspectives, discussion, and stories as expressed by participants, sometimes in light of what an invited expert had said and sometimes without any intervention from the outside.

Presentations were carefully scheduled so as not to take time away from small-group discussions and other activities. Experts were asked to accept this constraint when invited to share their knowledge of such diverse topics as world hunger, stereotypes about Africa, the African diaspora, nutrition in early childhood, U.S. foreign policy, environmental education in Thailand, treatment of death in different cultures, intercultural interactions, gender and economic development in Latin America, international perspectives on refugees, the state of civic education as revealed in a study of twenty-eight countries, and teaching and learning in China.[11]

As LATTICE developed, there was increasing support for the LATTICE belief that personal stories were one of the most powerful ways to help members connect with the thoughts and experiences of others, to become more aware of and sensitive to the diversity in the world and, for the teachers, in their own classrooms. These stories were especially significant when they contained what might be called a LATTICE moment, a critical moment when something was said or done in a LATTICE meeting by an international student that was so unexpected, striking, and memorable that it had an immediate impact on the way participants thought about the issues involved.

The nature of LATTICE discussion changed over the years. At first the emphasis was mostly on family life and cultural traditions. In general, these were topics that people from diverse backgrounds could talk about easily in a positive way. This served to build warm feelings within the group; LATTICE participants bonded and became a community. This allowed us to move on to more difficult, sensitive issues, such as race and gender, at first in terms that did not challenge the group too much, but thereafter with increasing depth and candor. Gaining confidence in one another, participants became more frank and willing to bring up matters about which all would not agree, particularly in the area of religion and politics.[12]

This effort turned out to be very timely after the attacks of September 11, 2001. LATTICE then spent multiple sessions on related issues, and especially on efforts to understand Islam better and to create better relationships between Muslims and others in our community. For the October 2001 session one month after the attack, Omar Soubani, who was chair of the board of directors at the East Lansing mosque, came to talk to the group. At the same session a panel of six LATTICE Muslim members answered questions about their faith.[13]

During such sessions we addressed some very sensitive topics that would have not been likely to be discussed in other venues (e.g., how is a terrorist different from a freedom fighter; under what conditions, if any, is racial profiling justified). In one session I moderated a panel discussion on the war in Iraq and its effect on LATTICE members, which led to heartfelt sharing of feelings and experiences. This discussion included one relatively new Lansing-area teacher who had been threatened with dismissal for talking to students about her involvement in antiwar activities. In another session that dealt with refugees, I was asked to help the group understand why a student from a Palestinian refugee family had the right to talk about her feelings of injustice.[14]

During this era a Jordanian couple (Motasem and Rana) became very active and enthusiastic participants in LATTICE and made exceptional contributions to this dialogue. They combined conservative Muslim practices with very outgoing and gregarious personalities and were therefore able to relate easily and well with people from other religions and nationalities. Their commitment to LATTICE was demonstrated one year when Motasem went home to Jordan for about a month. He was asked to bring back a book of Jordanian fiction in English translation that would be appropriate for children or adolescents and could be discussed in the LATTICE book club. It was not easy to find such a book. Motasem went to great lengths searching for a book and ultimately found a collection of short stories that seemed perfect, except that it was out of print. Motasem did not give up. He used some of his own money to help get this book reprinted, and then brought back enough copies not only for the book club but also to donate to the libraries of all the schools represented in LATTICE.[15] Subsequently, an Israeli couple arrived and played a similar role in LATTICE. Both the Israeli and Jordanian couples volunteered for the LATTICE planning team. Both participated actively and constructively in frank discussions of the Israeli-Palestinian conflict, the Iraq war, and terrorism.

In addition to the monthly sessions, LATTICE went on to generate all sorts of spin-offs.

Classroom Visits by International Students

MSU had had a long history of one-shot visits by international students to Michigan schools to talk about their home country. Although those visits had their place, visits by LATTICE members who already knew teachers well and had enjoyed much shared experience together were even better, for the teacher and the student could work together more easily in planning how the international student's experience and knowledge best fit into the teacher's curriculum.

Lattice Book Club

LATTICE members with seed money from Teach for Tolerance, Southern Poverty Law Center, started a book club that, in addition to the regular monthly sessions, met to discuss international children's and adolescents' literature and how it could be used in the teachers' classrooms. One memorable example was *Sadako and the Thousand Paper Cranes* by Eleanor Coerr,[16] where the strong initial appeal of the book to most of the American readers was counterbalanced by criticisms from three participants of Japanese or Japanese American origin.

Production of Video with Guidelines for the Replication or Adaptation of Lattice in Other Settings

Several school districts and units at MSU provided funds and in-kind support to make it possible to document the LATTICE approach to K–12 internationalization and include guidance for others to replicate it. The video was produced with leadership and technical expertise of one of the teachers at Haslett High School, one of the schools most involved in LATTICE. This teacher was known for his leadership in the school's award-winning cable TV channel, which broadcast sports, music, and other events at district schools. Once produced, the video was distributed widely, including all 120 federally funded Title VI international area studies centers at U.S. universities.[17]

Based on earlier experience by LATTICE leaders in South Africa as well as our South African students, a number of the spin-offs focused on that country.

Exchange with Teachers and Students in South Africa

LATTICE undertook its first effort to provide experience abroad for mid-Michigan K–12 teachers in 1999, when a Fulbright-Hays Group Projects Abroad award took fifteen educators from the mid-Michigan area for six weeks to visit schools and communities in Cape Town, Durban, and Richards Bay. The LATTICE members enjoyed visiting and teaching in schools, living with South African educators and their families, discussing history and politics with university experts, and experiencing a pilot South African LATTICE session with over one hundred participants. Journals written by participants plus notes from debriefing sessions documented what the teachers had gained from this Fulbright experience in terms of new knowledge, new personal relationships, new perspectives regarding race, ethnicity, gender, and class in South Africa, and deeper interest and understanding of these same issues in the United States. Following this Fulbright-Hayes trip, LATTICE went even further in bringing a group of thirteen racially diverse, middle school children from the Richards Bay area in South Africa to Michigan in an exchange that enriched the learning environments of LATTICE Lansing area schools.[18]

In 2003 LATTICE got to play host to one of the most extraordinary students it had sponsored in South Africa, the teenage poet Sibongeleni Zulu. Sally McClintock first met him in 1997. At that time he was a twelve-year-old who was already writing poetry in his personal journal. This was a boy who had lost one of his eyes in an accident and could not see well until LATTICE members arranged for an eye exam and glasses. LATTICE also paid his school fees. By 2003, he was studying mechanical engineering at the Durban Institute of Technology. While in Michigan he got to read his poetry at several mid-Michigan schools; visit MSU, Lansing Community College, and General Motors, as well as several churches; and meet with LATTICE members from twenty-two countries.[19]

Zulu Baskets as a Vehicle for Michigan Teacher Learning

This spin-off started when LATTICE got a grant from the Kellogg Foundation to bring two Zulu basket weavers from South Africa to the Lansing area to be artists in residence in local schools for three weeks. During that time LATTICE members learned that in northern KwaZulu-Natal province many parents were unable to pay the costs of their children's education. Among them were basket weavers who produced extraordinary work but could not earn money because there was no market for the baskets. This led Sally McClintock and other LATTICE members to launch a project to purchase baskets from Zulu artists and sell them in Michigan to pay the school fees.[20]

MSU's Preinternship Teaching Program and Other Study Abroad Programs in South Africa

Again building on LATTICE linkages, MSU's College of Education took about twenty MSU undergraduates in both 2000 and 2001 to South Africa for a credit program on education and society in that country. This program led to a still better program allowing students who had just received their bachelor's degrees at MSU to coteach in South Africa for six weeks in the summer before they began their required fifth-year internship in Michigan.[21]

Over the years, through its main sessions and spin-offs, LATTICE generated very strong commitments on the part of international students and teachers who bonded to the project and to one another.[22] When one of the leading LATTICE teachers, Margaret Holtschlag, became Michigan Teacher of the Year in 1999–2000 (and one of five finalists for National Teacher of the Year), she gave LATTICE credit for being the most important influence on her teaching.[23] In an article she had written earlier, she gave a striking example of why this was so, based on the life of an MSU student from Burundi:

> When Marie told about her home in Burundi, I forgot about myself completely as she told of a recent visit when she discovered that many people in her town had been murdered in the civil war. We saw her grief and her courage, and we wanted to know more.
>
> Marie's story came to mind many times throughout the following month. I wondered about Marie's reaction to the sensational news stories that clutter our newspaper while only small paragraphs mention the conflict in Burundi. I see Marie occasionally at school, as she supervises teacher interns, and we have become friends. She has joined my class in several lessons, including a simulation of the immigration process through Ellis Island. My students reacted at first with confusion, then understanding, when Marie took on the persona of an immigrant who could not speak English. Just as she had done for me with her story of home, she helped them to see their lessons through another's eyes.
>
> Instead of viewing the world from only my perspective, each LATTICE discussion challenges me not only to question my assumptions, but to view this world through another's eyes.[24]

Throughout the years in which LATTICE took place, the participating school districts demonstrated their conviction that the program was worthwhile professional development by paying for a substitute for each of the teacher participants for one afternoon per month. The university likewise made an unusual financial commitment to this project. A number of university units including the area studies centers and the dean of the graduate school provided substantial financial support year after year to cover, for example, modest stipends for the students so that there would be an added reason for them to attend the sessions consistently. All of this would have been insufficient to ensure the success of LATTICE, however, had Sally McClintock not been willing to volunteer her time without compensation—an indication that this work never quite acquired the university legitimacy that could have ensured full budgetary support.

The China Breakthroughs Engineered by Yong Zhao with Barbara Markle and Others

In the first ten years after Yong Zhao joined the college, his international outreach mushroomed in various ways even as his domestic work prospered as well. In particular, he moved onto the world stage by becoming active in the education activities of APEC (the Asia Pacific Economic Cooperation Forum) and then being called upon to organize the APEC Education Summit of 2004 in Beijing. This leadership led him to Jonathan Choi, a Hong Kong billionaire with philanthropic interests in China and elsewhere. In 2004 Yong received a major grant from Choi's Sunwah Foundation, a first step toward giving the college's China work a solid organizational and financial base. Initially, the grant underwrote the establishment of the U.S.-China Center for Research on Educational Excellence at MSU. In the beginning this center concentrated on developing a clearinghouse for exchange of education information between the United States and China and facilitating educational relationships between the two countries.

In February 2004, the center convened a four-day conference at the Skywalker Ranch in Northern California, which drew together thinkers who could generate creative, transformational ideas for school design. Following up on this conference, the U.S. China Center at MSU continued work on what became a network of early childhood, lower elementary schools now known as EGC, or Education for Global Citizenship, schools. The initial curriculum for these schools was designed by a team of experts from the United States and China, working at MSU. In 2005, the first EGC school was launched as the 3e International Kindergarten in Beijing, China, with the children spending half their day in an English-speaking environment with teachers using a Western approach, while the rest of the day was devoted to teaching and learning in a Chinese-speaking setting with teachers from China. In 2006, the second EGC school opened in Lansing. The philosophy of these schools is described on an MSU website:

In the EGC Schools model, we have combined the best of both Eastern and Western pedagogy in a learning environment that immerses students in both languages and cultures. This blending allows children to move between different cultures, languages and educational philosophies as part of their school day. In the Western classroom, students will be immersed in the English language and a child-centered learning environment. In the Eastern classroom, students will be immersed in a Mandarin Chinese language and a knowledge-centered, teacher directed environment.[25]

Now the 3e website contains a set of extremely positive parent testimonials for the school. Here are two examples:

Example A: When I arrived in Beijing, I looked at more than twenty different schools, both local (Chinese) and international. There is simply no other program like 3e, which is the only truly bilingual international school in Beijing. With 3e, we get the best of both worlds: full immersion in the Chinese language taught by Chinese teachers, and a first-rate international education. After two years, our son is now fluent in both English and Chinese, neither of which is his native tongue. Add to that the beautiful facilities, the caliber and dedication of the teachers, and the small class size . . . you just can't find that anywhere else in Beijing.

Example B: We came to China in 2011 when my children were 5 and 7 years old. None of us spoke or understood a word of Chinese. Thanks to 3e's curriculum that is fun, creative, interactive and effective; my children are now fluent in Chinese. In two short years, my children can also read and write Chinese characters. My eldest is even reading chapter books in Chinese! The English portion of the curriculum is equally fantastic. The teachers inspire learning and expertly integrate real-world problem solving skills. I feel strongly my children have blossomed at 3e in ways that they could not have at schools back home in the United States.[26]

Another major advance came in 2006 when the college, through Yong's efforts, was awarded one of the Confucius Institutes then spreading throughout the world to foster learning of Chinese language and culture. MSU-CI was the first online Confucius Institute in the world and the eighth Confucius Institute in the United States. Early on, it was selected as a Confucius Institute of the Year for three consecutive years, 2007–9. Although since then Confucius Institutes have become more common as instruments of Chinese cultural outreach and diplomacy, the MSU institute has remained unique in the extent to which it has worked online in teaching Mandarin to Americans. It pioneered in the first use of native Chinese speakers to tutor American learners online at a distance from China. According to its website, it was also the first to offer online Mandarin courses to high school students. These courses, known as "Chinese Your Way," were designed for students to work through video and interactive multimedia language software at the students' own pace. These courses have also been offered through the Michigan Virtual High School.

Still more striking were the online simulations that became the basis of a role-playing, language-learning game called ZON. In this game the learner is transported as an avatar to a virtual Chinese village, where in order to cope, the avatar must use Chinese language to communicate and accomplish basic tasks. It was launched in 2008. Still another important initiative of MSU's Confucius Institute has been to bring qualified native speakers of Chinese from China to teach, with special preparation at MSU, in American K–12 schools.

In December 2013 the council with oversight responsibilities for the MSU-CI held a meeting simultaneously at the Open University of China and at MSU to take stock of what had been achieved and to plan for continued work. It took place via live two-way video-conferencing between the two sites. Participants agreed that the MSU-CI would continue to focus on distance Chinese teaching; expand enrollments; develop resources to teach Chinese and Chinese culture in American K–12 schools; and undertake research on teaching methodology, curriculum design of Chinese courses, and distance online delivery. The council also noted that, by the end of 2013, about twenty-three hundred American students were registered for the online courses offered by MSU-CI. At the same time, the institute reported cooperating with more than twenty school districts in Michigan, offering face-to-face Chinese teaching from which over five thousand students were benefiting.[27]

Pragmatic Strategies for Study Abroad: Quest for Quality, Not Quantity

Building a study abroad program for purposes of internationalization in the College of Education has been a compelling, almost taken-for-granted idea. Although a no-brainer in principle, it has proved especially difficult to put into practice. Filled with requirements, the teacher education program for undergraduates in the college had little room for electives. The required courses, which often included fieldwork in local K–12 schools, did not readily lend themselves to study abroad. Since the leaders of the MSU program were reluctant to admit that any teacher education courses at universities abroad could be the equivalent in content, methods, and outcomes to MSU courses, taking a semester abroad was not feasible unless the student was willing to spend extra time to take all the required courses. Moreover, contrary to what outsiders tend to assume, very few of these required courses were actually taught in the College of Education. Most of the teacher education courses were offered by other MSU colleges. Adding to the barriers against study abroad in the college was the fact MSU education students tended to be strapped for money, often unable to afford the extra fees of study abroad or to give up any of the money they might earn in the summer, the period when most of the MSU study abroad courses have been offered.

Nevertheless, under the leadership of Anne Schneller, the college began to offer a limited repertoire of study abroad after the semester transition. Leading off in 1991 was a course on education and society first in Zimbabwe and then in South Africa. The switch to South Africa was made when the political and economic situation in Zimbabwe made it undesirable to take American undergraduates there. From the start, this course was carefully designed by Anne and John Metzler to overcome all obstacles and provide an exceptional experience to participants. It was offered as an overseas version of TE 250, Human Diversity, Power, and Opportunity in Social Institutions, the required course in social foundations that lent itself to study abroad because of its emphasis on diversity in race, ethnicity, and so on, and its attempt to demonstrate the importance of a concern for social justice in teaching. When this course was first offered, it was prized by MSU as one of a small number of very successful courses the university offered at that time in a developing region of the world and also a course that was able to attract African American students to participate in study abroad.[28]

Even though MSU already had a large study abroad program, the priority of sending undergraduates abroad increased sharply when Peter McPherson became the MSU president. With a strong interest in developing countries since his Peace Corps days, the new president announced that he wanted all students to do study abroad. Although unrealistic in the foreseeable future, this goal gave a big boost to MSU study abroad by giving the colleges the expectation that more such courses had to be offered and more students enticed to take them. Most MSU colleges responded by increasing their offerings substantially. But it was not clear how the College of Education could do this, for the reasons given above. Hence, the study abroad program in the college continued to be very small throughout the 1990s.

Ultimately, not having found a way to greatly increase enrollments, we tried to compensate for the lack of quantity by an emphasis on programs of exceptional value. The best example of this was the Preinternship Teaching Program offered for the first time in 2002. It came about because, in discussion of the internationalization of teacher education, talk inevitably turned to student teaching abroad. At Michigan State, this was an old subject of consideration. Student teaching abroad had, in fact, already been offered in the 1970s before the change to an integration-infusion approach. But examined more closely, what was done then did not meet the goals of the new five-year program of the 1990s. In those days the standard MSU teacher education program was highly fragmented and, from the perspective of today's practice, mediocre in various respects. Student teaching was managed separately from the rest of the program by a Division of Student Teaching within the college. And since at the same time the MSU Graduate Studies in Education Overseas (GSEO) program had close relations with many American International and Department of Defense schools overseas, it was a relatively simple matter to arrange for MSU students to meet their student teaching requirements by teaching in those schools. But teaching in those American schools was in no way an immersion experience of everyday culture in another country.

Moreover, as the MSU reform of teacher education proceeded, one of the fundamental goals of this reform was to weave student teaching and other field experience tightly into the program so that what was done in student teaching consistently reflected or at least was analyzed from the perspectives taken in university coursework. Supervision of this experience (which at MSU was more accurately described as field instruction) was greatly intensified over the earlier standard program. For these reasons, student teaching in American overseas schools was no longer encouraged.

However, as the integration-infusion approach took hold and the new five-year teacher preparation program was implemented, there were faculty members who once again advocated giving students opportunities to do practice teaching abroad. This time, however, the idea of giving time and credit for this as a partial or total substitute for the fifth-year internship was strongly resisted by the teacher preparation program coordinators. Having fought for field experience to be part of a tightly integrated program, with the internship taking place over the course of a whole year in a relatively nearby school affiliated with the university (where the students and their cooperating teachers could be visited frequently), the coordinators were not going to give up any part of this yearlong experience to a separate and difficult-to-monitor period of student teaching overseas. The result was stalemate.

Once again it was Anne Schneller who solved this problem, as she did so many others. She proposed to create a separate study abroad experience for student teaching while maintaining the one-year internship in Michigan. According to this proposal, additional study abroad would take place in the summer after students had received their bachelor's degrees for the first four years of the program but before the fifth-year internship. Students in this study abroad would spend most of their time as teachers in regular government schools of the host country, not private American International Schools. They would coteach together with the regular teachers, and if possible have homestays with the teacher's family. The trick was to find regular public schools in other countries that were operating in English during the MSU summer break.

South Africa not only met this criterion but was a country where Anne Schneller, Sally McClintock, and others already had the excellent relationships needed to make the program work. Building on LATTICE linkages in switching from Zimbabwe to South Africa, MSU's College of Education had already taken undergraduates in both 2000 and 2001 to South Africa for a credit program on education and society. In the Richards Bay area north of Durban, they combined home stays with learning about schools through observation, discussion, and a small amount of practice teaching.

With that foundation, in 2002 and 2003, the new Preinternship Teaching Program was launched, led by Anne Schneller and Margaret Holtschlag. Eighteen students spent six weeks in the Richards Bay area, earning master's degree credit. Each MSU student was assigned to teach in a regular South African class under a South African teacher. After a week of orientation to the community and intensive lectures and discussions with local educators, participants were judged ready to begin teaching. They moved in with their host families, generally the teachers at the schools where the students were assigned to teach. Students then received an orientation to their particular school and spent the first few days observing their class as well as other classes in the school. By the end of that week, most participants felt comfortable enough to begin coteaching with their collaborating teacher. Participants and collaborating teachers worked together to plan lessons and class activities. Since classes in these schools were typically very large by U.S. standards (often sixty, seventy, or more in elementary schools), the participants had to learn different techniques of classroom management as well as adjust to a different culture. The role of Anne and Margaret was to visit each school several times a week to observe and to consult with teachers and student teachers on how well the latter were doing.[29]

Service learning was also an integral part of this Preinternship Teaching Program. Each year, the MSU students worked on a project to benefit one of the South African schools (for example, tree planting, establishing a snack shop for the children at a school, painting and decorating a classroom block). This experience allowed the MSU students to participate in a South African community improvement activity along with parents, children, and community members.

From the start, the program was a huge success. This in-depth experience provided MSU students with deep insight into the challenges of teaching in South Africa in underresourced schools. Feedback from participants indicated that these experiences could profoundly influence their subsequent teaching in Michigan. We found that students who cotaught and had home stays with regular South African teachers in regular South African classrooms with upwards of eighty students and very few resources gained a self-confidence in teaching that would help them get and keep jobs once back in the United States. This success was documented in *Education Week*, the national newsweekly of record for K–12 education, in an article (December 11, 2002) on innovative programs abroad for student teachers in U.S. colleges and universities. Later the same program was offered in Australia and in Malaysia.

Once this stage was reached, there could be no comparison between this experience and the one offered thirty-plus years before. The difference was not lost on Dean Carole Ames, who was a strong critic of the way much of MSU study abroad was offered. She felt that there were many courses offered by other colleges in European locations, where the students stayed in dormitories or hostels, took their courses from MSU instructors, and therefore had pretty much the same experience as they would have had if the course had been offered on the MSU campus at home. In contrast, the dean wanted not just an immersion in a local culture, but one that would be "a stretch" for the students. She appreciated the preinternship program because it indisputably met her criteria. It proved to be a good omen for what the dean was prepared to do for internationalization in subsequent years.

Breakthrough Conference on Internationalizing Michigan Education

In spite of successes like LATTICE and the Preinternship Teaching Program, in meetings in Washington and elsewhere we were pressed to do still more for K–12 internationalization. In Michigan, Jim Kelly, who had been the driving force behind the National Board for Professional Teaching Standards, had become active in this movement, working with the Asia Society in Washington, DC. When he started lobbying MSU to do more, we came up with some ideas that we could discuss at a lunch we arranged in the Ann Arbor area for him, University of Michigan professor Phil Kearney, Barbara Markle, and myself. The meeting went well, but what exactly we would do was still unresolved. So while driving back to East Lansing with Barbara at the wheel, she and I discussed possible next steps. Suddenly, Barbara burst out: "We should have a conference!" Taken aback by how emphatic she was, I asked how on earth we were going to find time for this, given how busy we all were. After all, at times during the year, Barbara was already running conferences and time-consuming meetings nearly back to back. But she didn't hesitate a minute, declaring, "I can do it. It's not hard. I can do a conference like that with my hands tied behind my back."[30] And that was the origin of the first Internationalizing Michigan Education conference held at the Lansing Convention Center in 2007.

That conference turned out to be the sort of pivotal event that led to another breakthrough. Attendance and interest were high. Important guests had come from China, and participants were entertained by preschoolers from the immersion preschool Yong Zhao and colleagues had created in Lansing. The American preschoolers impressed the audience; they not only sang Chinese songs at the conference with what the Chinese guests asserted were excellent Mandarin accents, they got their instructions on stage from their adult leader entirely in Chinese. By 2011 Barbara and her team had organized five of these conferences, but it was the first one that had the greatest impact on our college, as reflected in changes the dean made in college priorities shortly after the event.[31]

Carole Ames Rallies to the Cause in a Big Way

One of the participants at Barbara's first conference was Carole Ames, dean of the MSU College of Education since 1993. Although Carole had been very supportive of me and the international work we were doing, international education had never been one of her top priorities until she went to this conference and saw how many of the movers and shakers of Michigan education were there. I'm not sure what went through her mind, but perhaps she took stock of a number of important signs of change and progress relevant to internationalization: the interest of the K–12 education community in internationalization, the pressure from the MSU central administration to give more priority to international work, the very strong international capabilities of our faculty, the various research and outreach accomplishments we had already put together, and the charismatic leadership of faculty members like Yong Zhao. From then on, strengthening the international dimension became one of Carole's strongest priorities for our college. For example, at a retreat for college administrators and the college faculty advisory committee, held only a few months after that first internationalization conference, our international efforts were one of only three points on the agenda for the whole day's meeting.

More was clearly needed. Although 25 percent of the faculty responding to our survey said they taught courses with substantial international content, there had been as yet no systematic content analysis that would reveal the extent to which the college's master's and doctoral courses embodied international perspectives and content. And even if the 25 percent figure was accurate, it meant that much of the curriculum had not been touched. Hence, when Dean Ames made internationalization such a high priority, plans were made to work on internationalization in much the same way that had earlier proved very successful in getting college faculty to use more technology in teaching. Central to this earlier effort in technology was a special course offered to faculty members. Each faculty member in the course had been expected to propose and work on a specific idea for using technology in a new way in a course that he or she would teach. Graduate students with expertise in technology took the course as well; their role was to assist faculty members with their project. This approach worked so well that a book was written about it.[32]

We proposed to do the same sort of course for purposes of internationalization. Each faculty member taking the course would be expected to do a project internationalizing some aspect of a course he or she would teach. Graduate students could take the course for credit if they were international students or other students with expertise related to internationalization so they could assist the faculty members with their projects.

The earlier technology course had also provided special financial incentives for faculty to take the course; similar incentives were proposed for the internationalization course. The dean initially agreed to all this, the course was scheduled, and John Dirkx was designated as the instructor. But because of the financial crisis of 2008, it was never offered, for lack of funding to cover the incentives. Hopefully, in the future it might still happen.

In any case, other initiatives were taken. Following the retreat of college administrators and faculty advisory committee at the beginning of 2007–8, in which internationalization was one of three main points on the agenda, Dean Ames asked me to organize faculty development opportunities in this area. After I consulted with eight other faculty leaders, the dean and I met again to discuss. We narrowed the ideas down to sponsoring a yearlong working group on internationalization of coursework and research. An orientation meeting was held to kick off the effort. Attendance was good, but participants were all over the map with issues and ideas, and not at all focused on thinking about how they might move ahead with a specific agenda for international research and international curriculum development as had been intended. Hence after this meeting, to clarify and simplify matters, the dean split up responsibility for these areas, with me heading up professional development for faculty on international research and Lynn Paine doing the same, but with more of a curricular focus, namely, figuring out what it would mean for faculty and students to acquire "global competence" and how to give them the opportunity to do this.

To do my part, I drew up a plan for a series of sessions throughout the year. Illustrating what we did, the following are six of the twelve topics we addressed in our series on "Lessons learned and new directions for international research in education":

- "Connecting with educational research outside the U.S.," led by visiting professors Sigrid Blömeke from Humboldt University in Berlin and Ruhama Even from the Weizman Institute of Science in Israel
- "Creativity in action: help Punya find IT in India," led by Punya Mishra
- "Using the writing process to facilitate healing among teen-aged orphans of genocide of Tutsis in Rwanda," led by Laura Apol and her collaborators
- "MSU prospects for international assessment in higher education," led by Sharif Shakrani, Teresa Tatto, Bill Schmidt, and Matt Wawrzynski
- "Creating a virtual water conservation game for science and environmental education in Jordan and the U.S.," led by Joe Codde, with participation from Dongping Zheng, Aroutis Foster, and Amita Chudgar

- "Prospects for MSU educational research in China," led by Yong Zhao and Lynn Paine

The sessions were intended to emphasize emerging work and opportunities rather than finished work, so that faculty could see what it took to launch such initiatives. This also helped make the sessions more fun. Fun was a big factor in the session with Punya when we advertised the session with a play on words based on the double meaning "it" vs "IT" for information technology. Signs were posted all over Erickson coaxing people in one tongue-in cheek way or another to come and find out what "it" was that Punya was up to. Actually the title was very accurate in the sense that Punya was hoping to travel extensively in India discovering, observing, and photographing creative or just unusual uses of technology in education or other related fields.

In a more serious vein than our flyers for Punya, the following is an excerpt from an email sent Jan 9, 2008, to all faculty as well as the listserv of internationally oriented students to encourage attendance at the session "Making the Most of International Conferences," led by Teresa Tatto, Lynn Paine, and Susan Peters.

What makes international conferences worthwhile—other than the undeniable pleasures of new places to visit? We will discuss making the most of this sort of travel with experienced international scholars from the college.

Take for example the World Congress of Comparative Education Societies, held only once every three years, most recently in Sarajevo, Bosnia, in September 2007. The College was represented by Teresa Tatto and Reitu Mabokela and doctoral students. Teresa has agreed to lead off Friday's discussions. . . .

Lynn Paine is just back from a major conference in Hong Kong which focused on the lesson study approach to professional development as practiced in various countries. This is the latest trip in her more than 30 years of work on education in Chinese-speaking countries. Susan Peters is another faculty member whose research and publications have been informed and advanced by participation in international conferences. For example, along with Reitu Mabokela, she led an MSU group of faculty and doctoral students to the World Congress of Comparative Education Societies when it was held in Cuba in 2004.

The questions for discussion include: (1) Which international research conferences have you found particularly beneficial in pursuing your research agenda? Why? What has been the impact? (2) For example, what have you learned from attending such conferences that you otherwise probably would not have learned? (3) To what extent have you kept in touch with scholars you initially met at international research conferences, and what have been the results and benefits of that? (4) What opportunities for publication have resulted from this participation? (5) From your perspective, what are the best international conferences to attend? (6) What advice do you have for others on how to make the most of these conferences?

Dean Ames Calls for an International Strand in the Five-Year Teacher Preparation Program

After giving internationalization increased priority, Carole Ames herself became the visionary who initiated two of the most important new initiatives of recent years: the Global Educators Cohort Program (GECP) and the doctoral study tours.[33] In 2007, the dean called a meeting with the associate dean for external and student affairs, the chair of the Department of Teacher Education, the dean of the Residential College for Arts and Humanities, and myself. None of us knew what the meeting was about. It turned out that the dean had an idea for internationalizing undergraduate teacher preparation, a part of our vision that had me stumped for a very long time. Influenced by the press for internationalization, she had decided that it was time for us to create a new strand within the five-year teacher education program that would prepare teachers for jobs in which international capabilities are especially important (e.g., school districts trying to internationalize their curricula, international baccalaureate schools, magnet schools, and American International Schools overseas).

In response to the dean, planning started immediately for the new strand, and before the curriculum design was even finished, recruitment of GECP students began for the following year. Soon the Global Educators Cohort Program was in full swing, providing a range of special opportunities to students, including tailored sections in required courses, extracurricular activities, and international experience.

Unlike the regular MSU teacher preparation program, in which students apply for the program during their sophomore year and spend the last two years of their bachelor's degree program and the year of internship meeting the requirements of the program, the GECP students apply for and enter the program as incoming freshmen and begin at that point to complete specialized coursework, engage in specialized practice teaching, and complete a global experience requirement. The coursework is a combination of courses that are required of all education majors but for which GECP students enroll in special, globally infused sections (e.g., a course on issues of diversity in education and a course on human learning), plus additional required courses that are GECP specific (a course on immigrant language and culture and a course on service learning for global educators). This required specialization coursework is completed during students' freshman and sophomore years.

By 2013, seventy-five students were entering the program each year, divided into three twenty-five-student "sections."[34] These sections remain intact throughout the students' GECP-required coursework in the freshman and sophomore years.

GECP students also are given specialized, global field placements to work with mentor teachers who are committed to global education and can support novice teachers as they begin to practice the global teaching envisioned by the program. Since it is difficult for novice teachers to translate their own global knowledge and competence into global pedagogical practice, opportunities for global teaching experience are therefore critical. To help meet this need, the College of Education offered nine different study abroad programs appropriate for teacher education students in the three years 2012–14, most of which provided students with teaching abroad opportunities that ranged from teaching a single lesson to a multiple-week student-teaching experience.[35] GECP students have also taken advantage of other existing MSU study abroad programs that at the same time can serve to complete general education requirements or disciplinary majors.

In spring 2011, support from various international units on campus and the College of Education enabled the GECP to offer a new short-term study abroad program in China. This program provided a low-cost study abroad opportunity for students who could not afford a lot of time away from a summer job or who were not able to pay the extra cost of a traditional study abroad experience. This idea got off the ground when Dean Ames coaxed our top China expert, Lynn Paine, into leading this program even though Lynn had no time that could be readily spared. The dean wanted a location that would be a "stretch" for the students, and China met that stipulation. It followed that for any such trip to China, Lynn was the logical faculty member to lead it. Lynn did manage to convince the dean that Margo Glew should go as well, since the trip would be more sustainable if it had two qualified leaders who could alternate from year to year. The first trip was so successful that it has since become an integral part of the program, with funding from both the College of Education and from Beijing Normal University.

In 2011, the MSU students who had participated in this trip the first year turned the tables when they got back to Michigan and insisted that MSU reciprocate by inviting their Chinese "buddies" (the preservice teacher candidates at Beijing Normal University with whom they had been matched in China) to come to MSU for a return visit. No money had been set aside for this, so Lynn Paine had rustle up money to cover expenses for the buddies while at MSU. But the results made it all worthwhile.

When the buddies got to East Lansing, they turned out to be spectacular representatives of their university, speaking amazingly good English and entering easily into substantive discussions—more so than many other more senior visiting scholars. Moreover, their MSU student hosts said, after the very first visit, that they had learned more in hosting their buddies than they had in China itself—and these students were ones who had already reported on how much they had learned in China! As reported by Lynn Paine: "Their argument—a familiar and powerful defense of comparative education as a field—was that it was in having to respond to questions from their buddies, or seeing US education through the eyes of their buddies, [that] they questioned their own assumptions about education in ways they never had, even when they were out of the country." Some went so far as to experience change in their career paths and their identities as a result of this exchange. And several even found jobs in China.[36]

GECP and the College of Education have also collaborated with the area studies centers on two externally funded projects to enable preservice and in-service teachers who mentor GECP student-teaching interns to travel abroad.

Breakthrough Goal of International Experience for All Doctoral Students

Dean Ames decided to set a goal of sending doctoral students to universities and other educational institutions in other countries for relatively brief periods to gain international experience. She had launched this idea with two pilot trips to China in 2009 and 2010. These China trips were hosted mainly by Southwest University in Chongqing.

With these successful pilots behind her, in a surprise move at an all-college faculty meeting in 2010, the Dean announced that the time had come to expand this program to other countries. Her motivation, she confessed, stemmed in part from having been appalled to learn that some doctoral students in the college did not have passports and had never been outside the United States. To expand the program, a competition was set up for faculty members to organize and lead the study tours, which were officially designated "Fellowships to Enhance Global Understanding." The result was three study tours in 2011 (China, Botswana, Vietnam), four in 2012 (China, Vietnam, Botswana, and Cyprus), and three in 2013 (China, Botswana, and Indonesia).[37] All these countries were ones with which we already had close relations, so that the tours could be organized on the basis of preexisting ties. The visits were made possible by the fact that they were heavily subsidized by the dean using discretionary funds that she had been able to accumulate over recent years—a very exceptional practice for a dean who was known for being very prudent and careful not to spend money in ways she considered unjustified.

In the first year of this competition, all faculty members at the annual college retreat were broken down into groups focusing on the region in which they were most involved or interested. I went to a well-attended session on Africa that began with a senior faculty member taking the floor to criticize the whole idea, saying that first we needed to gather evidence that the study tours would be more effective and/or less expensive than pursuing the same goals electronically through online linkages. But no one spoke up to support him. Everyone knew the decision had been made, and the initiative was going to move forward. And in my view, although the research proposed would have been good to do, it was high time to enable doctoral students to have an on-site international experience. Therefore, I welcomed the dean's proposal and did not want to see any delay in implementation.

In the same session, Deb Feltz, longtime chair of the kinesiology department, pointed to a written announcement describing the competition and said it was all about schooling in academic subjects and thus did not seem applicable to her department. But a further reading of the guidelines made it clear that the tours had to recruit from doctoral programs across the college and not just from one or more related programs. To make sure the tours were inclusive in this sense, another participant in the session argued that at least one of the tours should emphasize, not just academic subject matter, but rather education of the whole child or person. If so, a study tour with that emphasis could be especially suitable for a kinesiology department known for its emphasis, not on specialized training of elite athletes, but on sports and fitness for everyone as an integral aspect of holistic development.

In the subsequent preparation of proposals, this was one of the ideas pursued. Feltz herself submitted a proposal to do a tour in Botswana in collaboration with one of her former students, a Botswanan in sports psychology with whom she continued to have close relations. Later Evelyn Oka, professor of school psychology, was looking for a way to be involved and the Botswana project proved an ideal choice for her as well.[38] When this Botswana fellowship was first offered in 2011, it was designed to enhance students' knowledge of physical and psychological child development, along with educational philosophy, curriculum, structure, and policy in the cultural context of a southern African country. MSU students learned about the challenges facing Botswana's children, youth, and families as well as its social services. Participating were four doctoral students from kinesiology, seven from curriculum and instruction, two from school psychology, and one from educational psychology—six men and eight women in all.

In 2012, Leps Malete, University of Botswana faculty member and Feltz's former PhD student, further enriched the content of the study tour with a new series of lectures and discussions. These included not only UB faculty but also leading national athletic figures and representatives of organizations working to support youth development in Botswana. For their part, three of the kinesiology students from MSU led a workshop on first aid, coaching, and skills development for Botswanan coaches, athletes, and teachers. These student-led events were intended to strengthen the growing relationship between the University of Botswana and the MSU College of Education.

Another country added in 2011 was Vietnam. This visit included educational institutions and sites across the three major regions of the country: north, central highlands, and south. In Ho Chi Minh City the students visited the War Remnants Museum with its "sober portrayal of the Vietnam War, the University Place that housed South Vietnamese leadership during the war, and the Ho Chi Minh Museum that covers the life and career of the famed leader." For an experience more focused on professional education, the annual report noted:

> Perhaps the highlight of the tour was our visit with school and university staff who participated in the school and community development projects directed by Dr. Chris Wheeler from MSU. In these visits, participants were able to see firsthand the impact of these projects on selected families within the villages that were involved. Tour participants visited several homes of families involved in the project and were able to observe such projects as converting pig waste to methanol for fuel for cooking, organic gardening, and controlling dengue fever through careful collection and use of rain water. (9)

A second Vietnam study tour followed in 2012. Also in 2012, still another country was added—Cyprus, where the visit focused on peace education, based in part on research on peace education by Michalinos Zembylas, who following his PhD at the University of Illinois was a faculty member in MSU teacher education for one very successful year. In addition to these two new countries, the successfully piloted China study tour continued in 2011, its third year. Among its sixteen participants were doctoral students from the University of Washington, Seattle, as well as MSU; the nine students from MSU were in teacher education, curriculum and instruction, educational policy, measurement and quantitative methods, K–12 administration, education psychology and technology, and higher education. Then in 2012, the fourth year for this study tour, the MSU group broadened its itinerary to include GM Shanghai and BaoSteel in Shanghai as well as Southwest University and Beijing Normal University and other educational institutions—all in the interests of learning not only about China but also about globalization in general and its impact on education and society.

Conclusion

Ironically, even before these last three breakthroughs took place, MSU was already receiving attention and publicity for its work in internationalization of K–16 education—two prestigious awards, the first being the Goldman Sachs Higher Education Prize for Excellence in International Education in 2004 and the AACTE Best Practice Award in Support of Global and International Perspectives in 2006. The Goldman Sachs prize was made public (together with four other such awards outside higher education) with a full-page announcement in the *Financial Times*, November 29, 2004. Even though we were thrilled with these awards, we knew that what we had done was just a start and there was much more to do. More work followed as described in this book. And even now there is still much more to do.

For example, our achievements in study abroad are still modest. It has always been difficult for students who are cramped for money and in a very tightly sched-uled, packed curriculum to find the time and money to study abroad. But to do this and adhere to the teacher preparation program's standards of quality is still harder. How do we assure program leaders that the overseas assignments are tightly linked to coursework at MSU, that the whole teacher education experience is coordinated and coherent, that the field experience overseas is in the hands of mentors who work with students as intensively and effectively as the field instructors at MSU do? Part of the problem is that cross-national or cross-cultural immersion experience of this sort is still not seen by most MSU college administrators, program leaders, other faculty, and students as an essential part of learning to teach—perhaps desirable, but not essential.[39] Once they are convinced, with further work on the integration-infusion approach I am confident these problems will be solved.

Engaging Internationally Oriented Students to Create New Channels and Broaden Existing Ones

I deally, students themselves—international students and U.S. students with strong international interests—are viewed as one of the main resources for internationalizing schools of education. At MSU, the college has benefited enormously from the presence of these students, given their rich and diverse aspirations, experiences, and perspectives. But once again this view of internationalization has not been one that developed easily or naturally or is shared universally among the faculty even today. Many international students have felt they were not listened to or respected enough. Faculty commonly did not involve them as much as domestic students in class discussions. And a certain number of faculty tended to see international students more as problems than as assets.

These experiences and attitudes are readily understood when examined from a Bourdieu perspective. Seen in this light, international students are generally lacking in the capital needed to give them the status and legitimacy that would command attention throughout a U.S. school of education. Even U.S. students have little such capital compared to faculty, and international students lack the knowledge and experience of American education that is generally the currency of schools of education. The artificial borders between U.S. education and education in other countries and the ethnocentricity of U.S. studies in education have kept U.S.

LIPING MA (China)

Can internationally oriented students break through the boundaries that resist the infusion-integration approach and create new spaces for internationalization? Can they help make good on the promise of this approach to greatly increase the numbers and types of educators influenced by international efforts in education? In this regard it is instructive to examine the case of Liping Ma, a scholar of education who came to MSU from China as a doctoral student, and how she was able to carve out new territory for international inquiry in education.* A book based on her dissertation became a benchmark for the significance of international research in education, even though it was done by a student who started without any capital with recognized value in American fields of educational inquiry. Nevertheless, in the end she legitimized a new view of teacher knowledge. And even more important for the topic at hand, her story also represents the ideals of the integration-infusion approach pursued at MSU since 1984.

Liping Ma came to the United States from China in 1989 to do graduate study, first at Michigan State University and later at Stanford. In China, with only eight years of basic education, she was sent to a mountainous region during the Cultural Revolution, where she taught for seven years and then served as school principal and county teaching and research coordinator. She educated herself to the point where after the Cultural Revolution, she passed a test for admission to a university master's program. Determined to continue her studies in the United States, she arrived at MSU with only $30 in her pocket.

She found a graduate assistantship in MSU's National Center for Research on Teacher Learning. In coding data for the center, Ma was surprised at the difficulty U.S. elementary school teachers in the sample had in answering questions about how they would teach topics like division with fractions. Mary Kennedy, the director of NCRTE, took an interest in this, and gave Liping enough money to go to China to collect pilot data from Chinese teachers to see if Liping's conjectures about what they knew were right. These initial data proved to be of interest and were the beginning of what became her dissertation and book.

Although Ma's research interests were a great fit for MSU, her family was not happy in Michigan. She therefore transferred to Stanford, where former MSU professor

Lee Shulman took a keen interest in her preliminary investigations of teacher knowledge in mathematics. For her dissertation, although she did not consider herself either a comparativist or a mathematics educator, she collected data from a small comparative sample of Chinese teachers. With these data, she analyzed what it means for elementary school teachers to have a "profound understanding of fundamental mathematics."

A postdoctoral fellowship at Berkeley, with Alan Schoenfeld as her mentor, enabled Ma to turn the dissertation into a book.[†] Although she had been afraid that U.S. teachers would be offended by her conclusion that weak knowledge of mathematics was a widespread problem, the book in general was very well received, not only by teachers and mathematics educators, but most surprisingly by mathematicians. Even before it was published, the manuscript was being circulated and discussed by influential mathematicians and mathematics educators. Roger Howe's review of the book in *Notices of the American Mathematical Society* and Richard Askey's in *American Educator* were particularly influential. By 2003, the book had sold more than forty-six thousand copies.[‡] In some respects this dissertation research has had more influence than some of the well-funded large-scale comparative studies of mathematics achievement.

According to Fang and Paine,[§] the book influenced some groups more than others. Scholars in comparative education, in particular, paid little attention to this extraordinary example of comparative research. This was unfortunate since publication of this book illustrates important questions about the nature and future of international, comparative education: Should comparative education be walled off from efforts like this? Or should we instead judge the value of comparative education by how much it strengthens the efforts of educators and researchers more generally, whether or not it appeals to those who traditionally identify themselves with the prevailing orthodoxies of CIES? These are questions that challenge the state of comparative education when posed within a Bourdieu framework.

NOTES

* Schwille, 2004; Fang & Paine, 2008.
† Ma, 1999.
‡ Schwille, 2004.
§ Fang & Paine, 2008.

professors from trying to learn as much as they might from international students about the vast array of experiences and educational arrangements outside the United States. In short, the place envisaged by the integration-infusion approach for international students in the college constituted a direct challenge to more orthodox points of view.

Fortunately, some of our international students were so strong that they became leaders in our internationalization efforts in spite of these boundaries and constraints. I selected five who were especially deserving of leadership profiles: Liping Ma (China), Martial Dembélé (Burkina Faso), Qasim Al-Shannag (Jordan), Dwi Yuliantoro (Indonesia), and Bella Tirtowalujo (Indonesia).

Taking a College-Wide Perspective

The number of international students in the College of Education at the MA and PhD levels has remained large over the years, although with considerable variation. The official reported enrollments across the four college departments were 186 in 1983, 156 in 1992, 200 in 2000, 215 in 2008, and 292 in 2012. However, the figures for 2000 and thereafter appear to be inflated by online students and other anomalies in the reporting system.[1] The number of countries represented was typically about forty. In line with the integrated infusion approach, the ideal would be to have student representation from all parts of the world spread more or less equally across the college's departments and programs. However, in reality, the representation of regions of the world and representation across the college's departments have varied greatly over time.

The number of students from particular countries at any one time depended on a number of factors: the need in the home country for educators with advanced degrees in education, the wealth or lack of wealth of the country, the willingness of donor agencies to fund long-term students in the United States, the political conditions of the country, and previous MSU outreach to the country. Earlier in the 1970s, Iranians were a major presence, but after the Islamic Revolution, they faded from the scene. Students from the Middle East in general were a big group in the 1980s, but fell off as universities in that region became staffed at the desired levels. As the years went on, the balance shifted more and more toward East Asia, with larger groups of Chinese, Taiwanese, Koreans, and Japanese. Currently, students from China are by far the largest nationality group. African representation, which had been reduced over the years by lack of funding, remained important to the college, given the prominence of African studies and African projects across the university. During all these years, students from Latin America were poorly represented in comparison with these other groups.

Recruitment of excellent international students was a big challenge that we struggled with throughout the period in question, but never were able to develop an entirely satisfactory approach to. Fortunately, our pool of international students improved anyway. As the College of Education's reputation grew on the world stage, the applications from students abroad got better and better. The college had had many international students in the decades before the integration-infusion approach was adopted in 1984. At that time, as far as we know, proactive recruitment of individual students was limited. In those years it was relatively easy to attract international students. The admission of international students throughout the university operated mainly on the passive principle of receiving applications and reviewing them, not so much in going out to recruit. Instead, many students were sent by international development projects (e.g., from Thailand) in which the university and college were engaged. Thus, we had plenty of international students. The problem that continued into the early years covered by this book was that many of the students had limited success in reaching the high standards of doctoral study, and it appears that these standards were often not reached even though the students in question received degrees.

The philosophy of integration-infusion implied a different approach if international students were to be a resource and become colleagues who would add to the college's strengths. But a new approach proved very difficult to achieve, for various reasons. The first challenge pertained to factors out of our control. Admission of international students to MSU and typically to other U.S. universities as well was much more complicated and daunting than in Britain, for example. A Malaysian who was a good prospect for graduate study in the UK could expect to be taken in hand by the British Council, which would facilitate the entire process of application, admission, visas, and so on. The same person, when considering the United States, was much more on his or her own, facing various requirements that were difficult to understand and could vary from university to university. At MSU the situation was especially bad in this respect. Applications were received and initially reviewed by the university's centralized admissions office and then sent to the departments. Then at the department level, the decision making was usually in the hands of persons with limited special knowledge of other educational systems, and more frequently than one would like, in the hands of persons who regarded international students as potential problems rather than potential assets. Msu did not have the system of peer universities who hired one or more people to specialize solely in evaluation of international transcripts, thus compensating for lack of competence among faculty. At msu the first level of evaluation in the central administration was solely to determine whether the applicant had the equivalent of the U.S. degree required for entry into a master's or doctoral program. No other judgment about the value of the degree the applicant had earned was made until the application was forwarded to the college and also to the applicant's department, where the chances of it being evaluated by anyone with in-depth understanding of educational qualifications and credentials in the applicant's country were small.

As the infusion-integration approach developed, some small channels were created to make the passage from interested person in another country to admitted student easier. The expertise of faculty could be called upon, but in the regular course of events this did not happen as much as it could have. Our office was always somewhat out of the administrative loop of admissions, but over time managed to actively recruit a sizable number of outstanding students, often in alliance with internationalists like Lynn Paine, Chris Wheeler, Yong Zhao, and Punya Mishra. As with many other challenges that we could not reduce to routine solution, Anne Schneller took much of the responsibility for individualized international student recruitment. Her previous work with the Institute for International Education (iie) in New York, which was responsible for managing Fulbright programs, and her knowledge of other sources of funding for bringing international students to msu proved invaluable.

From time to time we took special steps. In 1999–2000, I met individually with twelve key faculty members who had many international contacts to ask them to think of one thing they could do that would be useful in student recruitment. Two of these conversations proved especially useful. One was with Yong Zhao and then with his department chair, Dick Prawat, to encourage a recruitment trip to China. This trip took place and brought in a number of highly regarded applications. Another meeting with Chris Clark, building on Anne Schneller's previous contacts with iie in New York, led to increased contacts with that organization and increased applications as a result.[2]

Throughout this period, we were always alert to the exceptional prospect and the need to help bring the prospect and the department together. Sometimes this

MARTIAL DEMBÉLÉ (Burkina Faso)

When Martial Dembélé came to MSU as a doctoral student, his command of oral and written English was close to impeccable. Although English was his third language (the others were French and a local lingua franca in parts of Côte d'Ivoire and Burkina Faso), Martial wrote English better than a large number of our graduate students who were native English speakers. Such fluency was highly unusual for a person whose parents were farmers in a francophone West African country and whose own early years were spent in a non-English-speaking environment. In fact, when I first began to read his written work and did not know him as well as I did later, the writing was so polished that I suspected that he must have gotten some final editing help from a native speaker. Before long I learned this was not at all the case.

I first remember meeting Martial at the Ohio University symposium for African students on African education that we went to regularly every year in the late 1980s and early 1990s, traveling in an MSU van with a group of our own African students. When Martial and I ran into each other at this symposium, I was delighted to find he was looking for a PhD program in teacher education, having almost completed a master's degree at Pittsburgh, under the guidance of Mark Ginsburg and Seth Spaulding. Although he could have stayed at Pitt, he wanted to concentrate on the study of teaching and teacher education. He also needed to find money for his studies and living expenses.

I told him that Michigan State was the place for the specialty he had chosen, but the only way he could get the assistantship he needed to support himself was to visit MSU and meet professors who had assistantships to offer. I promised to set up a schedule for such a visit. To allow him to make his case in an environment that at the time was unfavorable to giving assistantships to international students at the beginning of their doctoral studies, we gave him a rigorous schedule very similar to the taxing interviews we ordinarily used to fill faculty positions. Martial had to give a talk and had individual meetings with faculty who might offer him an assistantship. He was an instant hit! As is usually the case with people who meet Martial, the faculty were impressed by everything about him, and soon he was offered an assistantship by Sharon Feiman-Nemser in the National Center for Research on Teacher Learning (NCRTL). It was the perfect fit for a person of his interests and abilities. He kept it until completion of his PhD in 1995.

His assistantship brought him into a research group that played a pioneering role in research on the mentoring of novice teachers. His thesis was a revealing study comparing two teachers in the same school and how they mentored student intern teachers. One teacher was extremely systematic in planning and implementing a curriculum of learning to teach for the interns, while the other believed in a more conventional sink-or-swim approach for interns to learn from their own mistakes. Both teachers were effective in their own teaching, but, as the thesis demonstrates, they were not equally effective as mentors.

Martial also did very well in earning his own way at MSU. Unlike many international students, after he left Pittsburgh, he did not have the advantage of receiving a scholarship from external sources. But within MSU he was exceptionally successful in receiving recognition for his talent and ambition in the form of work opportunities and fellowship aid. As far as I know, he was the first MSU international student in education to receive both a graduate assistantship and fellowship funds from the university during his first year (earlier, the university did not allow the use of state funds for fellowships for international students).

Although I was not Martial's adviser, I continued to take a close interest in him and found that, in spite of having grown up and been educated in such different cultures and circumstances, we had much in common, both in our interests and the way we thought about things. These common points of view were consistent with an idea I had had for some time. I wanted some of the best international doctoral students to continue to collaborate closely with their advisers after graduation. But in spite of my hopes and efforts to model such a relationship and get other faculty members to follow suit, the practice did not catch on although in Martial's case, it did. We built a close collaboration and friendship that has continued until the present day, with Martial, his spouse, and children becoming, in effect, part of my family. Starting as a student, he became my principal collaborator for African work, especially during the ten years of the Guinea project (1993–2002).* In fact, one of the reasons for undertaking the Guinea project was to follow up on some of the ideas for teacher development that Martial had acquired in the doctoral program. In the end, I learned as much from him as he did from me.

I was especially interested in a project he organized in Burkina Faso immediately after graduation from MSU. He got grants from the Rockefeller Foundation and the Spencer Foundation to finance this work. His goal in the project was to demonstrate that practicing primary school teachers in a West African context could, with appropriate support, do research on their own practice. This was something that Martial told me he had wanted to do, almost from the day he arrived at Michigan State, that is, work directly with Burkinabè teachers at the grass roots on the improvement of their teaching and thereby initiate the sort of practitioner research that has proved to be a powerful tool of professional development and school improvement in other parts of the world. He was inspired not only by the teacher study group at MSU led by Helen Featherstone, but also by the work that Lynn Paine and Liping Ma had done in China as well as related literature on Japan. This all meant that, unlike many doctoral students from countries where doctoral degrees are uncommon, he was not thinking that with his PhD he would immediately step into a high-level policy job or other elite position where he would have little contact with practicing teachers. Instead he was willing to take the risk of having to demonstrate his capabilities where it would be most difficult—in schools and classrooms. For the holder of a doctorate to work intensively with primary school teachers in this way was unheard of in Burkina Faso at the time. Since his grant funds were limited, Martial used all the money for the expenses of the project and the other participants. For his part, he donated an enormous amount of time, receiving no salary from the grants.

The project followed a coaching model that Martial developed as a result of his dissertation research: at first the research support team took the lead in designing projects and collecting data with help from the teachers, but then gradually the teachers took more and more responsibility until they were able to carry out their own individual research projects. After four and a half years, this project came to a very successful conclusion. The series of progress reports that Martial produced contain a candid and blow-by-blow description of the problems encountered and the results achieved. A dissemination workshop was held in December 1999 in the capital city to discuss the results of the teacher projects; the teachers themselves were in demand to discuss what they had done in in-service meetings with other teachers; and the project was reported on by Martial and one of the teachers at a meeting of Spencer Foundation grantees in New Orleans in April 2000.[†]

Much earlier, when Martial was still a student, I took my first trip to Guinea (Conakry) in 1993 with a mandate to help develop a World Bank program to improve the quality of primary education. When I found that the primary education director in the Ministry of Education wanted to do a new kind of professional development, giving teachers more responsibility for their own development, I immediately thought of Martial's interest in this sort of program and got him to join me in this effort. We worked on this program for ten years, during which I developed more and more respect and admiration for Martial's talents. So in 1996–97, when I took a sabbatical, it made sense to spend four months of it living in Burkina Faso and working with Martial while continuing to make periodic visits to Guinea.

In our work together since 1994 I have been able to learn a great deal more about Martial's many strengths, which help account for his great success. As articulated in a letter of recommendation I wrote for him, these include the advantages of being highly organized and able to balance and reconcile multiple responsibilities; a good sense for what needs to be done next in a project; attention to punctuality at all times; concern for and a prodigious memory for details; remarkable powers of observation and sensitivity to the feelings of others; the ability to make sound inferences and judgments about other people's performance; the tendency to be assertive, confident, and at the same time modest, polite, and pleasant; an unwavering capacity to get along extremely well with others and to show consideration for everyone regardless of rank; an excellent sense of humor; good user's knowledge of computers, including fast, accurate, and elegant word-processing skills; financial trustworthiness and fastidiousness in accounting for money; enthusiasm for research; and not least, eagerness to learn about virtually everything.

One of Martial's most heartfelt goals was to put these qualities to good use in his home country, continuing after the teacher practitioner research, but after several years he found there was no job that would draw fully on his interests and capabilities, which in my view were best suited to a faculty position in a well-functioning research university. Given the lack of opportunity to make the best use of his talents in his home country, it is not surprising that Martial Dembélé is now very well established in international development circles and has become a tenured professor at the University of Montreal.

NOTES

* See, e.g., Schwille, Dembélé & Diallo, 2001; Schwille, Dembélé & Balde, 2002; Dembélé & Schwille, 2006; Schwille & Dembélé, 2007.
† First Practitioner Research Communication and Mentoring (PRCM) Invitational Conference, "Research on Practice: The Sharing and Dissemination of Research," organized by the Spencer Foundation in New Orleans at the time of AERA 2000.

QASIM AL-SHANNAG (Jordan)

In 1997 Jordanian doctoral student Qasim M. Al-Shannag was nominated at MSU for the Homer Higbee International Education Award, given to international students who have made extraordinary contributions to the university.* Qasim was the nominee of the LATTICE project. The project's planning/steering committee (itself composed of international students, area K–12 teachers, and MSU faculty and staff) selected Qasim for nomination because he embodied the contributions of MSU international students to this project in a most exemplary and exceptional way.

The main purpose of LATTICE has been to increase the teachers' understandings of complex international realities. The basic assumption of the project is that getting to know international students on a continuing, in-depth basis in a study group changes the teachers' ways of thinking, as short-term workshops and other encounters cannot do.

Qasim turned out to be a perfect choice for LATTICE, an international student who participated wholeheartedly and enthusiastically in its activities while expressing artic-ulate ideas and beliefs from his own culture and background that challenge the points of view of most of the American teachers as well as many of the other international students. As a PhD student in science education, he brought to the project a strong background in elementary and secondary teaching in Jordan. He had been president of the Jordanian Chemical Society, which was working to increase knowledge about chemistry among young people (e.g., by creating mobile chemistry labs).

When interviewed as a prospective LATTICE participant in April 1995, Qasim said one of his motivations for joining was that he had experienced so many negative stereotypes of Arabs since coming to the United States, particularly in the period right after the Oklahoma City bombing. "We are not like this," he kept saying and explaining. He then went on in LATTICE to demonstrate in many ways by personal example that "we are not like [those stereotypes]." He was extremely conscientious and devoted to the project, missing only one session in two and a half years. He also helped lead the project as a stalwart member of the planning committee.

But his major contribution was in simply being himself, dynamic, irrepressible, devout, and immensely personable. Even though his life at MSU was unusually hard due to financial cutbacks in the Jordanian government scholarship program that sent him to MSU, Qasim did not let this affect his community spirit. He got along well with everyone. He enjoyed meeting and interacting with both the K–12 teachers and the international students from many other countries. He loved sharing his country's food, culture, religious traditions, and so on, while learning about the customs of others. The impact of his appealing personality was part of the reason for teachers and students from other countries being able to learn from him when he expressed points of view that politically, culturally, and religiously were at odds with their own. The genius of Qasim was that he had a personality and attitude that made teachers more receptive to learning truths about misunderstandings between Muslims and non-Muslims that otherwise could have been difficult to accept. This was all the more important for many LATTICE participants because Qasim was the first Muslim they had ever had a chance to know well.

In short, Qasim was a devout, observant Muslim and a loyal Jordanian who frequently and politely explained what all this meant to him. This was most vividly exemplified early on in our program when we had an MSU scholar from the university's Kresge Art Museum come to one of our sessions to discuss examples of Islamic art. One of the paintings was of the Prophet ascending to heaven. According to the scholar, this portrayal was acceptable and respectful in the Muslim country where it was painted. But for Qasim it was not at all acceptable to him or others of his particular Muslim tradition to sit and view a representational portrait of the Prophet. As a result, he was visibly shaken in this LATTICE session by the conflict between his religious beliefs and his desire to be a cooperative, congenial member of the group—wanting to leave and not wanting to leave. Since the speaker and the other participants were caught unawares, this was a dramatic learning experience for all concerned. The teachers present indicated how much this affected them as they began to wonder how they could better avoid offending in unknowing ways children of diverse beliefs in their classrooms.

One of the best remembered of Qasim's stories was about the birth of his son. The birth of babies to LATTICE members was always noted in a short celebration. In this case, when the planning committee was talking about such an event and how birth rituals differ from culture to culture, Qasim began to talk about his wife being pregnant with their second child and said that, when his MSU colleagues had planned a baby shower for him, he did not know what a shower was or what to wear. He then went on to talk about how the birth would be different from what he experienced in Jordan. In particular, he looked forward to being in the delivery room, which would have been impossible at home. The planning team was struck by all this and asked him if he was willing to talk about it at the general LATTICE session. He was.

Once the baby was born, Qasim again talked about his experience and how it deepened his feelings about his wife and mother. In preparing to tell the story at LATTICE, he had taken pains to find out how his wife felt about all this. He had gained new respect for women when he saw what pain they went through at childbirth and knew he would not have had the same experience in Jordan. His marriage had been arranged, he said; in the beginning it had not been a love match. Now, however, it was different; he had become devoted to his wife. Although he was entitled to have more than one wife, he said, after this experience he would not take another wife. And he even called his mother in Jordan to tell her he now understood how difficult it must have been for her to give birth to him. All this left the LATTICE group moved and teary eyed. Qasim had everyone, it seemed, in the palm of his hand. As someone said later, from then on every teacher in the room would vividly remember that discussion—a source of insights rather than stereotypes.

As in the case of many other LATTICE international students, the project led Qasim to make visits to local schools. When he visited Everett High School in Lansing, he walked up and down the halls, pointing out to other members of his group the differences between what he was observing and what he had experienced in Jordan, including everything from class size to discipline and the kind of work teachers do. This conversation was not long, only a few minutes. The LATTICE moment does not have to be long. Later, after further LATTICE discussions, Qasim gave a copy of the Koran to several schools who were represented in the project. One of the teachers who took it to her school said she had never seen one before and was surprised that it was in English and that it was remarkably like the New Testament in some ways.

The impact of such stories is one of the reasons that explain why Margaret Holtschlag, Michigan Teacher of the Year in 1999–2000, said publicly a number of times that LATTICE had been the biggest influence on her teaching.[†] This powerful aspect of internationalization spreading out to K–12 educators could not have happened without students like Qasim.

NOTES

[*] Much of the content of this section was documented in a letter I wrote September 10, 2003, recommending the LATTICE project for an award and in an earlier recommendation I wrote for Qasim in support of his nomination for a Homer Higbee Award.
[†] AR eval 1999–2000.

DWI YULIANTORO and BELLA TIRTOWALUJO (Indonesia)

Indonesians, I have discovered, usually come in dyads, triads, and groups. They can work well alone, but the social support they thrive on is seldom far away. This has been a big advantage for internationalization, where in any activity, one enthusiastic Indonesian participant may lead to another and then another. In our college the key to forming such a chain of students has been Dwi Yuliantoro. He stands out as one of a few international students who during the period covered by this book have acted as gifted ambassadors linking their home countries to MSU. He has put his outgoing personality, openness to other cultures, and enthusiasm at the service of a number of the college's most significant internationalization efforts and in particular has been instrumental in bringing more extraordinary students like himself to MSU.

Indonesia is an immense, important country with the fourth largest population in the world, a vast expanse of over six thousand inhabited islands whose distance from west to east is longer than the United States coast to coast. It has had a rapidly growing economy. For years it was a concern of mine that until recently, the college had almost no students from Indonesia. When Dwi arrived as a Fulbright master's student, the first Indonesian student I got to know well, it was such a welcome breakthrough, especially since he soon threw himself into a personal campaign to bring more students from his country. And this paid off with a number of extraordinary individuals.

Before coming to East Lansing, Dwi had had diverse professional and work experiences in Indonesia, notably as a teacher of English. He had worked in both the private and the university sectors. He was involved in exchange programs, including a youth exchange between Indonesia and Canada. But in spite of his cosmopolitan spirit, Dwi remains very much wedded to his home country and likes to tell about and promote it. His hometown allegiance is to the cultural capital of Yogyakarta, even though he spent the first twelve years of his life in Jakarta. He identifies strongly with his roots in the Javanese communities of central Indonesia. In fact, during his first semester at MSU, homesickness was a big problem for him. But after one semester, he conquered this in a big way, becoming his true outgoing and congenial self, a student who is extremely fond of others in the MSU community, as they are of him.

After finishing his master's, he decided to stay on to do a doctorate. At first he was thinking of a PhD in higher and adult education (HALE), but after he went home the summer of his first year, he was convinced that he wanted to do his doctorate in teacher education. During that summer he had a chance to lead a professional development program for Indonesian teachers at the preuniversity level. He found this effort so rewarding that he decided to study for further work of this sort rather than concentrating on preparation for administrative roles in education.

At MSU Dwi became known as one of the most enthusiastic participants in a range of extracurricular activities. He was not only one of the most committed participants in LATTICE but also one of the most highly regarded leaders among the students in this project. In addition, he has done other volunteer work in area schools and at the East Lansing mosque.

Another of the key links in our growing chain of memorable Indonesian students and alumni is Bella Tirtowalujo. She came from Jakarta, the immense Indonesian capital that, by one measure, is one of the three largest metropolitan areas in the world. She was born there, not one of the millions of people who have moved to Jakarta but trace their family's roots and cultural identity to other parts of the gigantic Indonesian archipelago. Unlike Dwi, she is a member of the Christian minority, whereas Dwi belongs to the majority Muslim population. Nevertheless, like Dwi, she has played a big role in the leadership of the Indonesian students in our college, for example, in working on the annual Indonesia cultural festival at MSU. At the same time, she can be seen Sundays as one of the regulars in the choir at All Saints Episcopal Church in East Lansing.

Bella and Dwi are bonded to non-Indonesian students as well as their Indonesian compatriots. They started a small but multinational group who rented a four-bedroom apartment together, becoming a model for what I would like to see all international students experience in their living arrangements at MSU. For example, one year their apartment was home to a Mexican and a Palestinian from Israel as well as Dwi and Bella. Then Dwi moved on and a Tanzanian took his place. The next year it was a Colombian who replaced the Palestinian, who went away to do his dissertation research. In this apartment, each of the students took on cooking responsibilities for the group, and together they engaged in leisure activities as well, including movie nights in the apartment. Since the Tanzanian had never been to the States before, the group took charge of keeping him from spending all this time at his books, as he was inclined to do, and introduced him to a new country and new experiences, like bowling. In addition to the four students living in the apartment, their social world attracted others, including two U.S. Latinos who like Bella were teaching assistants in the social studies component of teacher education. Although each person was a strong member of this group and all were male except Bella, it was Bella who was their leader.

Dwi and Bella joined together in an ambassadorial role. For example, they began to lobby for one of our doctoral study tours to go to Indonesia. With their encouragement and offers of help, Laura Apol was readily convinced to apply to be the faculty leader of this group, a proposal was written, and the doctoral study tour was off and running—a phenomenal success. To plan and carry out this tour, Laura, Dwi, and Bella relied on their extensive network of MSU alumni back in Indonesia who are always up for any way to connect with and support their alma mater.

At the beginning of 2013, influenced by our high regard for the Indonesian students, my wife and I decided to spend a month in Indonesia, a country I had never visited. It was of course Dwi to whom we turned first for advice. When I told him six months in advance of our intent, he got so excited that I had the impression that he would have liked to put us on a plane right away and arrange for a red carpet and dignitaries on our arrival. It was a metaphor for what actually happened. Dwi, Bella, and our other Indonesian students shared their networks and insights with us to make for one of the most memorable and valued trips we have taken.

When the Global Educators Cohort Program (GECP) was created, Dwi became the indispensable graduate assistant who, working with the coordinator, had a strong impact on the program. He was responsible for organizing GIFT, the Global Initiative Forum for Future Teachers, a gathering of GECP students for discussions and presentations modeled in various ways on LATTICE. At the end of 2012–13, when Dwi gave up this responsibility, Margo Glew, the coordinator of GECP and Dwi's supervisor, wrote the following: "It is a bittersweet time as Dwi started working with me on the day we began efforts to develop this awesome global program. He worked with me in 2007–08 as we conceptualized, recruited for, and implemented our very first cohort of students. He has been my colleague, my helper, my sounding board, and my friend and while I am so happy for him and his accomplishment I will really miss him!"*

Dwi's leadership in GECP was also attested to on the Web by one of the GECP undergraduates, Ashley Maloff, in a piece titled "GECP Says Good-bye to Dwi." She wrote, "During my time in GECP, I had the opportunity to meet and work with a very special person, Dwi. Dwi quickly became one of the people that I knew I could turn to for advice, encouragement, and a listening ear throughout my educational journey, and I now consider him to be a colleague, mentor, and lifelong friend. Dwi helped to make Michigan State feel a lot less like 'just school,' and a lot more like home."[†]

This quotation is testimonial to the success of the integration-infusion approach, where international doctoral students are strongly involved in the studies and life of undergraduates and can even make MSU feel more like home for American undergraduates. Dwi may be exceptional. But even with all his leadership skills and ability to relate positively to people of all ages and backgrounds, his impact on the college would have been less if it were not for the talents and efforts of the other Indonesians who, like Bella, made up the Indonesian chain that helped hold our international community in the college together and pulled in students who had had no international experience.

NOTES

* Email from Margo Glew to me and other GECP colleagues, April 3, 2013, Subject Dwi farewell.
† Retrieved from the MSU Global Educators Cohort Program blog.

was easy. An email out of the blue could launch the whole process. This happened with the Japanese student Takayo Ogisu, who, though previously unknown, wrote an email to me expressing interest in graduate studies. In contrast to the many emails received that contained no sign of either exceptional qualifications or reasons why MSU would be well suited to the student, Takayo presented her qualifications and interests, which centered on the study of education and development in Cambodia, in such a way that I was immediately convinced she was a person we should try to attract. I got Avner Segal, the faculty member in charge of the doctoral program in the teacher education department, and Chris Wheeler, who had worked in Cambodia, to help make sure we followed up on Takayo's interest. As a result, we were able to bring the college one of those rare students who rose to every challenge, answered questions in class that no one else could answer, and wrote better English than many of her fellow students who were native speakers of English. She told me later that she had been attracted to MSU initially because she had attended the national CIES meetings earlier and had concluded from the sessions at which MSU people were presenting that this was probably the place for her.

Meeting with Students and Bringing Them Together

In the transformational era of the 1980s, MSU was striking out in new directions, attempting to be different from other schools of education in its engagement with reform and practice, building on a strong research base. The philosophy of integration-infusion called for international students to be fully part of this effort, and I was strongly supported by Deans Lanier and Ames to be the advocate for these students. To achieve this, the integration-infusion approach emphasized collaboration, teamwork, and collegiality across all borders. However, groups of students from disparate countries did not by themselves naturally form the sort of engaged community that was needed and that would benefit the students and the college. Left to themselves, international students faced many obstacles in a large college that traditionally revolved around domestic American concerns in spite of the importance of various international projects. To support and engage these students adequately and to create a community among them and like-minded Americans called for special steps. Over the years we tried out many ideas to make this happen. Some of these steps became regular events in our yearly cycles, and others worked well for a number of years, but petered out after a while when conditions changed. One of the most effective approaches we have taken was the LATTICE project. Originally, we thought of it merely as a means of giving teachers international perspectives, and in part for this reason we paid students a small stipend for attending. But then, although continuing to pay the stipend, we realized that LATTICE was equally effective in bonding our students from diverse countries among themselves and forming the community we were aiming for.

To increase communication among international students and help form a stronger international community within the college, in 1993 we established a listserv for these students plus other students or faculty members who were interested. This listserv still exists today and is used frequently. In 1993 listservs were still in their infancy. Fortunately, we had an American PhD student, Vickie Banks, who had established herself as the guru of listservs and who was one of the earliest people in our college to see this precursor of social media as an area of research. She gave freely of her time in making our listserv a success. The listserv proved invaluable in providing information to students, but it has always been less successful in terms of students and faculty members engaging in conversation with one another. The struggle to do better at the latter was already evident in my 1994 report to the dean: "When I was away . . . in Sweden and the Netherlands, I sent messages back to the network in order to model for students the ease of communication through email. At present nearly all international students are on the network, and with few exceptions are reading their email regularly. We have been less successful in fostering conversation."[3] The 1995 report again elaborated on our experience in this regard: "We have continued to reinforce and improve [the listserv] this year so that a steady, but not overwhelming stream of communication is maintained with our international students, including notices about graduate assistantships, scholarships, new courses, immigration issues, special co-curricular activities for international students, as well as messages of personal interest. I also sent out a separate message to internationally oriented faculty suggesting ways in which they could help strengthen this network, but so far we have not had the response I had hoped. On the other hand, I meet international students in the hall that I either don't know too well or that I have not seen for some time, and find that they are keenly aware of and interested in messages that we have been sending out."[4]

The Office of International Studies in Education also served as a place where international students could seek assistance and advice for all sorts of problems—academic, financial, and personal—when their departments and advisers had not been able or willing to be helpful. In earlier years, when we did not have much financial aid for international students and it was hard for them to get assistantships, I spent a lot of time with them for this and other reasons. In my annual report to the dean in 1996 I put it this way: "I continue to spend a lot of time meeting with international students to discuss academic issues and other problems. These include selection of advisors and doctoral committee members, selection of courses, choice of research areas, bibliographical search issues, search for assistantships and other sources of financial aid, preparation of resumes and letters of application, need for letters of recommendation and other sorts of mentoring needs that are not being met by the students' advisors."[5]

Especially memorable among these students was Deng Zong-Yi, a very intense and intelligent young man in physics education from China, who came with nowhere near enough money to keep him going even for the first year (as theoretically required by U.S. immigration), and who therefore used to stop by my office on a weekly basis to see if I had found a job for which he was likely to be hired. It was frustrating to have to say no for many weeks, but I assured him that once he got his first assistantship, it would become easier and easier to find such jobs, and as in many other such cases, this turned out to be true. Deng got the assistantships needed to finance his PhD and went on to be a faculty member at two very good institutions: the National Institute of Education in Singapore and the University of Hong Kong.

As the years passed, our students became more and more successful in the competition for the external funds to finance their degrees, even though the opportunities for obtaining scholarships and fellowships are very limited once the student enters graduate school, and this is especially for case for non-U.S. citizens. Among the U.S. citizens we had special success with the Fulbright-Hays and Fulbright dissertation awards. The College of Education was awarded nine between 2004 and 2012. In 2006, when there were only about one hundred Fulbright-Hays awards for the whole United States, we had our best year. MSU as a whole nominated eighteen students and won four fellowships. Three of them were in the College of Education, awarded to Steve Backman for research in Lesotho, Aliah Carolan in Paraguay, and Nils Kauffman for Moldova. In same year Sakeena Elayan, a Palestinian student in educational administration, and Annah Molosiwa, a teacher education student from Botswana, won Margaret McNamara fellowships from the World Bank. Just nine of these World Bank fellowships were awarded across the United States for all areas of study; MSU was only institution to get more than one.[6]

Creating a community of internationally oriented students through social events proved as challenging as gathering around issues of academic and career interest. We worked on both from the beginning. Already in 1984–85, my first year as assistant dean, I made a special effort to interact with students across the college. As faculty adviser for the International Student Association (ISA) in the college, I helped organize an orientation and reception for new students in the fall and a series of six brown-bag lunches in the spring, covering such topics as how to get assistantships and how to prepare for comps. We also started a tradition of entertaining international students in our home (e.g., dinner for about thirty people to honor new international graduates of the college, a brunch for new and former ISA officers, a wine and cheese party for the new student orientation, plus smaller gatherings).[7]

But our longest run of social activities—the continental breakfasts in Erickson Hall—came later, motivated by our mediocre success with other social gatherings. They were held occasionally during the 1990s. Then we had the idea of starting the year with a bigger breakfast at our home. The home breakfast started ostensibly as a celebration of my sixtieth birthday on August 27, 2001. But the real reason in my mind was that featuring this event as a birthday might get more students to come.

And indeed this breakfast at home was such a success that we decided to do it every year at the beginning of the year to welcome internationally oriented students back to campus and to greet new students. But since we did not have enough money in our university accounts to have the home breakfast catered and paid for by the university, Sharon and I covered the cost ourselves. We figured out a menu that did not take too much time to prepare and did not cost a lot. We opted for special breads, bagels, jams, cream cheese, herring, Swedish hard bread, cheese (always Jarlsberg, Havarti, and cheddar), fruit, oatmeal, and plenty of coffee or tea. At first Sharon and I did all the preparations ourselves, but gradually over the years students began to volunteer to help set up and clean up, and as a result we were soon counting on their help. We invited college administrators, faculty, staff from the college, as well as colleagues from the building next door, which houses all the university-wide international offices. Eventually about one hundred people showed up each year. These breakfasts were notable, among other things, because our dean, Carole Ames, and the dean of international studies and programs, Jeff Riedinger, both made a point of coming, as did other administrators and faculty. This created an opportunity for students to meet and talk to people they otherwise did not often see.

After this initial bash, we continued by serving a much more modest monthly continental breakfast in Erickson Hall (the education building). These monthly breakfasts also got their start in 2001 when 9/11 called for intensified efforts to provide a more supportive environment for the international students who had to deal with the draconian new efforts to monitor and control their access to and movement within the United States. The monthly breakfasts were harder to sustain than the annual breakfast at our home. But after a while, a core group of international or internationally oriented American students with whom we had the closest relationships made a point of coming on a regular basis. For these breakfasts we stuck to even cheaper food paid for from a university gift account: bagels, special breads, jams and jellies, butter, cream cheese, orange juice, coffee and tea. But occasionally the breakfast took a special turn. In 2008, as part of India week at MSU, faculty member Punya Mishra wanted to do a breakfast with Indian food prepared by our Indian faculty and students.[8] It was a great success! And after this success, the Korean students, with their competitive spirit, offered to do one with Korean food.[9] It, too, was very successful. I remember it well because there was this delicious bulgogi, and I was told it had been prepared by Soo-Yong Byun, a postdoc who worked with me in our international teacher education research.

Surprised, I asked him if it wasn't unusual for a Korean male to prepare such a dish. "Oh no," he replied. "Nowadays we have to know how to cook. Otherwise, no one wants to marry us." It was once again, as so often happened, an opportunity to learn, without even intending to, a lesson about cultural change in a most pleasant way.

Since creating a real sense of community to include international students as well as other students and faculty demanded more hospitality than just monthly breakfasts, I tried to do as much socializing with students as I could. In truth, it was one of the practices that made my job so enjoyable. The year 1994–95 was a good example, and I reported as follows to the dean: "Sharon and I did a good deal of entertaining this year, mostly at our own expense, on behalf of the College and to create a sense of community, friendship and concern for students, faculty and visitors. This included but was not limited to the following: watching Cameroon-Brazil World Cup match on TV at our house (all African students invited), dinner at home for visitors from the Guinea Ministry of Education (plus African student guests), birthday party for me (mostly Latino and Latin American faculty), dinner for Malaysian visitors (plus Malaysian students), Thanksgiving dinner (African and Asian students and visitors), St. Lucia's Day Swedish smorgasbord (for internationally oriented faculty), Christmas dinner for Peter Dzjimbo, Dean of Faculty of Education, University of Zimbabwe, and our colleague Susan Peters (both on leave, passing through on way to California), and New Year's Day dinner (two African students, plus faculty member Joyce Cain)."[10]

Jian Wang, a Chinese student at MSU, now a tenured chaired professor at Texas Tech, wrote, as follows, to affirm the value of the community that we were striving to create: "People often call the place home that they miss most long after they left it, they always rely on for support wherever they need, and they often show off their connection to whenever they have chances. Michigan State University is such a home to my family and me. Almost everything we have achieved and felt proud of doing ever since we came to US is directly and indirectly tied to Michigan State University and people over there."[11]

Social events were good, but for the community we were trying to create, our regular coursework and advising had to be made to work for international students. But until recently this was achieved only to a variable degree. Still, international students were often surprised to find faculty who made themselves available and interacted with students on a relatively egalitarian basis, inviting students to express themselves openly. For example, Kamila Rosolova of the Czech Republic had this to say, when asked what the benefits of coming to MSU were for her:

You have access to information, lectures I would never, ever find them in my home country. When I saw the authors' names on published articles, they could be here. And these people are really accessible. You can talk to them. You are okay. You feel you are a partner in this environment. You feel you are not going to be humiliated by any professors. You are equal in the community. It's okay to ask things, say what you think. Actually they expect you to do that.[12]

One of our very successful ventures in facilitating the scholarly interests of students was the African Educational Research Group, formed by African students in collaboration with a few faculty in the early 1990s. The purpose was to meet and discuss the students' research ideas and efforts. The group started in early 1990–91, inspired by the experience our students had in attending the African Educational Research Symposium at Ohio University. In 1990, eleven students made presentations at this conference. In 1991, another eleven students together with Anne Schneller and me made the trip to this annual Ohio event, and in 1992 we went with six students, along with a visiting professor from the University of Zimbabwe. We generally rented a university van in order to take all the MSU participants together. In fact, it was in the van on the way back from the conference that the idea for the AERG was first proposed and discussed.[13]

Two years later, before the Tenth Annual African Educational Research Symposium at Ohio University in 1994–95, a student who had participated in this conference in the past posted the following message on our listserv to encourage others to attend: "For the MSU crew, the fun of bonding together on this 7–8 hour trip is exceptional. How many people have really had the opportunity of sharing a car for 7–8 hours times two with Jack or any person of that status. I guess very few. So you can imagine the opportunity the Ohio Conference provides you to gain information, share ideas in an unthreatening context and atmosphere 'MSU van' with Jack."[14]

Through those same years, AERG continued to be active on campus. In 1992–93 it met on average about twice a month to discuss student work and to talk to visitors with African experience. A similar Asian group was started that same year. In 1993–94, thirteen students made presentations to the Asian Group and eight to the African Group, with additional invited presentations from faculty and outside visitors.[15]

Kedmon Hungwe from Zimbabwe, now on the faculty at Michigan Tech, recounted his participation in this and other student research groups as follows: "I found the College of Education to be a lively learning environment. I have wonderful memories of the different research groups. From an international perspective, I enjoyed participating in a research group with faculty and students with research interests in Africa. There were other research groups in my department to choose from. At one time I was participating in three groups."[16]

One of the most important contributions these students could make was to the teaching of students in MSU's five-year teacher preparation program, where they helped make the point that expertise in teaching is not confined to the United States. Internationally oriented students also became graduate assistants, helping to mentor the teacher preparation students during their yearlong fifth-year internship in the schools (see, e.g., dissertations by Jian Wang, 1998, and Martial's brother, Gaston Dembélé, 2005). They also brought their international perspectives to the teaching of on-campus courses for this program. The most notable example of this was TE 250, Human Diversity, Power, and Opportunity in Social Institutions, which was coordinated for years by Chris Wheeler, who was a key person in our international efforts. TE 250 was a large, required social foundations course that has been taught entirely in sections (up to twenty sections) by a mix of faculty and graduate assistants. From 2000 to 2007, when Wheeler was coordinator, twelve international students taught in this course and seven other TAs who were U.S. citizens also were chosen to teach, in part, because of their exceptionally strong international interests and backgrounds.[17]

The intensive coordination and mentoring that characterized this course produced benefits for instructors and students that can be illustrated with excerpts from a letter of recommendation I wrote for Aliah Carolan when she finished her PhD. This was a U.S. student who came with very strong international interests and experience. She had not only been a Peace Corps volunteer but had begun to do international research as an undergraduate. As a doctoral student she was selected for a Spencer Research Fellowship, one of the most competitive and sought-after sources of funding and special support for our students. Her dissertation required extensive fieldwork in a rural area of a developing country.

In the letter of recommendation, I described her teaching experience as follows:

Aliah has also excelled in actual teaching experience at Michigan State. She was a teaching assistant in one of the required courses in our teacher preparation program, TE 250 Human Diversity, Power, and Opportunity in Social Institutions. This course examines issues of culture, identity, diversity and equity in and outside schools. This is a challenge because so many of our students come to this course from relatively homogeneous cultural and social class backgrounds and therefore are not as committed and knowledgeable about social justice issues in education as we would like them to be. The course is notable in that, in spite of being a very large course, it is entirely taught in small sections by instructors who meet frequently and work closely together. It is also exceptional for a course of this size in the emphasis given to service learning assignments for the students. The course has also served as an initial test bed for increased internationalization of our teacher preparation program, with support and funding from our Title VI area studies centers. In my view this course has been the best place in our college to gain higher education teaching experience, in part because for years, until his retirement, it was coordinated by Chris Wheeler, who had very high expectations, very high standards of teaching both for himself and the teaching assistants in the course, took great pains to prepare and mentor the assistants, and yet allowed them considerable autonomy to adapt the syllabus to their own particular interests and strengths. Although I have not taught in the course, I know that Aliah did well, both from talking to Chris and from the fact that assistants who do not measure up are not rehired in later years.

Another major milestone was passed when a few doctoral students began to direct college study abroad programs. There had been opposition to students doing this because it was thought they would not have enough authority to act in loco parentis and deal with excessive drinking or other problematic behavior or even just laxity in meeting course expectations. The first student to overcome this hurdle was Steve Backman, an American student with much experience in Africa. He already had had relevant international experience at Brigham Young University and had none of the difficulties predicted for student leaders of programs.

Our flagship preinternship teaching program in South Africa, after being launched by Anne Schneller and Margaret Holtschlag, has also been led by two students. Corvell Cranfield from South Africa took over this program in the country where it was created, but with the added challenge of moving it from the Richards Bay region to Cape Town. That meant lining up the South African schools and teachers who were keys to the program's success. His leadership kept this flagship course in excellent shape, attracting sufficient students each year. Kurnia Yahya, a Malaysian student, also directed the program when it was introduced to Malaysia.

The results of all this work with students came to fruition in academic achievements, especially the dissertations, which are one of the best indicators of the degree to which we have achieved a college-wide integration of international perspectives. A few examples for each of the college's four departments and one college-wide program are sufficient to illustrate this point:

College-Wide Educational Policy PhD Program

- U.S. student Nils Joseph Kauffman (2009). "Empty Pedestals: Creating a National School System [in Moldova] in an Era of Globalization."
- U.S. student Todd Drummond (2011). "Predicting Differential Item Functioning in Cross-Lingual Testing: The Case of a High Stakes Test in the Kyrgyz Republic."

Department of Teacher Education

- Brazilian student Eduardo Santos Junqueira Rodrigues (2007). "Students' Communicative Practices around Writing and Digital Technologies: An Ethnographical Study of an Inner-City High School in the Northeast of Brazil."
- U.S. student Loukia K. Sarroub (2000). "Becoming American, Remaining Arab: How the 'Hijabat' Negotiate Life in Two Worlds." Later published as *All-American Yemeni Girls: Being Muslim in a Public School* (Philadelphia: University of Pennsylvania Press, 2005).

Department of Counseling, Educational Psychology and Special Education

- Kenyan student Anne M. N. Mungai (1997). "An Investigation of the Study Habits of Female Students (High and Low Achievers) in Rural Primary Schools in Murang's District, Kenya."
- Zimbabwean student Robert Chimedza (1999). "Effects of Different Communication Methods on the Comprehension of Stories by Deaf Students in Zimbabwe: Implications for Classroom Communication and Academic Achievement."

Department of Educational Administration

- Kenyan student Mary Mokeira Ombonga (2008). "Understanding

Experiences of Girls in a Center of Excellence in Kajiado District, Kenya: An Exploratory Case Study."
- U.S. student James M. Lucas (2009). "Where Are All the Males? A Mixed Methods Inquiry into Male Study Abroad Participation."

DEPARTMENT OF KINESIOLOGY

- U.S. student Shannon R. Siegel (1999). "Patterns of Sports Participation and Physical Activity in Urban Mexican Youth." Co-recipient of the 1999 College of Education Outstanding Dissertation of the Year Award.
- Mexican student Maria Eugenia Peña Reyes (2002). "Growth Status and Physical Fitness of Primary School Children in an Urban and a Rural Community in Oaxaca, Southern Mexico."

Conclusion

In spite of all these efforts, our goals for supporting international students have never been more than a partial success. We have no way of knowing how many students were disappointed, frustrated at MSU, and left dissatisfied. We do know that our special activities never attracted more than a minority of all international students, and in spite of my desire to get to know as many of our 150-plus international students as possible, there were always too many that I knew not at all. Keeping this channel of internationalization flowing to the benefit of all the international students and internationally oriented U.S. students as well as to the college was a never-ending challenge.

CHAPTER 10

Two Streams Less Connected with the Main Channels of Internationalization

ometimes international work does relatively little to serve the overall internationalization goals of the college. Such streams of international work can be substantial and important, but for one reason or another they fail to merge with the other streams to strengthen the currents of infusion and integration. One such case in MSU's College of Education was the professional development and master's degree offered to teachers in American International and Department of Defense Schools in all parts of the world. This program went on for decades and took more faculty members to other countries for work than any other program or project of the college. But given this volume, we had to ask how much this program gave faculty members an understanding of other countries outside the American schools in which they taught and, even more importantly, how much of what the participants learned came to influence their teaching and research back in the United States in the direction of internationalization.

Another such case is the college's support of the Japanese Saturday School in Battle Creek. Starting in the late 1980s, the college hired Japanese graduate students from MSU to teach as graduate assistants in the Battle Creek school. This could be done because the Battle Creek Saturday School was sponsored by the Lakeview Public School District as part of the community's overall economic development efforts, which brought a substantial number of Japanese companies to the Battle Creek area. The college's contribution was therefore considered outreach and public service not unlike other projects serving public K–12 systems. Moreover, this effort was, it appeared, an opportunity to examine globalization as it affected a Michigan community and to learn from the experiences of Japanese families in Battle Creek. In this way it was not unlike learning from the experiences of American families served by the American International Schools in which MSU provided professional development. However, examination of this experience over the years has shown that, with few exceptions, neither MSU faculty nor students took much advantage of our access to this site to do the research needed to strengthen our internationalization efforts.

Graduate Studies in Education Overseas (GSEO)

MSU started the GSEO program in 1972. In the early years, MSU faculty were sent directly to the larger American International Schools or Department of Defense schools to offer MSU courses to teachers right within their own school. Initially the program was not in the College of Education, but operated out of the Kellogg Center for Continuing Education under the MSU dean of lifelong education. But in 1987–88, the program was transferred organizationally to our college because the courses it offered were education courses. Then, after a year or so, it was physically moved to the College of Education and installed in remodeled premises in Erickson Hall that had once belonged to the university's TV and radio stations. At that time, Bruce Burke, a longtime College of Education faculty member, was appointed as senior faculty consultant, responsible for long-term planning, development, and assessment in this program. Sandy Bryson was maintained as program manager in charge of daily operations. Sandy, who earned a doctorate from our college, had spent virtually his whole career working on MSU international projects. He was a master in sending faculty members to teach throughout the world, as well as in managing whatever else came up in the GSEO program.

When GSEO first came into the college, Bruce and Sandy reported to me. But shortly after Carole Ames became dean in 1993, she put GSEO in a separate Office for Academic Outreach so it could take responsibility for all the college's off-campus courses, international or domestic, with Bruce and Sandy continuing as the principal managers. Bruce Burke soon proved to be especially creative in finding new ways to market the international program and make it work. Later when he retired, Susan Melnick, who had taught at GSEO sites at many locations around the world, took his place as assistant dean for academic outreach.

In 1984 before GSEO was incorporated in the college, the *Report of the Task Force on International Activities* had identified GSEO as an area of promise in implementing the integration-infusion approach.[1] GSEO was already the international activity in which College of Education faculty were most engaged. That year GSEO courses were offered at thirty-two locations. Two degrees could be earned by the teachers at the schools in those locations, a master's degree and an educational specialist degree. Unlike other institutions that offered similar programs, such as the University of Maryland, the college strongly felt that the program should be staffed by persons from MSU and not local hires. This was intended to ensure that the courses would be of the same quality as those offered on campus. Therefore, ordinarily the persons sent were East Lansing faculty, although as years went on, there was some use of retired faculty and doctoral students as well.

In 1987–88, the year GSEO became an organizational part of the college, it delivered courses in twenty-seven overseas sites with twenty-six College of Education faculty and five advanced doctoral students teaching. But by the time of the next year's report, GSEO was facing a "rapidly changing, unstable and competitive" environment and as a result had opened up negotiations for "new master's degree centers as replacements for possible reductions in GSEO operations elsewhere."[2] The reason was, after a couple of decades of school-based professional development, a great majority of the teachers in the larger schools, the main sites for GSEO in earlier years, had master's degrees, and so enrollments in MSU courses declined. In response, the college, under the leadership of Bruce Burke and Sandy Bryson, redesigned the program so it could be completed through several periods of summer study at special centers established for this purpose, with some coursework at a distance during the academic year. In order to make MSU master's level courses and degrees more readily accessible to international schoolteachers at smaller as well as larger international schools, the first such center started up at Valbonne, France, in summer 1991 and the second in Bangkok in 1992.[3]

When the Bangkok Center was opened in 1992, student credit hour production increased 12 percent. Offerings were broadened to include portfolio assessment, health education, physical education, and, in one of the efforts to serve administrators, a course in philosophy of education for administrators. Already by 1991–92, the annual report reported that a total of forty-eight different College of Education faculty members had had the chance to teach internationally for GSEO during the previous three years, equal to about a third of the tenure-stream faculty at that time.[4] And in 1993–94, the annual report stated that GSEO was serving about five hundred educators in its annual program, including 120 active master's degree candidates.[5] In 1997–98, GSEO was still doing business outside of, as well as at, the two main centers. That year it offered fifty-four courses taught by twenty-eight professors in eleven different countries in Europe, Africa, and Asia, including countries as diverse as Brazil, China, Egypt, Indonesia, Korea, and Madagascar.[6]

The two centers operated successfully for years. But eventually, better technology facilities were needed, and therefore a new center was established first in Switzerland and then in Ireland, and the Valbonne center gradually phased out. As a result the Department of Counseling, Educational Psychology and Special Education (CEPSE) was able to start a new overseas MA in educational technology and instructional design in Leysin, Switzerland, in summer 1999.[7]

The idea that GSEO should contribute to internationalization had long been advocated. For example, the 1984 task force report put it this way: "The College should continue to offer its instructional programs overseas but employ revised procedures to ensure that in the selection of both sites and faculty, the development of the international expertise of the College and its faculty take equal place with the interests of overseas clientele in offering programs."[8]

From time to time the promise of GSEO to contribute to internationalization was demonstrated though not on a regular, routine basis. Jim Gallagher taught science courses in GSEO that capitalized on location to help teachers learn about the local geophysical and biological environment. One such course was taught in Kenya in the early 1990s on the changing ecology of East Africa. In 1987–88 GSEO made it possible for seven faculty members to lecture at universities in China.[9] And in another of the few instructional attempts to make the program a more effective vehicle of internationalization, faculty member Sandra Hollingsworth offered a course in Taiwan in the early 1990s in which teachers studied Chinese education, teacher education, and culture, in hopes of promoting internationalization of the international school curriculum.

In September 1995, Moore, Bryson, and Pinheiro from the college reported on research to "assess the impact of GSEO overseas teaching assignments on faculty professional development." It was based on a survey of all College of Education faculty who had taught for GSEO in the preceding three years. The survey was sent to thirty-nine faculty members, of which thirty-three, or 80 percent, responded. Of the thirty-three faculty, three had had only one GSEO assignment, twelve had two to five assignments, and eighteen had had more than five assignments. The overall conclusion was to "confirm that GSEO experiences have contributed significantly to faculty professional development and have had an impact on the acquisition of professional knowledge as well as contributed in useful ways to international awareness and responsiveness to students from other cultures."[10]

But when examined more carefully, the results seem mixed and not so conclusive. More specifically, when asked whether GSEO had influenced their career direction, twenty-one, or 64 percent, said no, while twelve, or 36 percent, said yes. Nevertheless, almost all of the respondents (thirty-two, or 97 percent) claimed that GSEO experience had contributed to their professional development. In response to a question about whether GSEO had had an impact on their research, only eleven said it had had some impact, and of that number only eight had done professional presentations or publications directly related to GSEO. Significantly, all eight of these faculty members had had more than five GSEO assignments.

As far as global awareness was concerned, fifteen, or 45 percent, of the respondents asserted that GSEO experience had helped them to understand global issues "to a great extent," fourteen "to some extent," and the remaining four "to a little extent." This finding should be interpreted with some caution, given that the most endorsed reason for participating in the GSEO program was "interest in travel."

The GSEO program undoubtedly had a major positive impact on the college for many years, primarily because it was a great incentive for faculty, who not only enjoyed the opportunity to spend time abroad, but also found the teachers in American International Schools to be stimulating and rewarding to work with. Nevertheless, the sense persisted among college faculty and administrators that this program had not contributed to the integration-infusion approach by influencing the content of on-campus courses, giving faculty opportunities and professional development, leading to other international efforts, and so on. The reason for this is that it was almost entirely confined to the world of American International Schools and Department of Defense schools. The program therefore operated largely in accordance with American norms and practices and offered limited opportunities to become immersed in the culture and living conditions of the host country. Over the years, there was discussion of how to change this, for example, by extending faculty trips to include work in the host country's national education system, but we could never work out financing for this in any widespread way, and, moreover, faculty usually felt pressed to get back to

East Lansing for other work after finishing their teaching. The one indisputable contribution GSEO made to integration/infusion was the recruitment of doctoral students from those schools (e.g., Shirley Miske, who now has her own firm to do international development projects, came to MSU from being assistant high school principal at the International School of Hong Kong).

Carole Ames, feeling all the pressures on faculty to do more with less, eventually decided that GSEO was no longer of sufficient value to the college and closed it down, with new admissions ending in 2002. One of the reasons was that it was still basically an expatriate program that had failed to contribute sufficiently to overall internationalization.

Teachers for Japanese Saturday School in Battle Creek

Paul Williams had a problem. Williams was superintendent of schools in Lakeview School District in Battle Creek, Michigan. In the 1980s, Battle Creek had put on a successful campaign to attract Japanese plants to the area. By the late 1980s, thirteen Japanese companies had opened plants in the vicinity. At the time Japanese managers and their families were sent to Battle Creek to live for a number of years to staff these firms. The community through its economic development commission, Battle Creek Unlimited, went out of its way to make them feel welcome. The children needed a way to keep up and be able to return to school in Japan without falling behind. As a result, the Lakeview School District in Battle Creek started a Japanese Saturday School, cosponsoring it with a parent committee and their companies. Japanese Saturday Schools exist in many locations, providing instruction on Saturdays to enable Japanese children outside the country for a limited number of years to keep up with Japanese language and with mathematics at the level taught in Japan. However, it was difficult to staff the Battle Creek school with teachers inasmuch as the number of hours of teaching was so limited that it was not economically feasible to bring the teachers from Japan. Since Williams was one of the most gung-ho alumni of the MSU College of Education, he brought the problem to the college, thinking that perhaps hiring Japanese students to teach would be the answer. Although these students according to U.S. immigration policy could not work for employers outside the university, the fact that the Saturday School was sponsored by the public school district and offered in district facilities made it possible to consider appointing the students as university graduate assistants.

The rationale was that the collaboration with a Japanese school sponsored by a public school district could be considered part of normal MSU outreach. We started offering this service in 1987–88, when we employed six graduate assistants for the Saturday School.[11]

Another reason for doing this was that the school and community could be a site for research on globalization and its effect, especially in education. Or at least it could have served as a site for producing papers by graduate students, especially in K–12 administration. But, with few exceptions, little of this happened. One exception was in 1991–92 when two MSU doctoral students did their research practicums at Lakeview. Through textbook analysis, classroom observation, and teacher interviews in Battle Creek, Mako Sato compared the Lakeview K–6 mathematics curriculum and teaching methods to the Japanese national curriculum, while Akihito Kamata assisted the district in the organization and interpretation of Michigan assessment data.[12] A still more important exception that illustrated the potential of this site for such work was the dissertation of Amy Damrow. She did a remarkable and unique ethnographic study of one Japanese youngster's experience both at school and at home, first in Battle Creek as an expatriate in school and then back in Japan, where Damrow followed him to finish her data collection. The abstract to her dissertation highlights the interest of this study as follows:[13]

> Two story lines run through the dissertation. The first allows us to learn something about a boy as he goes to school and makes friends during a time of ecological transition; the other invites us to reflect on the systems of which he is a part in both the United States and Japan. I consider daily life in three particular schools, the ways that schools structure childhood, and the challenges border-crossing children face as they navigate implicit and explicit expectations. The study examines how friendships are conceptualized and experienced in different ways in different contexts.

Other than these exceptions, providing teaching assistants for the Battle Creek Japanese Saturday School should be seen as a service to the Battle Creek community and its Japanese residents, a means of financial support and on-the-job experience for MSU Japanese students (and therefore a way of recruiting these students), and finally a modest source of revenue for the college. For the most part the program operated smoothly in spite of having to reconcile very different systems—from calendar to expectations. Our most challenging learning experience in figuring out how to do this was when the graduate assistants got fed up with the fact that they were spending more time than the assistantships officially required—ten hours a week on average for quarter-time appointments. Given the time taken in transporting them to Battle Creek, the time spent teaching there Saturday mornings, and preparation, their claims were justified. But the resolution was not clear-cut due to the fact that at MSU, each college was supposed to have its own policy for GA work expectations, and our college did not have anything that quite fit this situation. We let this situation get out of hand, and the students got very upset. In response, the MSU ombudsperson and other university authorities were soon telling us what we had to do. The students had to be given vacation time, but it was up to us to say how much. The students also had to be compensated for the extra time, but it was up to us to figure out how much. The result was ultimately a rather elaborate letter explaining the contract with students and laying out the expectations in detail, including the required extra compensation and vacation time.

Conclusion

GSEO was important to the college because for so many years it gave faculty members international experience on all the populated continents, making it a strong source of satisfaction for these professors. The college was able to offer master's degree work to teachers in American International Schools and DoD schools, a target population that our faculty found rewarding to work with. These teachers were also a pool from which good doctoral students were drawn. And finally, for many of these years, it was a significant source of revenue for the college. But while contributing so much to the college in these ways, GSEO never proved to be as effective as we hoped in contributing to internationalization of the college in terms of its research and teaching back on campus.

The Japanese Saturday School in Battle Creek was similar in its benefits and drawbacks. The financial benefits helped us support Japanese graduate students at MSU and even to recruit them from Japan in the ongoing search for the students who were most qualified for our programs. The program was also needed by the community of Battle Creek, which for economic development reasons looked for ways to support the local Japanese community. When the college provided support, its reputation benefited in turn. However, our hope to encourage research on

Japanese Saturday School, its students, their adaptation to Battle Creek, and the ramifications for the community in general—all with the goal of better understanding globalization and its effect on Michigan schools and communities—was realized only to a small degree. And yet as the program continues, the opportunity to do more of this research remains.

International Visiting Scholars, a Source of Internationalization That Could Exceed Expectations but Often Did Not

G iven the college's reputation as a top school of education and one that was very active internationally, it was to be expected that many colleagues around the world would want to come for a visit. So over the years, we have had a great many international visiting scholars, usually individuals, sometimes groups. Many visits are for a week or less but others have lasted from several months to a year. Over the years we put a lot of effort and resources into being a good host. It was our policy that if we told colleagues that they were welcome to visit, we needed to make sure the visitors were lined up with whatever they needed to accomplish their goals. The secretary in our office spent a lot of time setting up schedules, including the challenging task of persuading reluctant faculty to set time aside for the visitors. In other universities, many visitors have been left to fend for themselves, but in my view this risks a bad experience, which, in turn, does the university's reputation no good. Adequate support means ensuring access to the faculty in the visitor's areas of interest, plus opportunities to observe university classes and visit k–12 schools.

This chapter examines the question of how much and under what conditions the college's internationalization efforts benefited from the visiting scholars it hosted. Looking back, I remain skeptical that the college and its international programs have benefited sufficiently from these visitors. But there were exceptions, visitors who played important roles or responded in ways that were extremely beneficial to the college. By all accounts, the most important long-term visitor to our college over this twenty-eight-year period was Harry Judge after he retired as chair of the Educational Studies Department at Oxford. Another important visitor was Sigrid Blömeke from Humboldt University in Berlin, who played a very important role in TEDS-M, a seventeen-country study of teacher education.

Taking a College-Wide Perspective

Judge and Blömeke were not the only visitors to make noteworthy contributions to the college. Another visitor who was much less well known than Judge or Blömeke but who left a very positive impression was Hiroshi Takahata from Japan's Shimane University. He spent a year with us studying our teacher education programs in exceptionally serious and systematic fashion. Even though he had a hard time communicating in English, he nevertheless was able to learn and do what he wanted. Whenever he came to my office to get my advice, he always had a carefully prepared agenda that indicated clearly what he knew and what he wanted to find out. But the most impressive indication of the impact of this visit came a few years later when Hiroshi wrote that he wanted to come back with two colleagues for a follow-up. We learned that, among other things, they wanted to give a colloquium to discuss how their university's teacher education had been influenced by and benefited from what he had learned earlier at MSU. This colloquium was one of the most satisfying experiences we ever had with a long-term visiting scholar.

Still another noted visitor was Kabiru Kinyanjui, who visited from Nairobi, Kenya, for five weeks in fall 1992, funded by a grant that Anne Schneller had applied for.[1] Kinyanjui was a noted educational and social researcher, a program officer with the Canadian International Development Research Center (then one of the most effective agencies for educational research in developing countries). Unfortunately, this visit turned out to be grueling for our visitor. In order to get the grant to finance the visit, we promised he would visit all the Big Ten universities who were members of the Midwest Universities Consortium for International Activities (MUCIA), and this turned out to be much harder to do than we had thought, in large part because the weather was very bad that year. In the season of severe thunderstorms, in order to deliver on our promise of visits to the other Big Ten universities, we had had to schedule Kinyanjui on the small planes serving the university towns he had to visit (the University of Minnesota, located in a major metropolitan area, was an exception). The turbulence he had to put up with was unusually bad. Thinking of all those bumpy, unpleasant rides, I was feeling very guilty by the time the visit was over. Nevertheless, Kinyanjui made it clear he was impressed with what we were doing to mentor our African students compared to what he observed at other MUCIA universities he visited.

LEADERSHIP PROFILE

HARRY JUDGE (England)

Harry Judge was commissioned by the Ford Foundation in the early 1980s to study American graduate schools of education. In the little book he wrote about his results,* he characterized the scene as one with a few elite schools like Harvard, Stanford, and Chicago that modeled themselves on graduate schools of arts and sciences and avoided involvement in actual K–12 schools. On the other hand, most education schools ("plebeian" he called them) were much more involved in K–12 schools but generally were not doing much creditable research.

After publication of this report, Judge was told that MSU, under the leadership of Judith Lanier and Lee Shulman, was different and was becoming strong in research while at the same time building up its relationships with K–12 schools. To find out more about this unusual dual strength, Judge came to MSU, struck up a strong relationship with Dean Lanier, and remained close to MSU for years to see how its efforts at reform of teaching and teacher education were faring at local, state, and national levels. For some years, he was often on-site at MSU as a visiting professor, including three years in which he was appointed half-time. During that time, among other things, he launched a project, funded by the Spencer Foundation, for research on the relations between universities and teacher education programs in the UK, France, and the United States.† It was also the era of the Holmes Group, a coalition that was organized by Lanier and other leading deans of education in 1986 as a force for reform from the inside.‡ Judge became increasingly influential and heavily committed during these years as one of the most important consultants to the Holmes Group.

Judge's philosophy of teacher education can also be seen not only in his continuing presence and voice in U.S. reform efforts, but also, surprisingly, in work he did in

Pakistan for the Aga Khan Foundation and Aga Khan University, which paralleled positions taken by the Holmes Group. This was his one and only major detour from his Western roots in a career that otherwise extended out of Britain, in the main, only to the United States and France. Incidentally, this involvement in Pakistan also led me to take a continuing interest in the Aga Khan Foundation and Aga Khan University. The unique nature of Aga Khan University and why it attracted Judge's interest and guidance is explained in an article written by Judge's successor at Oxford, Richard Pring:

> The Aga Khan University was established in the early 1980s in Karachi, Pakistan. It was, in many senses, unique as a university foundation. From the beginning it was intended to be "world class," and yet it did not start with the subject or mission which one would normally associate with a world class university—the study of history, of law, of sciences, or of theology. The creation of the university was primarily to meet the social problems of a developing country where many were deprived of basic necessities for a fulfilling life—health care, medical treatment and education. These services required professional knowledge and preparation, albeit in the context of appropriate research. The first courses therefore were in community health care, quickly followed by the establishment of a medical school. Already there was an underlying conception of the relation of theory to practice. Theory cannot be developed independently of practical involvement—the "making sense of the situation" which one is in and experiencing.[§]

So when His Highness the Aga Khan decided it was time to add education as a field of study and practice to medicine at the AKU, he established a task force in 1988 and appointed Harry Judge as chair to recommend an appropriate institutional framework for programs with a mission analogous to that of the medical school. The report of this task force argued against establishing a conventional university faculty of education, reflecting Judge's view that such faculties across the world had been failures as far as influencing elementary and secondary schools in the directions that were needed. Instead the AKU Institute for Educational Development (IED) would be created within a complex of Aga Khan primary and secondary schools, albeit with a building of its own, in order to create a context in which theory and practice, research and the wisdom of practice, researchers, teacher educators, and practitioners could all be brought together in a fruitful mixture from which would emerge better research, better practice, and the basis for better teacher education.[ii]

The Universities of Oxford and Toronto became partners in the realization of this vision for the AKU in Karachi. Having influenced the vision of the task force, MSU was also originally slated to be a partner. But a condition was to find a U.S. donor to pay MSU's costs, and as it turned out, even with the help of Jeremy Greenland, the very effective education program officer at the Geneva headquarters of AKF, no such donor could be found to underwrite MSU's participation. In Harry's case as well, he did not play an on-site role in the implementation of the vision he had inspired, but his imprint remained on an IED that became increasingly important in Pakistan and other countries.

After the IED was established in 1992, its first program was a MEd for practicing teachers from affiliated schools who spent two years at the IED studying to become master teachers with the ability to mentor other teachers in their school of origin or another similar school and become change agents at the grassroots level. The emphasis was on whole-school improvement. Throughout their whole collaborative field-based program, the teachers in this program worked continually with students and teachers to learn this new role and to meet its ambitious demands. In a 2006 book on the program, it was noted, for example, that "the M.Ed. programme aims to prepare reflective practitioners and so has an explicit focus on action research, maintaining reflective journals and encouraging a critically questioning stance towards own practice and to all knowledge."[#]

For anyone familiar with the educational reform efforts undertaken by MSU in the 1980s and early 1990s, it hardly needs to be said how much this AKU story resembles the philosophy and presumptions of educational reform advocated by Judge, Dean Lanier, and others whose efforts centered in East Lansing.

Nothing in Judge's background predestined him to play such an important role in the globalization of teacher education and work for a radical transformation of faculties of education.** Born in 1928 to a relatively modest, but not underprivileged family (his father held a white-collar job in the railway system), Harry Judge was a scholarship student at Cardiff High School for Boys in Wales. He went on to win a competitive place at Brasenose College at Oxford, where he came back later and was still serving at the end of his career. Earlier (1954–59) he had served as a history teacher in two grammar schools with a good reputation for their strongly academic curricula. At the same time, he did a PhD outside education by writing a thesis in French history. Then in 1961, at the age of thirty-three, he was interviewed for headmaster of another grammar school, located in Banbury, a job that changed his life. During this interview, he was given no warning of the difficulties he was going to face at a time when the different types of secondary schools in England were under strong countervailing pressures. There was pressure from those who wanted these schools to amalgamate in some way as well as from those who were unalterably opposed to such a blending. Banbury, with its secondary modern schools as well as the more prestigious grammar school, was very much a case in point. By 1965 Harry had become convinced that the only way out was to consolidate all these schools in one comprehensive school and not yield to the opposition and anxieties such a move would incur.

> I was convinced, and did not afterwards look back, that the only solution would be a bold one. Unless one school was created as rapidly as it honestly could be, then the corrosive uncertainty would spread, tentative plans would proliferate but never come to fruition.[tt]

The plan did come to fruition, and Harry became headmaster. His success in this and other ventures soon vaulted him into the thick of national education politics and policymaking. In 1971 he was named by Margaret Thatcher, then secretary of state for education and science, as one of seven members of the famed James Commission on Teacher Education and Training, which had been given just one year to do its work. During that year Harry continued as headmaster of the Banbury Comprehensive School, but in fact his responsibilities on the commission came close to being full-time. He had to spend four days a week in London or visiting colleges and universities across the country. And as planned, in one year the tight deadline was met; the commission members met with Mrs. Thatcher for dinner on January 24, 1972, to discuss the results of their work.

Harry's part in the commission's labor was soon to be rewarded. Later that same year, in what his noted colleague A. H. Halsey called an "unprecedented promotion for the head of a comprehensive school,"[tt] Harry was plucked out of the world of practice to become director of educational studies at Oxford as well as a professorial fellow at his old college, Brasenose. As director he continued to make his mark as a reformer, leading his department through a period of major change, from emphasis on the academic social science aspects of education to grappling with issues of teaching and curriculum, and working on teacher education with regular schools outside the university. In his 1984 book, Harry pointed out that these changes were inspired not by the research model practiced in U.S. graduate schools of education, but rather by the teaching hospitals affiliated with university faculties of medicine. In advocating these changes Harry foreshadowed the leadership he provided in MSU reform efforts in the 1980s and 1990s.

In spite of these achievements, in a continuing reminder of the barriers facing persons who had not made their whole career as a university scholar, Harry was never given an Oxford chair; it was only after he retired that his successor benefited from the directorship of the Educational Studies Department becoming a statutory chair. Nevertheless, at MSU, as in the United States more generally, this slight mattered not at all. Harry Judge was held in very high regard for his wisdom and insight regarding teacher education reform and for his unmatched brilliance and wit in expressing his ideas. The return, within the United States, on the intellectual capital of such an Oxford don turned out to be very high indeed.

NOTES

* Judge, 1982.
† Judge et al., 1994.
‡ Forzani, 2011.
§ Pring, 2008.
‖ Farah & Jaworski, 2006.
Shamim & Farah, 2006.
** The biographical details that follow are drawn both from the Judge (1984) history of English secondary education following 1944 and from the 2008 *Oxford Review of Education* issue no. 3 in Judge's honor.
†† Judge, 1984, 78.
‡‡ Halsey, 2008.

SIGRID BLÖMEKE (Germany)

Sigrid Blömeke became a full professor at Humboldt University of Berlin at an unusually young age in a system at the time not known for support and promotion of women. At the time she was not known to us at MSU. We found out about her only when we were working on the IEA TEDS-M international teacher education research. She came to our attention when we were looking for people to invite to our first meeting of experts to give us advice on designing the study. In reviewing the cvs submitted in this case by the German IEA General Assembly member, we came across Sigrid's cv, which detailed her research on teacher education. She stood out as having the sort of research interests and qualifications we were looking for. We therefore invited her to the first meeting; she came and immediately made an exceptionally positive impression. It turned out that she was not only knowledgeable and competent in research on teacher education but passionate about it. Our positive assessment of her competence and relevance increased steadily from then on to the end of the study and thereafter.

Sigrid became the TEDS-M national research coordinator for Germany, and she represented Germany in the earlier P-TEDS study as well. When she started to work on TEDS-M, there was a good deal of skepticism and resistance to it in Germany, one of the most important countries to include. Sigrid herself told us at the time there was no way that all sixteen German states would agree to participate. But in the end, because of Sigrid's ability to secure approval and support from the relevant authorities, all the German states did participate. It was a splendid and very welcome achievement.

But representing Germany and German views was only one part of Sigrid's role in TEDS-M. She was so important to overall work on the study and fit so well into the TEDS-M and P-TEDS teams at MSU that, after some time, she decided to accept the invitation to come to MSU as a visiting professor to work more closely and continuously with us. Since her P-TEDS work had made her a key member of that project, at MSU she worked intensively with Bill Schmidt's group as well as the international team. Her MSU office was located in the same office area as Bill Schmidt, Richard Houang, Lee Cogan, Jacqie Babcock, and other members of Bill's team. In all, she spent two years (2007–9) at MSU and became in all ways an integral part of our college, well known, well liked, and well respected by everyone she met. She had the opportunity to show that the international as well as the German research she worked on had significance even for those in the college whose work had been purely domestic, helping them think more internationally and start to align themselves with the integration-infusion approach.

Sigrid had a strong impact on the quality and rigor of P-TEDS and TEDS-M work. When the TEDS-M national centers were given permission, unusual in IEA studies, to publish national reports before the international reports were released, the German reports, not surprisingly, were among the first out the door. They were impressive—solidly and fully analyzed and demonstrating the academic quality of TEDS-M at its best. There were two volumes, each nearly four hundred pages long.* Written in German, they showed that IEA studies had gone beyond the limitations of English-only reporting—starting to overcome what Bourdieu would identify as a questionable marker of what counts as legitimate knowledge in educational research.

Sigrid became more than a colleague. We learned that back in Germany she was a passionate sports fan—of soccer but even more of basketball. But when she arrived at MSU, we found there was a big gap in her sports knowledge. She already knew a lot about the NBA, but very little about college sports. With encouragement from her friends at MSU, she developed into a true Spartan, continuing to follow coach Tom Izzo and his team even after she went back to Germany. It was harder to get her interested in American football, but we did our best. Dean Carole Ames and Associate Dean Cass Book started by taking her to a game, but it was such a Spartan wipeout of a sacrificial nonconference lamb at the beginning of the season that they all got bored and left at the end of the half. The next time was better; we got her invited inside the president's box so she could enjoy the perks of that, including the elaborate spread of snack foods and an opportunity to meet MSU president Lou Anna Simon as well as the famous mascot Sparty himself.

My wife Sharon and I also got to be friends with Sigrid, and today she is one of our closest. She joined our dinner group, people like Chris Wheeler and Richard Houang who were largely from the college and who went out to eat every Friday night. We learned that Sigrid had other virtues of which we had been unaware, such as a love of beer and an ability to explain to poorly informed Americans what to look for in a beer. Friday nights were also the occasion of much discussion of all manner of things, but mostly heated discussion and arguments over politics and university news.

In her second year at MSU, since Sigrid had to give up her apartment in downtown East Lansing, we invited her to live in our house, sharing it with us for the first semester and then having it to herself when we were on sabbatical in Gothenburg during spring 2009.

Our close professional and personal relationship with Sigrid continued after her two years at MSU as a visiting professor. She has come back to work regularly for short periods of time. Mostly, she has collaborated not with the quantitative types who had been her colleagues on TEDS-M, but with Lynn Paine, who turned out to be a kindred spirit with whom Sigrid developed a strong intellectual bond manifesting itself in writing and publication together.†

Overall, then, Sigrid Blömeke represented an ideal type of visitor for an integration-infusion approach. She collaborated on and strengthened some of the most important research in which MSU was engaged. She formed strong professional alliances with some of our best faculty. She became a fan not just of Spartan sports but of many other aspects of MSU as well. But perhaps most importantly, as far as internationalization was concerned, she was by herself a channel to educate us about educational research in Europe and thereby overcome the long-standing tendency of American educational researchers to ignore or discount educational research in non-English-speaking countries. She was also willing to patiently explain many other aspects of her experience and life as a German in the new Europe. She herself was always proud and delighted to show that she did not fit the stereotypes of Germans in general and of the German intellectual elite in particular. Contemptuous of such markers of culture as Bourdieu would have identified for this elite, such as a love of opera or strong interests in the high culture of art museums and the like, Sigrid had grown up in a small rural village where her family and villagers were not investors in this world of cultural capital. Instead Sigrid became the fanatic sports fan that she is and a lover of spending her time fishing and hiking in the remote and rugged world of Norwegian nature. Nevertheless, she was hardly a fish out of water in most of the discussions that preoccupy academics outside their fields. She was very well informed about politics, the economy, the media, and everything else that could be defined as intellectually as serious as opera and museums. In short, would that we could have many other visiting professors like her who could make such major and far-reaching contributions to our integration-infusion approach.

NOTES

* Blömeke, Kaiser & Lehmann, 2010a, 2010b.
† E.g., Blömeke & Paine, 2008.

At the beginning of the new century, another special visitor was Panom Pongpaibool, the secretary-general of the Thailand National Education Commission (NEC), who was also president of the MSU Alumni Association in that country. Much earlier in the 1960s MSU had had a major USAID project to help build up the NEC, which had been established in the Office of the Prime Minister in 1958 as the office with primary responsibility for educational policy in Thailand; that project brought many Thai students like Panom to MSU for graduate study. Starting in the mid-1980s, Panom himself became especially important to MSU as a key supporter of the work Chris Wheeler and colleagues did in Thailand. When Panom was the head of the NEC, that organization was our main partner for the BRIDGES research. Panom came back to MSU first in January 1988 and then again in October 2000, in the latter case so we could celebrate all the achievements of these Thai partnerships and he could receive an outstanding alumni award.[2]

In summer 1999 another important visitor in a position to influence policy came from South Africa. It was Jairam Reddy, former vice-chancellor at the University of Durban, Westville, and chair of South Africa's National Higher Education Commission. He came to MSU as a visiting scholar to do research on higher education.[3]

If we look across the most successful visitors, it becomes clear that they possessed the sort of capital that had widespread appeal in the college among those whose commitment to internationalization was limited, such as faculty working in teacher education research and reform. This was especially true of those visitors who were invited to come and teach regular MSU courses, such as Miriam Ben-Peretz of Israel and Constantinos Papanastasiou of Cyprus. Both of these visitors had collaborated with MSU faculty well before their visit. Ben-Peretz was well known in teacher education circles, with a strong connection to MSU's Sharon Feiman-Nemser. Papanastasiou was Cyprus's principal representative in IEA research, including the landmark TIMSS 1995. It was that study that brought him together with Bill Schmidt. His link to MSU was strengthened when his daughter Elena came to MSU to do her PhD. While Elena was in this program, both her mother and father spent a year at MSU, during which Constantinos taught in the Measurement and Quantitative Methods program. Eventually, after Elena completed her PhD, she succeeded her father as the IEA General Assembly member from Cyprus.

Otherwise, numerous visitors came and went without drawing much attention to themselves or bringing great benefits to MSU. In 1987–88, for example, OISE hosted visitors from Australia, China, England, Indonesia, Israel, Jamaica, New Zealand, Norway, Saudi Arabia, Scotland, Sri Lanka, Switzerland, Thailand, and Zimbabwe. One of our busiest years was in 1993–94, when there were thirty-eight international visitors from eighteen countries, not including a group of thirty Thai principals who visited in August 1993.[4]

Initially, all this hosting of visitors was done for free. But after some years, it became clear that the college did not benefit from all these visits. Although visitors ordinarily expressed great satisfaction and gratitude for how they had been treated and what they had been able to do, many were never heard from again. So when budgets became tight, our office adopted a policy of charging visitors a modest fee for administrative support. Only visitors that the college especially wanted to encourage were hosted for free, and then usually only in cases where the visitor could not afford to pay.

Whole delegations also arrived with some frequency. In May 1988, we had delegation of ten outstanding Chinese elementary and secondary school teachers. In 1993, as mentioned above, thirty-two Thai principals visited as a group. Upon return from her Fulbright in 1998, Ann Austin hosted eleven South African higher education leaders at MSU in March 1999. The following year a course on educational supervision was designed and offered to eleven Saudi Arabian educators at MSU in July 2000, funded by the Saudi Ministry of Education.[5]

These group visits proved to be so much work that we had to insist after some years that at least part of the special costs of hosting them had to be reimbursed. For example, to enable guests to circulate conveniently in our huge and complex campus and surrounding area, we had to hire students to escort and drive them in university vehicles.

Conclusion

After spending a great deal of time hosting visitors over the years, we learned that most of these visits, while of value to the visitors, did little for MSU in return. Subsequently, we tried to accept fewer unless clearly warranted, and began to charge a fee to help defray the costs. Even then our control was limited, since many visitors came as guests, not of the college or one of its departments, but of individual faculty members. Nevertheless, there were major compensations even if on average we gained little from visitors: we had a few visitors like Harry Judge and Sigrid Blömeke who made major contributions to the college. And others made themselves welcome by simply being very engaging and stimulating to have around. They added a lot to the social events we sponsored for faculty and students. The bottom line was that the goal we had set, to have a small number of visitors at all times (at least one or two) and more from time to time to enrich the life of the college, was a target to be maintained, but on condition that they were sufficiently vetted before an invitation was issued so we could be confident they would live up to expectations of benefiting the college.

CHAPTER 12

Finding Enough Money and Support Staff to Feed and Expand Channels

Nowhere in the university is the dependence on external and other soft money more apparent than in its international work. At MSU such funding has always been less bountiful than among some of its peer research universities. But now other major public universities are generally pretty much in the same leaky boat, deprived of the resources to which they had become accustomed by the reductions in public funding for higher education. Little can be done if budgets are limited to hard money. The necessity of international travel and a way to support faculty and students in spending substantial periods abroad make this international work difficult to start and hard to sustain. And if funding is scarce, staff will be scarce. In our case, the leadership of Anne Schneller and other nonfaculty with extraordinary international expertise was key to starting and continuing international work of all sorts.

Taking a College-Wide Perspective

In the 1980s, at Michigan State, outside the College of Education, there were two primary sources of external international funding: USAID and the U.S. Department of

Education Title VI funding for international resource centers.[1] Both have remained important down to the present time, though less sufficient and predominant as the years went on. And in any case, unlike other units at MSU, they never in the twenty-eight years addressed by this book provided sufficient international funding for the College of Education. The college had almost no Title VI funding during this period, although it benefited indirectly from MSU's Center for the Advanced Study of International Development and the area studies centers funded by Title VI. It did have some important USAID projects, including the very beneficial BRIDGES project discussed above. But although it continued to compete for projects that fit with the college's vision (e.g., ones focused on teacher education), it became clear that USAID projects came with many constraints and risks that could easily undermine or cut short the benefits.

LEADERSHIP PROFILE

ANNE SCHNELLER

Anne Schneller is a perfect example of how internationalization can be advanced in many ways by a leader who is not a faculty member. Without a PhD and classified as an academic specialist in international outreach, she brought to her position in the MSU College of Education unequaled international experience and knowledge that in many respects went far beyond the capabilities of others in the college, including faculty. When she eventually moved to an MSU position outside our college in 2007, she had spent fourteen years living and working in Africa, twenty years serving in the College of Education, and five years working in the MSU African Studies Center. Without her leadership, for example, the College of Education would have had virtually no study abroad program and no way of showing that the college had responded to President McPherson's top international education priority—getting as many MSU students into study abroad as possible. Most likely, without her strengths and accomplishments, MSU would not have won the prestigious 2005 Goldman Sachs Higher Education Prize for Excellence in International Education.

As the prime force behind study abroad in the college, Anne knew how to write proposals to help faculty get approval of new study abroad programs, recruit students effectively for these programs, advise faculty on all aspects of planning a study abroad experience, and, not least, on the basis of her own ten years of running programs in southern Africa, prepare faculty to deal with all the problems that can arise on these trips. In recruiting students Anne was a master at coaxing students and parents into a first international experience and helping them realize that study abroad participation, while challenging in some respects, did not warrant the anxiety and trepidation it initially produced in families where both parents and children had not done anything of the sort. Anne's interventions in study abroad were especially critical at moments when faculty members were either unwilling or unable to do everything that was needed by way of preparation, thereby making possible programs that were ultimately successful and to the credit of the faculty member and the college.

Anne herself was the creator and codirector of the College's flagship study abroad program—the preinternship teaching program in South Africa. The issue that led to this program was the desire of a few faculty and others in the College to provide practice teaching abroad to gain international experience. This had been possible in earlier decades when the teacher education program was much more loosely organized and it sufficed to find an American International School abroad to host, and a collaborating teacher to supervise, the student's practicum. But after creation of the new five-year program of teacher education, discussions between the teacher education program coordinators and advocates of study abroad for teacher interns were at a stalemate, due to resistance in the new and more tightly organized programs of teacher education with their insistence on a full-year internship in a single school close enough to be integrated with the university components of the program. To address this stalemate, Anne came up with the idea of developing a program with student teaching in South Africa in the summer before teacher preparation students began their fifth-year internship in Michigan. She was the main designer of this program, which built on existing LATTICE linkages with South African schools in KwaZulu-Natal. The program allowed participants to coteach in regular South African schools with South African teachers. These teachers generally also served as the participants' hosts for homestays. Evaluation of this program has since indicated that it was a life-changing experience for many of the students. In addition, we found that such a distinctive and challenging experience could facilitate finding one of the scarce teaching positions in Michigan after year five.

Another important part of Anne's job was to look for external funding for our internationalization efforts. Alert to any possibilities for external funding, she wrote all or part of many proposals. While we were fortunate to have many colleagues who were good at getting and using external funding, none had the breadth and depth of Anne's knowledge of international funding agencies and how they work. She provided indispensable leadership in many aspects of proposal preparation, including maintaining relationships in funding agencies; tracking forthcoming RFPs; identifying possible faculty members who fit opportunities; telling them about these opportunities; writing up their qualifications; drafting institutional capacity statements emphasizing international strengths; recruiting partners in other universities, nonprofit Washington firms, and overseas universities; developing and revising budgets; and generally figuring out how to deal with the difficult special regulatory requirements of USAID and similar funding agencies.

Anne also worked closely with faculty in all four departments to keep them informed of international opportunities and to help them take advantage of these opportunities. She provided backup support for international projects throughout the college. She was a key contact and support person for many of the college's international linkages with individual scholars and research institutions worldwide. Finally, she was one of the few people in our college who worked hard to keep in touch and maintain good relations with our international alumni.

Still another of her responsibilities was to support international students and internationally oriented American students. Here she built on her vast network of international contacts to recruit outstanding international doctoral students. Our office tracked international doctoral student applicants as much as time allowed in order to identify the most promising applicants and help match them with available financial support. Anne was proactive in seeking out good prospective students, especially those who came with external funding. For example, one year to improve our tracking process she went through all the international applications in the college with at least one GRE score of 650 or higher, and then displayed on a single chart other strengths of these applicants, plus any signs that might indicate invalid GRE scores. She kept in touch with applicants who had special international interests and helped those who had particular problems with the admissions process. She arranged visits to campus for some of the most promising prospects. In addition, she put together special mailings, for example, to all Peace Corps offices around the world in an effort to recruit returning Peace Corps volunteers who had served as teachers. By the time the new students she had recruited arrived, they and Anne had often become good friends. A number stayed at her house until they were able to find a place to live with suitable accommodations or apartment mates.

Another of Anne's contributions was to help current international students address their academic, financial, and personal problems and to make the university a more caring, homelike environment for them. Anne was always available to these students to assist them with academic, immigration, or financial problems; help them find lodging when they were new to MSU; help them locate sources of funding for tuition, living expenses, or conferences where they were scheduled to present papers; write their letters of recommendation; and arrange other special events for international students. Her office on the second floor of Erickson was a gathering place for international students and like-minded American students—a good number regularly brought their lunch and joined her there for the meal.

For important conferences such as the national and regional meetings of the Comparative and International Education Society, she helped organize and coordinate participation by both faculty and students. In addition, from the beginning she was one of the leaders in our extremely successful LATTICE study group of MSU international students and Lansing area K–12 teachers. She was able to write a grant and codirect the resulting Fulbright Group Project Abroad project, which took thirteen LATTICE Lansing area K–12 teachers to South Africa for four weeks in 1999 at very little cost to the participating teachers.*

Anne's international contributions have not been confined to MSU business. During her missions or residence in Africa, she served, for example, as consultant for the Ford Foundation in Nairobi, field coordinator for the Institute of International Education (IIE) in Zimbabwe, and adviser to the dean of education at the University of Durban–Westville in South Africa. Anne, on her own time and initiative, also undertook highly visible public service activities that were beneficial to our international reputation. For example, she took vacation leave one year to be an invited participant in an international team of observers deployed by the Jimmy Carter Center to monitor the elections in Zambia (one of two such elections she observed). When she got back to MSU from this trip, she gave a well-received brown-bag presentation on this trip to interested persons from across the university. Similarly, in connection with her responsibilities in South Africa, she always found time to provide much-needed material assistance to poor schools in that country. One year she worked through Laura Apol to acquire at no cost over two thousand brand-new library books and was successful in getting a small grant from the Rotary Club in Richards Bay, South Africa, to ship all these books for use in one of the poorer schools in that area.†

Anne was able to do all this in part because she was exceptionally well known and well connected nationally and internationally to institutions and individual leaders in international development and international exchange. This included the World Bank, USAID, various Fulbright offices, the Academy for Educational Development, and various other important Washington firms and agencies. Having worked outside MSU for fourteen years on site in Africa, her knowledge of, and contacts on, that continent were of enormous value to maintaining MSU's reputation as a premier institution in international education and in African studies.

Amazingly efficient and effective, Anne brought to her job not only her long and extraordinary experience, but also her exceptional ability to communicate, collaborate, empathize, and negotiate at all levels of the university and outside with people of great diversity. If we managed to create some sense of community among the internationalists in the college, connected outside the college to others throughout the world, it was Anne's presence and efforts that made it all stick together. The integration-infusion approach cannot work without those who, like Anne, can work across various boundaries and have the capital necessary to successful internationalizing.

NOTES

* AR ISP 1998–99.

† Schwille memo nominating Anne Schneller for Distinguished Academic Specialist Award, October 1, 2002.

Our most successful year for diversifying funding was 1992–93, when the international work of the college was supported from each of the following sources: Ford Foundation, Rockefeller Foundation, Spencer Foundation, Toyota Foundation, World Bank, United Nations Development Programme, National Science Foundation, U.S. Department of Education, U.S. Information Agency, USAID, Fulbright programs, the Canadian federal government, America-Mideast Educational and Training Services, Midwest Universities Consortium for International Activities, MSU Foundation, and other internal MSU grant competitions. In 1992–94, support for international work in the College of Education was obtained from a total of twenty-two foundations and agencies of the U.S. federal government, the UN, foreign governments, and other donors.[2]

In the nomination of Anne Schneller for the university's distinguished academic specialist award in 2002, we again took note of what we had been able to accomplish in our search for funds for the college's international work. Over the previous two years the Office of International Studies in Education had generated proposals with collaborating departments and faculty for over $20 million in external funding. Among the major pieces of that effort were the following: a World Bank–funded program to help teams of teachers in Guinea carry out their own school improvement projects (cumulative MSU funding at that time over $1.2 million); continuation of sole-source MSU funding for further technical assistance in Guinea for new World Bank program over the next ten years (detailed plans approved by World Bank, but then derailed); new Ethiopia USAID project to provide staff development for teacher-training colleges (subcontract projected at $688,000 over five years, but not totally realized); new IEA cross-national study of teacher education(the initial estimate of needed MSU funding was about $5 million); open-ended USAID dot-com competition (although we got MSU included in the successful bid of a consortium headed by Education Development Center to become the principal supplier of educational technology to USAID projects around the world, we never got any funding from it); open-ended USAID competition for EQUIP (Educational Quality Improvement Program). In this latter case, we did get a good deal of funding for Egypt and Pakistan projects before they ended prematurely. But as can be seen from this list, the state of international funding for the College of Education at any one point in time was very much a mixed bag; initial commitments, especially from USAID, too often failed to materialize. To be adequately funded therefore meant deliberately participating in more proposals than would be funded. And even among funded proposals, we were often faced with a shortfall between the initial promise and the amount received.

In addition to the traditional sources of government and foundation funding, the ability to generate funding from other sources made an activity more attractive. For example, study abroad was funded by student fees; the GSEO by its clientele—individual teachers, schools, and their higher administration (e.g., Department of Defense Dependents Schools); Japanese Saturday School by the companies served; and LATTICE by the school districts and MSU itself.

In short, diversifying and increasing external funding was always a priority, though difficult to achieve. The college managed to put together a credible track record of fund-raising, although never as much as it could use. In 1995, the Office of International Studies in Education submitted a special report on funding as part of the university's Academic Program Planning and Review.[3] At that time this report indicated that multiyear external funding for international work in the College of Education was $5,904,531, or $40,167 average for each of the college's 147 tenure stream faculty members. Just the *annual* funding at that time was more than $2 million, or $14,373 per tenure stream faculty member. At those levels, the College of Education ranked second among MSU colleges in external funding for international work. In 1999–2000 external life-of-project funding for international projects in the college totaled over $11 million ($9.5 million for TIMSS and $1.7 million for other projects).[4]

By far the college's greatest source of external funding for international work during this period was NSF support for the IEA studies TIMSS 1995 and TEDS-M 2008. In total this funding amounted to well over $20 million. At the same time, progress was made in increasing foundation funding. Here, too, the greatest success occurred with one of the IEA studies, in this case TEDS-M. Thanks primarily to the efforts of Bill Schmidt, the national part of TEDS-M was funded by a combination of grants from the Gates Foundation, Boeing, General Electric, and the Carnegie Corporation of New York.

Another major rainmaker for the college was Yong Zhao. Initially, his large grants were for domestic projects, but then he broke new ground with a major multi-million-dollar grant from Sunwah Foundation in Hong Kong to sponsor the U.S.-China Center for Research on Educational Excellence. Later, Yong was instrumental in bringing a Confucius Institute (CI) to MSU, funded by Hanban (the Office of Chinese Language Council International).

Another more recent source of funding was developed through the efforts of Punya Mishra. The contract for a partnership with the new Azim Premji University in Bangalore meant that MSU had the opportunity to form an institutional partnership that would not be subject to all the threats that make such partnerships fragile and working in one of the world's most important countries, where earlier the College of Education had been little involved.

More recently, the college has benefited from a new source of funding with advantages the college has never enjoyed before. Around 2005, a wealthy MSU donor couple (one of whom was a College of Education alumnus) inquired about the possibility of their funding MSU work in Africa. They were inspired to make this offer by MSU's accomplishments in Africa and reputation. After extensive discussions, this initiative became the Tanzania Partnership Program, a cross-college effort to find new ways to strengthen rural villages in Tanzania. Drawing on faculty expertise in education, agriculture, human health, animal health, and environmental sciences, this work began in two target villages in Tanzania.[5] The donors promised to fund this program in perpetuity with an endowment. This was an exceptional opportunity for MSU to take a long-term approach to issues of development in Africa that cannot be adequately addressed in projects of three to five years. With this unprecedented support, the university should be able to develop new practices and discover new insights that otherwise would not be possible.

Support Staff

In addition to faculty, a strong international program, especially one that takes an integration-infusion approach, requires substantial staff support. Otherwise, faculty are left to do work that they would rather not do, or cannot do, or for which they are paid more than persons who might do it instead. As the core of the college's effort, until 2009 the Office of International Studies in Education enjoyed the services of an academic specialist in addition to a secretary and myself. This was the position initially filled by Anne Schneller and then for shorter periods of time by Gretchen Neisler and Cheryl Bartz. They helped get new initiatives started, proposals written, budgets drafted, faculty mentored for international work, while at the same time providing all sorts of support activities for internationally oriented students. This position was eliminated in 2009 as part of a reduction of some seventy support staff in the College of Education to help meet a university-wide budget reduction—a huge blow to the international office. Fortunately, this position was restored after my retirement. In addition to this core support for the Office of International Studies in Education, large international initiatives have added much more staff funded by special grants and contracts. Both Bill Schmidt and Yong Zhao kept sizable staffs funded through soft money.

Over the years the international expertise developed under these conditions was phenomenal. The GECP is a case in point. According to Lynn Paine, for example, the GECP would never have worked without creating a full-time coordinator's position and filling it with Margo Glew, who brought to the job both strong teaching experience and an in-depth background in international work. She had earned her doctorate in teaching of English as a second language. As Lynn recalls: "I am sure GECP couldn't have come into being, nor thrived as it had, if it had had to get going by resting on existing resources/folks simply adding to their tasks. . . . [Margo] is clearly the point person, [who] allows this program not to be diffuse and, as sometimes happen, eventually dwindle into some sort of entropy as different individuals, sharing responsibility, get drawn off into other initiatives."[6] Other extraordinary examples are easy to cite. Sandy Bryson worked for over forty years on MSU international business; most of this time was spent in management of GSEO. In our college he managed all aspects of sending faculty abroad for that program. Anne Schneller brought into the college knowledge resulting from all her years of living in Africa. As already mentioned, she served in our office for twenty years and was one of the most efficient staff members that I have ever encountered. The two people who succeeded Anne, Gretchen Neisler and Cheryl Bartz, were also great assets to the office.

Nevertheless, staff support for the Office of International Studies in Education suffered over these years from successive budget cuts and the dean's efforts to make the college more efficient. In 1990 two subsidiary offices were reporting to the assistant dean for international studies and programs (INET and GSEO). Between the two of them, there was a clerical staff of five full-time equivalent staff members, which was sufficient to provide backup at all times and to manage the workload at peak times. But as discussed above, GSEO was merged with management of domestic off-campus courses, and therefore no longer available to support other aspects of International Studies in Education.

Also, for space when the two offices worked together, two very large classrooms totaling two thousand square feet had been converted and devoted to international education, providing plenty of space for international visitors, students, and staff alike. But by 2004, this staff and space support had largely disappeared; the INET clerical position had been eliminated in a budget reduction. The remaining staff in our international support office dwindled to a half-time academic specialist, a half-time secretary, a quarter-time graduate assistant, and myself. Both classrooms had been put to other uses. The merged GSEO-domestic academic outreach program was assigned space elsewhere, and the Office of International Studies in Education was confined to cramped space on the fifth floor of Erickson Hall. Thus in spite of the priority given to internationalization during that time, it could be said that, in terms of the bureaucratic criterion of space, the office remained marginal relative to the rest of the college.

Conclusion

Flexibility in housing and staffing international efforts was both an advantage and a necessity for our integration-infusion approach. Individual faculty members and college departments, as well as administrators at the department and college levels, played a large role in how these issues were worked out. The Office of International Studies in Education was but one of the units whose support and capability were essential to the dispersed success of our approach to comparative and international education.

CHAPTER 13

Connecting to the Channels of Other Institutions through the CIES

O ne might assume that the integration-infusion approach pursued at MSU would lead to less participation in the Comparative and International Education Society (CIES) than would be the case in a university with a more traditional approach where priority is given to comparative education degree programs with a faculty focused on these programs and the kind of research most emphasized and presented at the CIES. But in the case of MSU, participation in the CIES has continued at a very substantial level and has grown to include faculty and students who would not otherwise be involved. Although funding was very limited, our office helped fund travel of students and faculty who were presenting an internationally oriented paper at either the CIES or the American Educational Research Association. Our goal was to participate in both the main comparative education organization, the CIES, at the national level and the much larger, more general, and mostly domestic educational research organization AERA. As far as internationalists in the college were concerned, we tried not privilege one too much to the neglect of the other.

CIES extended the channels of internationalization that existed within the college. It connected MSU channels with the international research of schools of education across the country, and to a lesser extent across the world. The annual reports from the Office of International Studies in Education document the extent of this participation in CIES meetings during earlier phases of the integration-infusion effort: in 1990, six faculty and five graduate students presented papers; in 1991, eleven faculty and six graduate students; and in 1992, nine faculty and ten students. We also hosted two memorable *regional* CIES meetings at MSU in 1993 and 2005. In 1993 the total attendance was 201 persons from thirty-eight colleges and universities. Of the 105 people on the program, 44 were from MSU and 61 from outside MSU. The September 2005 regional meeting attracted over one hundred participants, not as many as in 1993, but still enough to make it a success. Important peer institutions such as Penn State, Pittsburgh, and Indiana were well represented.[1]

MSU has also been well represented on the CIES board of directors: Lynn Paine (1991–94), Jack Schwille (1993–96), Teresa Tatto (1994–97), David Plank (1995–98), Susan Peters (2002–5), and Reitu Mabokela (2004–7).[2] Earlier Reitu Mabokela accepted CIES president Kassie Freeman's invitation to be the overall program chair and for MSU to cohost the 2003 CIES national/international meeting in New Orleans. She recruited MSU students as volunteers to help with organizing this conference, and as a reward they got assistance in attending the meeting. The leadership of Reitu and these students at this meeting greatly increased interest in the CIES at MSU.

The CIES under Teresa Tatto's Leadership

The peak of our CIES involvement was reached under Teresa Tatto's leadership when as CIES president-elect, she organized the CIES annual meetings at the Palmer House in Chicago in 2010. This was an ideal opportunity to bring to the attention of conference participants some of the diversity and strengths that up to that time had characterized the infusion-integration approach at MSU. Sixty-one persons at MSU (faculty, students, and very recent graduates) were listed on the program. A sizable number of the participating students had been volunteers working on the program throughout the year with Teresa and Inese Berzina-Pitcher, the conference coordinator.

After the meeting we asked all sixty-one MSU participants what they got out of CIES, and received forty-one replies.[3] Here are examples of what they said:

> When looking back to the moment when I agreed to coordinate the conference, I know that I made the right decision. . . . It was a chance for us to show what MSU

and our college is all about and what we bring to the CIES. We succeeded in that. People loved the conference. It has been very rewarding to hear so much positive feedback about the conference. I am very thankful for all the help and support we received from our student volunteers. We could not have done it without them. It was amazing to witness their dedication and work ethic throughout the year and then to get to know them more on the personal level in Chicago. (Inese Berzina-Pitcher, originally from Latvia, also coordinator for TEDS-M)

Making the decision to volunteer for a conference when I had no idea what CIES really was, or what my responsibilities would be, took a huge leap of faith, and adding more "volunteering" to my schedule seemed like a sure way to short circuit plans to succeed academically this semester. But I can't imagine my experience as a graduate student without having been able to work so closely with MSU faculty, staff, and graduates who demonstrate such intelligence, grace, and camaraderie to the larger international community. Watching the event unfold as MSU's vision of public scholarship, reflected in months of hard work here on campus was a bit surreal; so many names and ideas that had only been papers, data, text, had suddenly come to life. As I stood in the Empire Room at the Palmer House at dinner, I seriously thought about what the conference would look like when the legacy was passed down to future scholars, with no doubt that I and my fellow MSU volunteers would be among the key decision makers. (Stacy Clause, doctoral student in higher education)

One of the comments we received was especially heartwarming in describing an MSU student's emotions when leaving this Chicago meeting to return to East Lansing. It brought to life in a sincere and personal way the sense of international community at MSU on which the integration-infusion approach depends.

While heading to catch my train at 5.00 in the evening, I was nostalgic about home because Chicago reminded me of Nairobi, the city I was born and raised in. It seemed as if everyone was rushing for something and headed in the same direction. I gathered the rush was on to catch the train. Regardless, I appreciated my little quaint town of Lansing, where I never have to deal with a rush hour or large crowds of people. All in all, I thoroughly enjoyed the conference. It was particularly special because it was organized by Michigan State University College of Education. So this doesn't just make me proud to be a College of Education student but a proud Spartan because at the end of the day it is about representing Michigan State University. (Betty Okwako, PhD student in teacher education from Kenya)

Conclusion

CIES meetings are the only place where a university with an integration-infusion approach can make its case face to face with colleagues from across the United States and across the world. Publications are important in giving this effort visibility and importance among those who identify with comparative and international education, but in a narrower way. Having watched MSU's interest and involvement in the CIES greatly increase over the years, with faculty members and students from the various programs and departments, I take this growth to mean that we are indeed making progress toward the vision of a college-wide international dimension.

CHAPTER 14

Summing Up

The stories of colleagues like Lynn Paine, Bill Schmidt, Teresa Tatto, Chris Wheeler, Yong Zhao, Barbara Markle, and Anne Schneller; students like Liping Ma, Martial Dembélé, and Qasim Al-Shannag, and visiting professors like Harry Judge and Sigrid Blömeke are ones of exceptional accomplishment. But they should not be seen as isolated, individualistic developments in MSU's pursuit of a broader, more inclusive comparative education. The annual international reports of the college in the 1990s documented broader indications of this success. For example, the report for 1994–95 encapsulates striking examples of this inclusiveness in the college's work for that year:[1]

> Teachers in China and the United Sates discussing videotapes of teaching in the two countries; American researchers at national meetings analyzing other MSU videotape clips of interactions between mentors and novice teachers in China, England and the U.S.; MSU researchers comparing the curricula in science and mathematics in over forty countries, based on detailed analysis of textbooks and curriculum guides; Thai rural schoolchildren briefing officials from Bangkok on local case studies the children had produced on environmental issues; Guinean school officials in West Africa learning new ways to work with teachers in a

small grants program for teacher-initiated school improvement projects; MSU faculty members serving as Fulbright visiting professors in South Africa and Zimbabwe; visiting MSU professor giving address titled "A Latino Perspective on International Initiatives in Higher Education" while on sabbatical in Mexico; teacher education professor using original texts from Socrates, Gandhi, Mencius and Dewey to teach newly internationalized philosophy of education course to American International School teachers at the College's GSEO center in Bangkok; faculty and graduate assistants back on the MSU campus teaching transcollegiate course on childhood and adolescence in China, Japan and the United States; joint faculty-student-practitioner committee interviewing international students for a year-long program in 1995–96 of international discussion and study with teachers from Haslett and Lansing school districts;[2] and PhD student from Zimbabwe presenting results of Rockefeller-funded dissertation research to special interest group of African students.

In September 1998, a letter went out to faculty colleagues with five bullet points making a succinct case for the success of the college's internationalization effort, which

- Represented diverse regions of the World
- Involved strong faculty from all four departments of our college
- Received much attention in donor agencies (U.S. government, World Bank, UNICEF), scholarly organizations, and in the case of TIMSS, the mass media as well
- Involved local K–12 teachers
- Built on the rich experiences of international students from many countries.

At a retreat for the dean's executive staff in 1988, I gave the college administrators my view of where the college might be internationally in the year 2000. Among the predictions I made at that time were the following:

At the end of the century universities in the U.S. and elsewhere have become more important than ever as sources of ideas, knowledge and social adaptability. But educational systems in all countries have difficulty keeping pace. Six out of seven of the world's elementary school students are in developing countries where the demand for education continues to outstrip resources. In all countries there is also the problem of preparing students for jobs that do not yet exist. . . . Cultural and social literacy now has to do not only with the traditions of the West, but also with international economics, the sacred writings and political ideologies of Islam, and the worldwide influence of Japanese art and design—to cite only a few examples. . . . Within the College of Education, it is increasingly taken for granted that faculty members will continually be in touch with developments in other countries. Whereas it used to take extraordinary efforts to sustain international activities, they have become as natural and integral to the College as were the national activities of an earlier era.[3]

Circumstances rarely fall into place in the optimal fashion implied by such a vision. Now more than a dozen years into the new century, what I predicted is still far from fully achieved. Like everything else in American universities, the integration-infusion approach will always be a work in progress. Even though we had been at it for twenty-eight years and the vision remained the same, namely, to build an international dimension to research, teaching, and outreach throughout the college, it was still the case that many of the college's activities remained relatively untouched in this respect. And the mixture of vision and opportunism did not always reach a happy conclusion. For sure, new opportunities to advance the vision continued to arise, but opportunities we had benefited from in the past also faded away. Nothing was or is immune from change, especially in an era of rapidly growing knowledge and technology combined with severe financial constraints. The composition of the faculty changed with retirements or moves to other universities and the resulting recruitment of new faculty. In fact, over half the college's tenure-stream faculty at the time of this writing have been recruited since the beginning of the Carole Ames deanship in 1993. Likewise, the composition of the graduate student body changed as the labor market and the appeal of particular fields of study varied over time. And knowledge itself was changing, increasing, transforming at an ever accelerating rate, while new technology of all kinds has made this sort of change inevitable. Internationalization is just one aspect of this frenzy, a response to all those interrelated trends we call globalization. Where all the channels discussed in this book will ultimately lead is unknown and at any one point in time unknowable.

Besides being unpredictable in the longer run, international work in the short run often carries risks of not turning out as intended, influenced more often than not by circumstances over which one has little control. Such risks and the associated extra load of making arrangements and taking precautions in doing international work are not to every faculty member's liking. There will always be faculty who are not willing or in a position to undertake international assignments or generate international projects. Just keeping upwards of 150 tenure-stream faculty as well as graduate students well informed about our international work was a task at which we succeeded only partially. For example, in my attempt to get people out for our international breakfasts, I drew attention to this failure in a facetious email I sent on November 18, 2009, to all faculty and staff in the college with the subject line: "Little family argument over international breakfasts":

> If you think this is one of those pesky emails you shouldn't have been sent, you can blame it all on a little family argument I had on Friday with [my wife] Sharon:

> JACK (*Friday afternoon, Nov 16*): "Our breakfast for international students was fantastic this morning. The Korean food was outstanding and we had very good attendance."
> SHARON: "Why don't I ever hear about these breakfasts?"
> JACK: "You have to look at the notices we put in front of all the elevators."
> SHARON: "Are you sure there was one on the third floor?"
> JACK: "Yes."
> SHARON: "I don't see them. I never take the elevators. I use the stairs to get exercise."
> JACK: "I don't see how you know what's going on in the college without reading notices in front of the elevators."
> SHARON: "I bet there are a lot of people who don't know about the breakfasts."

> This is not the first time we've had this argument, and I have to admit that as usual Sharon is probably right. So I'm sending this email right now to tell everyone the schedule of breakfasts for the rest of the academic year.

In spite of these cautions, which range from agnostic to pessimistic, as long as we have an all-encompassing vision to encourage and give legitimacy to international work, creating expectations about what could or should be done in a school of education, the directions that have been set are not easy to ignore and will, I believe, continue to influence the entire college. What has been done for the last twenty-eight years will evolve, and some previous accomplishments will no doubt fall by the wayside, but the expectations and momentum generated can give us grounds for optimism about the future of the integration-infusion approach. While degree programs can be abolished entirely, the integration-infusion approach is flexible enough to avoid any such instant death.

In short, after twenty-eight years of development, the integration-infusion approach is not an unqualified or complete success and never will be. It has not removed all borders and barriers. Administrators continue to protect their fiefs in ways that obstruct the integration-infusion approach, although not as easily as they did before. But is it better than a more conventional approach to international and comparative education? The answer, at least in the case of MSU, is yes. This approach has allowed MSU to do things and bring an international influence to bear in ways and areas that would not have been possible otherwise. It has contributed substantially to the field of comparative education as traditionally conceived while influencing the course of U.S. education more generally.

For evidence of how this approach has worked, it is useful to go back to the three overall goals used to describe this approach at MSU:

- International research to improve education in the United States and other countries
- Collaboration with educators and institutions in other countries to create educational conditions necessary to sustainable development
- Efforts to help U.S. educators become more internationally oriented

Since 1984 the college has made substantial progress toward each of these goals. Efforts to help U.S. educators become more internationally oriented include, among others, the continuation of the LATTICE project for seventeen-plus years with very little external funding, the introduction of a special strand in the five-year teacher preparation program to emphasize international knowledge and perspectives, the preinternship teaching study abroad that allows MSU students to experience teaching under authentic and challenging conditions in resource-scarce schools of countries in Africa and Asia, and the study tours to support the expectation that all doctoral students will gain international experience. This progress, plus other accomplishments, was recognized by the Goldman Sachs Foundation Higher Education Prize for Excellence in Higher Education in 2004 and the American Association of Colleges for Teacher Education Best Practice Award for Global and International Teacher Education in 2006.

Collaboration with educators and institutions in developing countries included work experience (not conferences) in twenty-two developing countries: Algeria, Botswana, Burkina Faso, Burundi, Cambodia, China, Costa Rica, Dominican Republic, Egypt, Ethiopia, Guinea, India, Indonesia, Jordan, Mexico, Mozambique, Myanmar, South Africa, Tanzania, Thailand, Vietnam, and Zimbabwe. As noted above, MSU's excellence in this work has been further recognized by the Azim Premji Foundation in India, which chose MSU as the main U.S. partner in the creation of a new university to focus on education as a field of study and on issues of development. But it is in research where the contributions of this approach are most visible and compelling. Appendix 2 lists thirty-two books with an international focus written by faculty and published between 1994 and 2013.

Overall, and perhaps most important, faculty and students throughout the college have been able to learn a great deal not only from what international and comparative education has to offer but also about the integration-infusion approach itself. We now know this approach is feasible; it works. We have learned what it takes. As shown in this book, we can discuss the various borders to be crossed or removed. We can show how a larger academic space (*fields* in Bourdieu's terms) can be developed in which comparative education is no longer a marginalized academic specialty competing against fields with more readily convertible intellectual capital. Instead the integration-infusion approach opens the way to new understandings of education, new processes of inquiry, new and productive cross-disciplinary interactions—all of which can be beneficial to educational policy, practice, and research in general.

Development of International Strengths among MSU College of Education Faculty, 1984–2012

Internationalist Faculty Members with Graduate Study in Comparative and International Education (or the Equivalent)

King Beach (1991–2002), PhD CUNY, joined the faculty as assistant professor for cognitive studies in education. He spoke Hindi and Nepali and had had six years of field experience in a remote Nepali village (research plus work). Later, adding to his study of school-to-work transitions in a rural setting, he also did research on street children in Nepal.

Joyce Cain (1986–95), PhD University of Illinois, an African American with a passion for international work, brought much-needed new perspectives to our internationally active faculty and became a leader in our African projects. After her untimely death, a CIES award was created in her memory.

Brendan Cantwell (2011–present), PhD University of Arizona, was a student of comparative higher education in his doctoral program with particular emphasis on internationalization and globalization of higher education. At MSU he teaches the comparative higher education course.

Amita Chudgar (2006–present), PhD Stanford University, was a doctoral student of former CIES president Martin Carnoy at Stanford. She is an economist of education whose research focuses on providing children and adults in resource-constrained environments (especially in India, her home country, and other developing regions) with equal access to high-quality learning opportunities irrespective of their background.

John Metzler (1987–present), PhD University of Wisconsin, was another serendipitous recruit, hired with a doctoral degree in education to be outreach coordinator for the university-wide MSU African Studies Center. Although his primary appointment has never been in the College of Education, he became an invaluable asset in our internationalization efforts.

Richard Navarro (1983–98), PhD Stanford University, was hired as a graduate of the Stanford SIDEC program for a tenure-stream position in teacher education. Navarro continued the influx of Stanford graduates begun by Lynn Paine and Mun Tsang. He was eager to join the leadership group for our BRIDGES project, where he worked on the Sri Lanka research.

Susan Peters (1985–2011), PhD Stanford University, became our leader in the effort to devote more attention to young people with disabilities in developing countries. She was especially active in southern Africa. On her first trip to Zimbabwe, she was able to demonstrate how people with disabilities are able to exceed expectations for what they can do. She played wheelchair tennis and basketball with young Zimbabweans, and worked to get them sports wheelchairs like hers.

Kristin Phillips (2009–12), PhD University of Wisconsin, an anthropology-of-education student of Amy Stambach, was hired because she was a perfect fit for our Tanzania Partnership Program. She had devoted two years of Fulbright-Hays dissertation fieldwork to the study of a Tanzanian rural village that was in many ways similar to the villages in which TPP has been working.

David Plank (1993–2006), PhD University of Chicago, was one of several faculty members who got their start at the University of Chicago Comparative Education Center. Although he was hired in an MSU position that did not call for international qualifications, his willingness to take on international leadership as well as his extensive background in Brazil, South Africa, and Mozambique made him an especially valuable addition to our integration-infusion effort. While at MSU, for example, he published a book in English and Portuguese on Brazilian education.

Riyad Shahjahan (2011–present), PhD University of Toronto, a faculty member in higher education, has done research on the role of international organizations (especially the Organization for Economic Cooperation and Development) in globalizing higher education policy. He has taken particular interest in why some ways of knowing are valued over others in higher education and how various factors have shaped the validation and dissemination of knowledge.

Mun Tsang (1985–99), PhD Stanford University, one of the most highly regarded students of Hank Levin, was selected to fill one of the two international positions created by Dean Lanier for the integration-infusion approach. It was designated for economics of education, complementing the sociology-of-education position filled not long after by Lynn Paine. For fourteen years he was a highly valued and productive faculty member who eventually left because we had no tenure-track position to offer his spouse, a historian of China.

Gilbert Valverde (1992–98), PhD University of Chicago, a valued research associate in TIMSS, was one of the last PhDs produced by the Comparative Education Center at the University of Chicago. We wanted him to stay at MSU, but he left for Albany when we failed to get a tenure-stream position that he could compete for.

See also leadership profiles for **Lynn Paine** (1985–present), PhD Stanford University, and **Maria Teresa Tatto** (1987–present), DEd Harvard University.

Other Internationalist Faculty Members Originally from Countries outside the United States

Margret Buchmann (1977–97), PhD Stanford University, a faculty member originally from Germany, focused on the study of teaching and teacher education. Her distinctive approach drew on an exceptional background in the history of philosophy and philosophy of education. A college newsletter in 1989 reported that, as of that year, she had been a visiting scholar at Oxford, Cambridge, and Tubingen, had published widely in European journals, and was in regular correspondence with European scholars regarding their work.

Sandra Crespo (1998–present), PhD University of British Columbia, is a mathematics educator originally from the Dominican Republic who has done international research on teacher education as well as curriculum and professional development work in her home country.

Richard Houang (1979–present), PhD University of California, Santa Barbara, is a psychometrician recruited for methodological strengths who later became one of the key and exceptionally productive researchers on Bill Schmidt's team and coauthor of many publications.

Reitu Mabokela (1999–2014), PhD University of Illinois, is South African by origin and wrote her dissertation on gender and higher education leadership in South Africa. Active in CIES, she made numerous contributions to the integration-infusion approach and became the assistant dean for international studies in education in 2013 before leaving for an international education leadership position at the University of Illinois at Urbana-Champaign.

See also leadership profiles for **Punya Mishra** (1998–present), PhD University of Illinois, and **Yong Zhao** (1996–2010), PhD University of Illinois.

Other Internationalist Faculty Members Who Developed Competence in Comparative and International Education through Project Experience or Closely Related Fields of Graduate Study

Ann Austin (1991–present), PhD University of Michigan, already was a highly regarded scholar of higher education when she joined our faculty. However, having had no international experience, she was eager to acquire some. The opportunity came with a Fulbright in 1988 to study the transformation of South African universities from a base at what is now Nelson Mandela University. Since that time Austin has maintained a strong relationship with that university not only for herself, but also for MSU colleagues and students.

Maenette Benham (1993–2008), PhD University of Hawaii, Manoa, has a passion for developing healthy and sustainable learning environments for indigenous learners and their families around the world. While at MSU she developed and taught the first version of an all-university undergraduate transcollegiate course titled Growing Up and Coming of Age in China, Japan and the United States. After leaving MSU, Maenette Kapaʻeahiokalani Padeken Ah Nee-Benham, a native Hawaiian, became the inaugural dean of the School of Hawaiian Knowledge at the University of Hawaii, Manoa.

Bruce Burke (1964–99), PhD Syracuse University, a leader in teacher education, devised creative new initiatives while serving as director of the Graduate Studies in Education Overseas (GSEO) program. Working with program manager Norris (Sandy) Bryson, he was instrumental in creating GSEO centers in Thailand, France, and Switzerland.

Joe Codde (1999–2014), PhD MSU, professor of educational technology, did his international work primarily in the Middle East and North Africa, where he acquired experience in Algeria, Lebanon, the United Arab Emirates, and Pakistan, focusing on teaching with technology and other school improvement issues. In addition, he has worked with the MSU Confucius Institute on its programs both nationally and internationally.

Lee Cogan (1993–present), PhD MSU, joined the Bill Schmidt team during the TIMSS 1995 era and made such important contributions that he was kept on as a full-time researcher and coauthor of many publications in that group.

Higinio Dominguez (2011–present), PhD University of Texas, is a mathematics educator with experience in the American Southwest and Mexico, focusing on learning mathematics in classes that include bilingual students, English learners, and immigrant children.

James Gallagher (1976–2006), DEd Harvard University, was a science educator noted for his work inside and outside the United States. He taught science education research and environmental education around the world (e.g., Australia, Brazil, Panama, South Africa, Taiwan, Thailand, and Vietnam) and was one of the leaders of the MSU environmental education and community development projects in Thailand and Vietnam.

Margo Glew (2007–present), PhD MSU, was hired in a new academic specialist position to build and coordinate the Global Educators Cohort Program, a special international strand in the five-year teacher preparation program. Earlier, Margo with a PhD in TESOL, had been working on second-language issues in MSU international units outside the College, including the Flagship Program for the Teaching of Arabic.

Kyle Greenwalt (2007–present), PhD University of Minnesota, did fieldwork for his dissertation in France. At MSU he has been a leader in the Global Educators Cohort Program and has done research on the students in that program.

Elizabeth Heilman (2002–present), PhD Indiana University, professor of teacher education, has taught social studies education, global education, and social science courses in the MSU general education courses for students from throughout the university. Her research interests include the study of citizenship, identity, and diversity in national and global contexts, as well as how people develop a sense of power, political efficacy, human connection, and responsibility to others.

Sandra (Sam) Hollingsworth (1989–95), PhD University of Texas, is a well-known and much-published researcher and practitioner of literacy education, with extensive experience of girls' education and reading reforms in developing countries as well as in the United States. While at MSU she made exceptional efforts to internationalize the professional development offered to American International Schools by the GSEO program.

William Joyce (1964–2009), EdD Northwestern University, was a social studies educator who became director of the MSU Canadian Studies Center and developed curriculum materials on teaching about Canada.

Muhammed Khalifa (2011–present), PhD MSU, is a native of Michigan who has studied school leadership in Middle Eastern and African Countries as well as the United States. He has also done research on the problems faced by African refugee students in the United States.

Michael Leahy (1986–present) is professor in and director of MSU's Office of Rehabilitation and Disabilities and author of more the 150 refereed journal articles, books, book chapters, and research monographs. National leader in his field, his collaboration with Sister Martha Hegarty, Daughters of Charity, Ireland, led to the development of a major MSU partnership working with all the universities in the Irish Republic and Northern Ireland.

Susan Melnick (1980–2012), PhD University of Wisconsin, was a faculty member in teacher education who became assistant dean for academic outreach programs and responsible for directing the GSEO program following the retirement of Bruce Burke. Earlier she was in wide demand for teaching GSEO courses worldwide. In her teaching she was especially concerned with issues of race, class, gender, and educational equity, both domestic and cross-national. She was also an exceptionally strong supporter and mentor of international students.

Steve Raudenbush (1984–98), PhD Harvard University, lacked international experience, but his advanced methodological capabilities (especially in hierarchical linear models) were much needed in our BRIDGES research in Thailand. He joined the BRIDGES team and quickly emerged as a leader.

Barbara Schneider (2005–present), PhD Northwestern University, holds the John A. Hannah Chair in the College of Education. A sociologist of education, she was formerly professor of sociology and human development at the University of Chicago. Her research focuses on how the social contexts of schools and families influence the academic success and social well-being of young people as they move into adulthood. While at MSU she has also become one of our leaders of international work, including a collaborative study of student engagement in Finland and the United States.

See also leadership profiles for **Bill Schmidt** (1969–present), PhD University of Chicago, **Chris Wheeler** (1979–2008), PhD Columbia University, and **Barbara Markle** (1988–present), PhD MSU.

Thirty-Two International Books Authored or Edited by MSU College of Education Faculty, 1994–2012

Note: MSU faculty at the time of publication are identified with an asterisk.

2012

Learning and Doing Policy Analysis in Education: Examining Diverse Approaches to Increasing Educational Access. Editor: Maria Teresa Tatto*. Rotterdam: Sense Publishers.

Policy, Practice and Readiness to Teach Primary and Secondary Mathematics in 17 Countries: Findings from the IEA Teacher Education and Development Study (TEDS-M). Authors: Maria Teresa Tatto*, John Schwille*, Sharon L. Senk*, Lawrence Ingvarson, Glenn Rowley, Ray Peck, Kiril Bankov, Michael Rodriguez, and Mark Reckase*. Amsterdam: International Association for the Evaluation of Educational Achievement.

2011

Education and Capitalism: Struggles for Learning and Liberation. Editors: Jeff Bale* and Sarah Knopp. Chicago: Haymarket Books.

2010

Teacher Education Matters: A Study of Middle School Mathematics Teacher Preparation in Six Countries. Authors: William H. Schmidt*, Sigrid Blömeke, and Maria Teresa Tatto*. New York: Teachers College Press.

2009

Catching Up or Leading the Way. Author: Yong Zhao*. Alexandria, VA: ASCD.
Reforming Teaching and Learning: Comparative Perspectives in a Global Era. Editors: Maria Teresa Tatto* and Monica Mincu. Rotterdam: Sense Publishers.

2008

Teacher Education and Development Study in Mathematics (TEDS-M): Policy, Practice, and Readiness to Teach Primary and Secondary Mathematics. Conceptual Framework. Authors: Maria Teresa Tatto*, John Schwille*, Sharon L. Senk, Lawrence Ingvarson, Ray Peck, and Glenn Rowley. Amsterdam: International Association for the Evaluation of Educational Achievement.

2007

Global Perspectives on Teacher Learning: Improving Policy and Practice. Authors: John Schwille* and Martial Dembélé with Jane Schubert. Paris: UNESCO.
Internationalisation and Globalisation in Mathematics and Science Education. Editors: Bill Atweh, Angela Calabrese Barton*, Marcelo Borba, Noel Gough, Christine Keitel, Catherine Vistro-Yu, and Renuka Vithal. Amsterdam: Springer.
Reforming Teaching Globally. Editor: Maria Teresa Tatto*. Oxford: Symposium Press.

2004

La educacion magisterial: Su alcance en la era de la globalizacion. Author: Maria Teresa Tatto*. Mexico City: Aula XXI. Editorial Santillana.

2003

Choosing Choice: School Choice in International Perspective. Editors: David Plank* and Gary Sykes*. New York: Teachers College Press.

Comprehensive Teacher Induction: Systems for Early Career Learning. Authors: Edward D. Britton, Lynn Paine*, David Pimm, and Senta Raizen. Dordrecht: Kluwer Academic Publishers.

2002

According to the Book: Using TIMSS to Investigate the Translation of Policy into Practice through the World of Textbooks. Authors: Gilbert A. Valverde*, Leonard J. Bianchi, Richard G. Wolfe, William. H. Schmidt*, and Richard T. Houang*. Dordrecht: Kluwer Academic Publishers.

Disability and Special Needs Education in an African Context. Authors: Susan Peters* and Robert Chimedza. Harare: Open University Press.

Higher Education in the Developing World: Changing Contexts and Institutional Responses. Editors: David W. Chapman and Ann E. Austin*. Westport, CT: Greenwood.

New Paradigms and Recurring Paradoxes in Education for Citizenship: An International Comparison. Editors: Gita Steiner-Khamsi, Judith M. Torney-Purta, and John Schwille*. Amsterdam: Elsevier.

2001

Apartheid No More: Case Studies of Southern African Universities in the Process of Transformation. Editors: Reitumetse Obakeng Mabokela* and Kimberly Lenease King. Westport, CT: Greenwood Publishing.

Política Educacional no Brasil: Caminhos para a Salvação Pública. Author: David N. Plank*. Porto Alegre: Artmed Editora Ltda.

Values Education for Dynamic Societies: Individualism or Collectivism. Editors: William K. Cummings, Maria Teresa Tatto*, and John Hawkins. Hong Kong: Hong Kong University Press.

Why Schools Matter: A Cross-National Comparison of Curriculum and Learning.

Authors: William H. Schmidt*, Curtis C. McKnight, Richard T. Houang*, Hsing Chi Wang*, David E. Wiley, Leland S. Cogan*, and Richard G. Wolfe. San Francisco, CA: John Wiley and Sons.

2000

Now We Read, We See, We Speak: Portrait of Literacy Development in an Adult Freirean-Based Class. Authors: Victoria Purcell-Gates* and Robin A. Waterman. Mahwah, NJ: Lawrence Erlbaum Associates.

Voices of Conflict: Desegregating South African Universities. Author: Reitumetse Obakeng Mabokela*. New York: Routledge Falmer.

1999

Civic Education across Countries: Twenty-Four National Case Studies from the IEA Civic Education Project. Editors: Judith M. Torney-Purta, John Schwille*, and Jo-Ann Amadeo. Amsterdam: International Association for the Evaluation of Educational Achievement.

Facing the Consequences: Using TIMSS for a Closer Look at U.S. Mathematics and Science Education. Authors: William H. Schmidt*, Curtis C. McKnight, Leland S. Cogan*, Pamela M. Jakwerth, and Richard T. Houang*. Dordrecht: Kluwer Academic Publishers.

1998

Toward School and Community Collaboration in Social Forestry: Lessons from Thai Experience. Authors: Maureen McDonough* and Christopher W. Wheeler*. Washington, DC: Academy for Educational Development.

1997

Many Visions, Many Aims (Vol. 1): A Cross-National Investigation of Curricular Intentions in School Mathematics. Authors: William H. Schmidt*, Curtis C. McKnight, Gilbert A. Valverde*, Richard T. Houang*, and David E. Wiley. Dordrecht: Kluwer Academic Publishers.

Many Visions, Many Aims (Vol. 2): A Cross-National Investigation of Curricular Intentions in School Science. Authors: William H. Schmidt*, Senta A. Raizen, Edward D. Britton, Leonard J. Bianchi, and Richard G. Wolfe. Dordrecht: Kluwer Academic Publishers.

A Splintered Vision: An Investigation of U.S. Science and Mathematics Education. Authors: William H. Schmidt*, Curtis C. McKnight, and Senta A. Raizen. Dordrecht: Kluwer Academic Publishers.

1996

Characterizing Pedagogical Flow: An Investigation of Mathematics and Science Teaching in Six Countries. Authors: William H. Schmidt*, Leland S. Cogan*, Gilbert Valverde*, Richard Prawat*, et al. Dordrecht: Kluwer Academic Publishers.

The Means of Our Salvation: Public Education in Brazil, 1930–1995. Author: David N. Plank*. Boulder, CO: Westview Press.

1994

The University and the Teachers: France, the United States, England. Authors: Harry Judge, Lynn Paine*, Michel Lemosse, and Michael Sedlak*. New York: Oxford.

Timeline: MSU Integration-Infusion Policy in Practice

S ince the content within and between chapters of this book is organized thematically, an overall timeline of relevant events and periods is provided below as a reference to facilitate reader understanding and to answer precise questions about what took place when and in what order.

Pre-1984 Internationalization and Later Events of Overall Importance

1945   President John Hannah, broadcasting on MSU radio, asserts that MSU has a responsibility for leadership in education worldwide.

1956   Appointment of first university-wide dean of international studies and programs

1960–67   COE faculty heavily involved in establishment of University of Nigeria at Nsukka

1962   Proposal for internationalization of College of Education (COE) submitted to whole college faculty

1963   Institute for International Studies in Education established within COE.

1972   Associate Dean Cole Brembeck serves as president of the Comparative and International Education Society (CIES).

1975–84   MSU Nonformal Education Information Center funded by USAID

1976   MSU receives federal funding to establish Institute for Research on Teaching (IRT), a critical event in the College's rise in research prominence.

1980–92   Judith Lanier serves as dean of COE.

1980–82   Drastic budget cuts across the University lead to abolition of Institute for International Studies in Education, elimination of degree programs in comparative and international education, and retirement of associate dean and institute director Cole Brembeck.

1983   The U.S. secretary of education, Terrell Bell, visits MSU to give IRT an award and to release report *Nation at Risk*, famous for use of international IEA studies to support its conclusions.

1984   COE task force on future of international activities in the College proposes adoption of integration-infusion approach.

1984–2012   Jack Schwille serves as assistant dean for international studies in education with responsibilities for implementation of integration-infusion approach.

1985   Recruitment of Lynn Paine and Mun Tsang for international positions in sociology of education and economics of education

1992   MSU switches from quarter to semester system, a change that requires redesign of all courses.

1993   Peter McPherson becomes MSU president and proposes early in his term that all MSU students do study abroad.

1993–2010   Carole Ames serves as dean of COE.

1994–present   From the first *U.S. News & World Report* ranking of schools of education by specialty until the present, the MSU COE ranks first in the nation in both elementary and secondary education.

2004   MSU receives Goldman Sachs Higher Education Prize for Excellence in International Education.

2006   MSU receives Best Practice Award in Support of Global and International Perspectives from American Association of Colleges of Teacher Education (AACTE).

International Research

1978–79   First MSU participation in IEA study (Second International Mathematics Study or SIMS). Jack Schwille and Bill Schmidt work on planning of study in New Zealand in 1978 and 1979 respectively. Schwille organizes international SIMS meeting at MSU in winter 1979.

1985–92   USAID BRIDGES research enables Chris Wheeler, Steve Raudenbush, and Mun Tsang to work in Thailand; Mun Tsang in Pakistan; Teresa Tatto and Richard Navarro in Sri Lanka; and Jack Schwille, plus alumnus Bob Prouty, in Burundi

1985   First proposal for MSU international research on teacher education, submitted to U.S. Department of Education. Not funded.

1985–90   Study group to plan and continue search for funding for international research on teacher education

1989–94   Lynn Paine and Michael Sedlak participate, under leadership of Harry Judge, in triadic study of universities and teacher education in England, France, and the United States.

1992   Paper by Raudenbush, Sang Jin Kang and Thai colleague on BRIDGES Thailand research awarded best article of the year in *Comparative Education Review*

1991–98   Bill Schmidt heads up MSU team for landmark IEA Third International Mathematics and Science Study (TIMSS 1995).

1997   Publication of U.S. National TIMSS report, famous for "U.S. curriculum is a mile wide and an inch deep" (Bill Schmidt et al., authors)

1997   President Clinton briefs the press in the White House Rose Garden on the 1995 TIMSS fourth-grade results.

1997	March 6, President Clinton, in speech to Michigan legislature, thanks MSU and Bill Schmidt by name for their TIMSS work and accomplishments.
1990–2003	Cross-national research on teacher mentoring and induction under leadership of Sharon Feiman-Nemser and Lynn Paine
1994–2002	Jack Schwille serves under Judith Torney-Purta on international leadership team for IEA second international study of civic education.
1999	The book *Civic Education across Countries: 24 National Case Studies* (Steiner-Khamsi, Torney-Purta, and Schwille, editors) receives Outstanding Book of Year award from the journal *Choice*.
2000	International conference at MSU, organized by David Plank, Barbara Markle, and Gary Sykes, to examine school choice reforms from international, national, and Michigan perspectives
2002–13	Teresa Tatto heads up leadership team for cross-national research on teacher education in seventeen countries (TEDS-M).
2002–7	Bill Schmidt heads up preparatory pilot study for TEDS-M, known first as P-TEDS and then as MT21, carried out in six countries.
2008	TEDS-M, the "airplane that skeptics said would never fly", is declared a success at meeting in Bergen, Norway.
2012	Last of seven volumes on TEDS-M published

International Development

1991	Senior Thai education officials visit MSU in search of a partner for environmental education project.
1992–2001	Chris Wheeler heads up leadership team for Education and Social Forestry Project in Northern Thailand.
1994–2002	Schwille and Dembélé are MSU leaders for World Bank funded project in Guinea to enable teachers to take more responsibility for their own professional development.

1997–2010   Chris Wheeler is MSU leader for Vietnam project Improving School Quality, Integrating School Reform and Community Development.

1997–99   Tom Bird heads up MSU teacher education work in Indonesia.

2004–6   Gretchen Neisler is MSU leader of USAID-funded project in Egypt for reform of teacher education, working with seven Egyptian universities.

2006   Joe Codde starts his international development work in various North African and Middle Eastern countries with educational technology project in Algeria.

2008–10   Reitu Mabokela is MSU leader of USAID-funded project in Pakistan for teacher education reform, working with fifteen universities.

International Partnerships

1985–86   MSU Conference on Education in the New Zimbabwe for Zimbabweans on study leave in North America

1989–2008   Chris Wheeler is MSU leader for institutional relationships with National Education Commission and Chulalongkorn University in Thailand and Can Tho University in Vietnam.

1998–present   Ann Austin is MSU leader for institutional relationship with Nelson Mandela University, Port Elizabeth, South Africa.

2007–present   Mike Leahy is MSU leader for institutional relationship with Irish universities to use assistive technologies to serve persons with autism or other intellectual disabilities. The first step taken toward this partnership was a 2007 MSU study abroad program in Ireland, focused on Disability in a Diverse Society.

2010–present   Punya Mishra is MSU leader for institutional relationship with Azim Premji University, Bangalore, India.

Internationalization of K–16 and Teacher Education

1990	Fulbright Group Projects Abroad takes twelve U.S. teacher educators to Zimbabwe for six weeks of work with Zimbabwean teacher educators
1991	First COE study abroad course in Zimbabwe, followed by annual courses first in Zimbabwe and then in South Africa
1994	Transcollegiate course, Growing Up and Coming of Age in Three Societies, taught for first time by Maenette Benham and three teaching assistants
1995–present	LATTICE project, established under leadership of Sally McClintock, continues as a professional development study group of MSU international students and Lansing area K–12 teachers.
1999	Fifteen LATTICE Michigan educators travel to South Africa for Fulbright Group Projects Abroad.
1999–2000	Margaret Holtschlag is Michigan Teacher of the Year. She credits LATTICE with being the biggest influence on her teaching.
2002	Preinternship teaching program offered for first time in South Africa, allowing MSU teacher education students to coteach for six weeks in regular South African schools
2003	Yong Zhao organizes APEC education summit in Beijing with grants from Sunwah and Hewlett Foundations.
2004–9	Grant of $5 million from Jonathan Choi's Sunwah Foundation for U.S.-China Center for Research on Educational Excellence at MSU
2005	Pioneering trip to China for executive directors of all sixteen Michigan education associations, organized by Barbara Markle
2005	First Chinese American immersion school initiated by MSU in Beijing, known as 3e International Kindergarten
2006–9	MSU, initially awarded a Confucius Institute in 2006, subsequently designated as a Confucius Institute of the Year for three years 2007–9
2007	First Internationalizing Michigan Education conference held at MSU, organized by Barbara Markle

2007   Dean Carole Ames initiates international strand in five-year teacher preparation program, known as Global Educators Cohort Program; Margo Glew hired as coordinator.

2008–present   After two years of piloting in China, Dean Ames in 2010 announces expansion of doctoral study tours funded by her office. Subsequently, the tours (known as Fellowships to Enhance Global Understanding) take place in China, Botswana, Vietnam in 2011; China, Vietnam, Botswana, and Cyprus in 2012; China, Botswana, and Indonesia in 2013.

International Students

1986–95   Annual conferences on Education in Africa at Ohio University; MSU African students and other interested students, faculty, and staff travel and bond together in a university van.

1990–98   African Educational Research Group meets regularly to discuss research interests of African students in the College.

1992–98   Asian Educational Research Group, modeled on African group, also holds regular meetings.

1999   Book on the teaching of mathematics by Liping Ma published. Based on work started by Liping at MSU, it had sold forty-six thousand copies by 2003.

2001   First of the annual breakfasts at Schwille house to start off new academic year, gradually increased to about one hundred people in attendance each year

International Visitors

1985   Cowden Chikombah, dean of education at the University of Zimbabwe, spends his sabbatical at MSU, funded by a Fulbright Scholar in Residence award.

1987–97   Harry Judge visits MSU frequently as consultant to Holmes Group, headquartered in East Lansing; appointed half-time MSU faculty for three years.

2007–9   Sigrid Blömeke is visiting professor, working on MT21 and TEDS-M.

MSU Contributions to Comparative and International Education Society

1991–2007   Faculty members on CIES national board of directors: Lynn Paine (1991–94), Jack Schwille (1993–96), Teresa Tatto (1994–97), David Plank (1995–98), Susan Peters (2002–5), Reitu Mabokela (2004–7)

1993   Midwest Regional CIES meetings held at MSU (201 persons from thirty-eight colleges or universities)

2000   CIES creates posthumous award for former MSU faculty member Joyce Cain, awarded annually at national meetings for Distinguished Research on People of African Descent

2003   Reitu Mabokela designated national program chair for CIES meeting in New Orleans

2005   Midwest Regional CIES meetings held at MSU (more than one hundred participants)

2008–12   Teresa Tatto serves four-year cycle as CIES vice president elect, vice president, president, and past president; she organizes annual CIES meeting in Chicago in 2010.

Other (GSEO, Japanese Saturday School)

1972–ca. 2002   Graduate Studies in Education Overseas (GSEO, aka GEO) program delivers in-service courses leading to master's degrees for teachers in Department of Defense schools and American International Schools

1987–88   Control of GSEO transferred at MSU from Lifelong Education to the College of Education

1987–88   First year of MSU provision of teachers for Japanese Saturday School in Battle Creek; continues to the present

Notes

Preface

1. E.g., Schwille, 1993, 1994.

Introduction

1. Thomson, 2012.

Chapter 1. Toward a Sociology of Comparative and International Education

1. See, e.g., Bourdieu, 1984, 2004. For a clear and balanced discussion in language easier to comprehend than the original, see Swartz, 1997, and Grenfell, 2012. This whole section relies heavily on these two interpreters of Bourdieu.
2. Bourdieu, 2004, 44.
3. Bourdieu, 2004, 44.
4. Maton, 2012, 54.
5. Kuhn, 1962. See also Furlong, 2013, for still another, different discussion of sociological vs. epistemological explanations of university fields of study, with emphasis on education.
6. Bourdieu, 2004, 34.
7. As many critics have noted, e.g., Pérez, 2008; Thomson, 2012, 77.

8. Pérez, 2008.

9. Moton, 2012, 51.

10. Moton, 2012, 52.

11. Bourdieu, 2004, 70.

Chapter 2. Differing Approaches to Comparative and International Education in Schools of Education

1. Bourdieu, 2004, 35.

2. The grand synthesis of research on teacher education, Cochran-Smith & Zeichner, 2005, is illustrative of this tendency since one might expect it to be exhaustive, whereas, in fact, it covers only research done in the United States.

3. See, e.g., Bourdieu, 1984.

4. Foster, Addy & Samoff, 2012, 711.

5. Anderson, 1977.

6. Altbach, 1991.

7. Kazamias, 1972.

8. Brembeck, 1975.

9. Crossley, 2000. For a "comparativist" to see other scholars in his own area as outside the mainstream is in itself a telling admission.

10. Tikly & Crossley, 2001, 561.

11. Foster, Addy & Samoff, 2012, 712.

12. Foster, Addy & Samoff, 2012, 711.

13. Foster, Addy & Samoff, 2012, 717.

14. Kubow & Blosser, 2016.

15. Raby, 2007, 2010.

16. Manzon, 2011, 211.

17. Bourdieu, 2004, 43.

18. Bourdieu, 2008.

19. Drake, 2011.

20. Drake, 2011, 189.

21. Drake, 2011, 197.

22. Heyneman, 2009.

23. Drake, 2011.

24. Drake, 2011, 197. When Drake calls attention to the fact that the University of South Carolina has adopted a similar approach, he incorrectly suggests that it has a specialized college-wide office for international education and MSU does not. In fact, MSU has

had an Office of International Studies in Education within the dean's office since the integration-infusion approach was adopted in 1984.

Chapter 3. The Changing Landscape of Internationalization in a New Era of MSU History

1. Thomas, 2008, 220.
2. Smuckler, 2003; Hinckle, Scheer & Stern, 1966.
3. For an overall timeline of events and periods relevant to the content of this book, see appendix 3.
4. This information and the following paragraph are from a small, but revealing file of documents from the 1950s and 1960s, which I was fortunate to receive from Charles Blackman, a longtime College of Education faculty member, when he retired in 1991. Blackman participated in the various discussions about the College's international role at the time and kept documents that had come into his possession. They will now be deposited in the MSU Archives.
5. This period and MSU leadership are the focus of a recent 2011 dissertation by Francesca Forzani at the University of Michigan, titled "The Work of Reform in Teacher Education."
6. Hanson, 1984.
7. A position endorsed by Phillips & Schweisfurth, 2008/2014, among others.
8. Hanson, 1984.
9. It should be said that before this period, Teachers College, Columbia set the pace for broad international involvement in a school of education. See the Teachers College website article "Shaping Education around the World." According to that website, TC Columbia has since the beginning of the twentieth century been "formally committed to an international focus that has helped shape and reshape education in the United States and around the world."
10. According to Mark Ginsburg (personal communication), Pittsburgh and Teachers College, Columbia are examples of universities with such a mixed approach.

Chapter 4. Faculty to Develop and Explore the Main Channels of Internationalization

To tell this story, part 2 draws heavily on my memory and the administrative files I maintained during the period in question. In addition, certain details are further substantiated by reference to specific documents, especially the annual reports submitted to the dean of education and the dean of international studies and programs. These reports are denoted by the abbreviations "AR eval" for annual report submitted to the MSU dean of education for evaluation of my performance, and "AR ISP" for reports submitted to the dean of international studies and programs for inclusion in an annual report on all of the university's international work. The latter was prepared for public release.

The content of the profiles is based primarily on the knowledge I gained in working the individual in question over long periods of time.

1. Hanson, 1984, vi.
2. From file copies; emphasis added.
3. Schwille & Kim, 2009.
4. The online questionnaire was one that could be answered in less than five minutes, although longer open responses were welcomed. Our response rate was terrific! Of the 126 tenure-stream and other key faculty surveyed, 84 percent responded. Admittedly, we hounded quite a few faculty members with multiple reminders to do this.
5. Memos addressed to International Education Study Group from Margret Buchmann (October, 17, 1989, Subject: Where we are heading) and Lynn Paine (February 19, 1990, Subject: Moving to Confucius and the challenges of classical education in a modern world).
6. The proposal we submitted in response to this invitation was submitted to Dean Ames, May 7, 1996, Subject: Theme proposal.
7. AR ISP 2001–2, AR eval 2001–2.
8. AR eval 2001–2.

Chapter 5. Creating and Benefiting from New Channels of International Research

1. AR ISP 1999–2000; Plank & Sykes, 2003.
2. To document these achievements, appendix 2 lists the thirty-two international books edited or authored by MSU faculty in the College of Education between 1994 and 2012.
3. Burstein, 1993.
4. Robitaille & Garden, 1989.
5. U.S. Department of Education, 1983.
6. See Klein, 2014, for a retrospective account of the history and importance of this event.
7. See all the IEA publications on TIMSS 1995 at www.iea.nl.
8. Schmidt et al., 2001; Valverde et al., 2002.
9. AR ISP 1993–94.
10. Schmidt et al., 1996.
11. AR ISP 1996–97, 1997–98, 1998–99; for TIMSS publications produced at MSU during

this era, see e.g., Schmidt et al., 1996; Schmidt, McKnight, Raizen, et al., 1997; Schmidt, McKnight, Valverde, et al., 1997; Schmidt et al., 1999; Schmidt et al., 2001; Valverde et al., 2002.

12. Schwille, 2011, 659.
13. Schwille, 2011, 659.
14. E.g. Bradburn & Gilford, 1990; Gilford, 1993; Porter & Gamoran, 2002; Chabbott & Elliott, 2003.
15. Torney-Purta et al., 2001.
16. Torney-Purta, Amadeo & Schwille, 2010.
17. The results were published in *Teaching and Teacher Education* and other relevant outlets (e.g. Tatto et al., 1993).
18. Lockheed & Verspoor, 1991; Levin & Lockheed, 1993.
19. Raudenbush, Kidchanapanish & Kang, 1991.
20. AR eval 1984–85; undated list in files classifying responses; the total adds up to twenty-nine responses, not twenty-eight, for unexplained reasons; also May 20, 1985, summary of responses to correspondence on international, comparative research on teacher education, author not shown.
21. During 1987 Harry Judge periodically sent memos to his proposed collaborators on the latest plans for the September 1987 meeting at Oxford as well as his ideas for a cross-national research project.
22. These discussions and proposals are likewise all documented in files containing a continuing series of memos and minutes of meetings.
23. Judge et al., 1994. See also Lemosse, 2008.
24. Section based in large part on chapter 4 in Schwille & Dembélé, 2007.
25. Feiman-Nemser, 1996.
26. AR ISP 1992–93.
27. AR ISP 1994–95.
28. Personal communication, Lynn Paine, September 2015.
29. Britton et al., 2003.
30. Britton et al., 2003.
31. Britton et al., 2003, 304–5.
32. Britton et al., 2003, 136.
33. See, e.g., Wang, Strong & Odell, 2004; and Wang & Paine, 2001, for a more in-depth analysis of these differences.
34. Britton et al., 2003, 42.
35. Paine & Ma, 1993; Schwille, 1993c.

36. "Contrived" in the sense of Hargreaves & Dawe, 1990.

37. Britton et al., 2003, 312.

38. Another MSU faculty member, Randi Stanulis, has also drawn on ideas developed in the five-nation study for her induction work in Michigan and Georgia.

39. Much of the following section is also covered in Schwille, 2011.

40. As documented in IEA standards document, Martin, Rust & Adams, 1999.

41. Three from MSU (Teresa Tatto, Sharon Senk, and myself), three from ACER (Lawrence Ingvarson, Ray Peck, and Glenn Rowley—replacing Adrien Beavis), and finally Hans Wagemaker (supported by IEA staff, notably Barbara Malak, Sabine Meinck, Ralph Carstens, Falk Brese, as well as Jean Dumais, our sampling and survey expert from Statistics Canada). As the project progressed, persons outside the core group of seven and IEA staff became increasingly important as well (e.g., Mark Reckase, an MSU psychometrician who had been a vice president of a major testing firm [ACT] and later a vice president of AERA; Kiril Bankov, the Bulgarian mathematician who had worked on TIMSS; Michael Rodriguez, a psychometrician at the University of Minnesota who got his PhD at MSU and had previously worked with Teresa; and finally Inese Berzina-Pitcher, the TEDS consortium coordinator at MSU, who was originally from Latvia).

42. All IEA national centers who are members of IEA are listed on the organization's website. However, centers may join individual IEA studies without becoming institutional members of IEA.

43. All of this tension and conflict could be readily examined further from a Bourdieu point of viewing, clarifying what was at stake.

44. Tatto et al., 2008.

45. For more detail, see her leadership profile.

46. Tatto et al., 2012; Ingvarson et al., 2013; Schwille, Ingvarson & Holdgreve-Resendez, 2013; Tatto, 2013.

47. E.g., Schmidt et al, 2010; Blömeke, Kaiser & Lehmann, 2010a, 2010b—the latter two volumes totaled eight hundred pages.

Chapter 6. Building New Channels for International Development Work

1. Hanson, 1984.

2. Hanson, 1984, 1.

3. Hanson, 1984, 29.

4. Later he became MSU president.

5. Http://www.globalspheres.org/bios/Alemu_Beeftu.pdf.

6. Overall sources for this section include the nomination of Chris Wheeler for Smuckler

Award for Advancing International Studies and Programs at Michigan State, January 27, 2004, as well as the proposal to extend Thailand project, October 14, 1999, titled "Possible briefing points for support of proposal to expand the Thailand Environmental Education Project."

7. For a brief history and synopsis of this project, see Gallagher et al., 1999. A still more extensive discussion can be found in McDonough & Wheeler, 1998.

8. AR ISP 1995–96, 1996–97, 1997–98, 1998–99.

9. AR ISP 1996–97.

10. J. Gallagher trip report, February 16, 1998.

11. First annual report to the Shell Foundation, June 30, 2002; executive summary of second annual report to the Shell Foundation, July 3, 2003; Wheeler memo, Improving school quality, integrating school reform and community development: Synopsis of the Education Component of the Shell Project, January 27, 2004.

12. Final report to the McKnight Foundation for the Project: Integrating School Reform with Community Development, May 31, 2010; Wheeler et al., 2007.

13. Final report to McKnight Foundation, May 31, 2010.

14. Concept paper, improving teaching and learning in Can Tho University's School of Education: proposal for linking staff development to community resources and community development, February 24, 1998; C. Wheeler letter to U.S. State Department responding to questions on MSU proposal for Can Tho—MSU linkage, June 28, 2001; C. Wheeler email to MSU colleagues, September 3, 2002, Subject: Linkage grant starts a new year.

15. Nomination of Wheeler for ISP Smuckler Award at MSU, January 27, 2004.

16. For further background on this section, see Schwille et al., 1997; Dembélé 1997; Schwille, Dembélé & Bah, 1999; Schwille, Dembélé & Diallo, 2001; Schwille, Dembélé & Balde, 2002, as well as my annual ISP and eval reports from 1993–94 to 2001–2.

17. AR eval 1994–95.

18. This whole description of the 1995 seminar in this section is based primarily on Schwille et al., 1997.

19. AR ISP 1998–99, AR eval 1998–99.

20. Schwille, Dembélé & Diallo, 2001.

21. Schwille et al., 1997.

22. Letter from Robert Prouty, Senior Education Specialist, West Africa Department, the World Bank to Carole Ames, Dean MSU College of Education, July 25, 1995.

23. In addition to file copies of our repeated revisions of plans for this new program, the planning work is briefly described in my blog "World of Jack."

24. See, in particular, Schwille et al., 1997; Dembélé, 1997; Schwille, Dembélé & Bah, 1999; Schwille, Dembélé & Diallo, 2001; Schwille, Dembélé & Balde, 2002.

25. AR eval 2001–2, 2002–3; memo from Schwille to Dean Ames, August 28, 2002, Subject: Proposals funded or in progress. Also Report on Activities for Ethiopia Teacher Strengthening Program, September 1–December 31, 2002, College of Education, MSU.

26. MSU was not included in a third consortium EQUIP-3, which focused on out-of-school youth and was led by the Education Development Center (EDC).

27. AR eval 2003–4.

28. AR eval 2005–6.

29. The section on this project draws on Henion & Geary, 2009, as well as AR eval 2008–9 and also a brief description of FOER from office files, June 29, 2010, no author given.

30. AR eval 1993–94.

31. AR ISP 1994–95, ISP 1996–97.

32. AR ISP 1997–98.

33. AR ISP 1998–99.

Chapter 7. The Fragility of International Partnerships Needed to Feed Channels of Internationalization

1. Chikombah et al. 1988.

2. AR ISP 1989–90, 1994–95, 1998–99.

3. AR ISP 1995–96.

4. See conference report (MSU, 1998).

5. AR ISP 1995–96.

6. AR ISP 1998–99.

7. AR ISP 1997–98, ISP 1998–99.

8. Flyer for Ann Austin presentation, December 2, 2008, on this initiative.

9. AR ISP 1990–91.

10. Much of this section was written for my travel blog, "The World of Jack."

11. In 2004 and 2011 issues.

12. "MSU and Wipro Limited Announce Graduation of First Cohort of 25 Teachers of MSU-WIPRO Urban STEM & Leadership Fellowship Program," News, Michigan State University College of Education, http://edwp.educ.msu.edu/news/2015.

13. *Southern Star*, May 3, 2008.

14. "Rehab counseling research goes global," *New Educator*, Spring-summer 2011.

15. Http://www.globalsciencecollaboration.org/public/site/PDFS/assistive/Leahy%20 M.%20The%20MSU-DOCTRID%20Hegarty%20Fellows%20Programme.pdf.

16. *New Educator*, Fall 2013.

Chapter 8. Preparing the Ground for Channels of International Content and World Languages in K–12 and Teacher Education

1. Merryfield, 1994; Schneider, 2003.
2. Hanson, 1984, v–vi.
3. Memo from Jack Schwille and Mun Tsang to Interim Dean David Cohen, January 15, 1990, Subject: Next steps in development of Master's program in international policy studies.
4. AR ISP 1993–94.
5. AR ISP 1994–95; see also Benham, 2004.
6. AR eval 1995–96.
7. Personal communication, Lynn Paine, December 2014.
8. Section based in part on LATTICE nomination for Goldman-Sachs Award, September 30, 2003.
9. Papanastasiou & Conway, 2002.
10. LATTICE nomination for Goldman-Sachs Award, September 30, 2003.
11. Also LATTICE Goldman-Sachs nomination, plus various LATTICE annual yearbooks.
12. LATTICE yearbook, 2002–3.
13. LATTICE yearbook, 2001–2.
14. AR eval 2002–3.
15. Also AR eval 2002–3 and LATTICE Goldman-Sachs nomination, September 30, 2003.
16. Coerr, 2004.
17. LATTICE, 2004.
18. AR ISP 1998–99, 1999–2000; LATTICE yearbook, 1998–99, 1999–2000.
19. LATTICE press release at time of November 25–December 8, 2003, visit.
20. LATTICE yearbook, 2000–2001.
21. These programs are discussed in more detail below in the section on the role of study abroad in our internationalization efforts.
22. More recently, however, it has become difficult to get teachers to join LATTICE because they feel so much pressure from reform mandates put in place since LATTICE was started.
23. AR eval 1999–2000.
24. AR eval 1995–96.
25. http://www.experiencechinese.com/index.php/programs/immersion, also http://www.3einternationalschool.org/en.
26. Http://www.3einternationalschool.org/en/community.
27. Http://www.myechinese.org/app/en/?p=238.
28. AR ISP 1993–94, ISP 1994–95.
29. AR ISP 2001–2, AR ISP 2003–4.

30. Conversation recalled in an email to two colleagues, April 21, 2008.

31. These conferences were variably documented in the *New Educator* (college magazine) as well as on the college website.

32. See Mishra, Koehler & Zhao, 2007.

33. Glew, 2014, was the primary source for the following account of implementation of the GECP strand.

34. Glew, 2014.

35. Drummond, 2014, 7.

36. Personal communication, Lynn Paine, September 2015.

37. Fellowship to Enhance Global Understanding (FEGU), College of Education, MSU, annual reports: 2010–11, 2011–12, 2012–13.

38. The information that follows was primarily drawn from FEGU annual reports for 2010–11 and 2011–12.

39. Personal communication, Lynn Paine, September 2015.

Chapter 9. Engaging Internationally Oriented Students to Create New Channels and Broaden Existing Ones

1. Official means reported by the MSU Office of International Students and Scholars. Comparison with other documents indicate discrepancies. For the year 2000, for example, we have a listing of 177 international students, while for 2001 the listing showed 159. The first year in which students were reported enrolled in the all-college online master's program was 2001, with an enrollment of 29.

2. AR eval 1999–2000.

3. AR eval 1993–94.

4. AR eval 1994–95.

5. AR eval 1995–96.

6. AR eval 2005–6; also handwritten notes used for my oral report at all-college faculty meeting, May 5, 2006.

7. AR eval 1984–85.

8. Email on Indian breakfast sent to listserv of internationally oriented students, March 15, 2008.

9. Email on Korean breakfast sent to listserv of internationally oriented students, November 8, 2009.

10. AR eval 1994–95.

11. This testimonial was on the OISE website, but is no longer available.

12. From flyer for recruitment of international students, May 2000.

13. AR ISP 1989–90, 1990–91, 1991–92, 1992–93.
14. No longer available.
15. AR eval 1992–93, 93–94.
16. Testimonial originally on OISE website, no longer available.
17. Personal communication, Chris Wheeler.

Chapter 10. Two Streams Less Connected with the Main Channels of Internationalization

1. Hanson, 1984, 25.
2. AR ISP 1989–90.
3. AR ISP 1990–91.
4. AR ISP 1991–92.
5. AR ISP 1993–94.
6. AR ISP 1997–98.
7. AR ISP 1999–2000.
8. Hanson, 1984, vi.
9. AR ISP 1987–88.
10. Moore, Bryson & Pinheiro, 1995.
11. AR ISP 1987–88.
12. AR ISP 1991–92.
13. Damrow, 2011.

Chapter 11. International Visiting Scholars, a Source of Internationalization That Could Exceed Expectations but Often Did Not

1. AR ISP 1992–93.
2. AR ISP 1987–88; file copy of Panom's itinerary for fall 2000 visit.
3. AR ISP 1998–99.
4. AR ISP 1987–88, AR eval 1993–94.
5. AR ISP 1998–99, 99–00.

Chapter 12. Finding Enough Money and Support Staff to Feed and Expand Channels

1. Wiley & Glew, 2010.
2. AR ISP 1992–93.
3. APP&R for submission by College of Education to central administration, January 9, 1995.
4. AR 1999–2000.

5. The education work is documented in Schwille & Roberts, 2014.

6. Personal communication, Lynn Paine, September 2015.

Chapter 13. Connecting to the Channels of Other Institutions through the CIES

1. AR ISP 1993–94, AR eval 2005–6; memo from Schwille to CIES Board of Directors, November 23, 1993, Subject: Midwest regional meetings at MSU.

2. Note that in 1995–96, three of the ten members of the board were from MSU.

3. These replies, including the excerpts below, were circulated to the listservs of internationally oriented faculty and students, May 4, 2010.

Chapter 14. Summing Up

1. AR ISP 1994–95.

2. This refers to the beginning of LATTICE as described earlier in this book.

3. *Educator: The College of Education Alumni Association Newsletter* 6 (2) (Spring 1989): 5.

References

Altbach, P. G. (1991). Trends in comparative education. *Comparative Education Review* 35 (3): 491–507.

Altbach, P. G., and E. T. Tan. (1995). *Programs and Centers in Comparative and International Education: A Global Inventory*. Buffalo: Graduate School of Education Publications in association with the Comparative Education Center, State University of New York at Buffalo and the Comparative and International Education Society.

Anderson, C. A. (1977). Comparative education over a quarter century: Maturity and challenges. *Comparative Education Review* 21 (2–3): 405–16.

Benham, M. (2004). Where can we collectively be that is greater than where we are now? *Hulili: Multidisciplinary Research on Hawaiian Well-Being* 1 (1): 35–52.

Blömeke, S., G. Kaiser, and R. Lehmann. (Eds.). (2010a). *TEDS-M 2008. Professionelle Kompetenz und Lerngelegenheiten angehender Primarstufenlehrkräfte im internationalen Vergleich*. Münster: Waxmann Verlag.

———. (2010b). *TEDS-M 2008. Professionelle Kompetenz und Lerngelegenheiten angehender Mathematiklehrkräfte für die Sekundarstufe I im internationalen Vergleich*. Münster: Waxmann Verlag.

Blömeke, S., and L. Paine. (2008). Getting the fish out of the water: Considering benefits and problems of doing research on teacher education at an international level. *Teaching and*

Teacher Education 24 (8): 2027–37.

Bourdieu, P. (1984). *Homo academicus*. Paris: Editions de Minuit.

———. (2004). *Science of Science and Reflexivity*. Trans. by R. Nice. Chicago: University of Chicago Press.

———. (2008). *Sketch for a Self-Analysis*. Trans. by R. Nice. Chicago: University of Chicago Press.

Bourdieu, P., and J. C. Passeron. (1970). *La Reproduction:* Éléments d'une théorie du système d'enseignement. Paris: Editions de Minuit.

Bradburn, N. M., and D. M. Gilford (Eds.) (1990). *A Framework and Principles for International Comparative Studies in Education*. Washington, DC: Board on International Comparative Studies in Education, National Research Council, National Academies Press.

Brembeck, C. S. (1975). The future of comparative and international education. *Comparative Education Review* 19:369–74.

Britton, E., L. Paine, D. Pimm, and S. Raizen. (2003). *Comprehensive Teacher Induction*. Dordrecht: Kluwer.

Burstein, L. (Ed.). (1993). *The IEA Study of Mathematics III: Student Growth and Classroom Processes* (Vol. 3). Oxford: Pergamon.

Chabbott, C., and E. Elliott. (Eds.) (2003). *Understanding Others, Educating Ourselves: Getting More from International Comparative Studies in Education*. Washington, DC: Committee on a Framework and Long-Term Agenda for International Comparative Education Studies, Board on International Comparative Studies in Education, Board on Testing and Assessment, National Research Council, National Academies Press.

Chikombah, C., E. Johnston, A. Schneller, and J. Schwille. (Eds.) (1988). *Education in the New Zimbabwe*. Proceedings of a conference at Michigan State University in collaboration with the University of Zimbabwe, jointly published by the African Studies Center and the Office for International Networks in Education and Development, Michigan State University.

Cochran-Smith, M., and K. M. Zeichner (Eds.) (2005). *Studying Teacher Education: The Report of the AERA Panel on Research and Teacher Education*. Mahwah, NJ: Lawrence Erlbaum Associates.

Coerr, E. (2004). *Sadako and the Thousand Paper Cranes*. New York: Penguin.

Cook, B. J., S. J. Hite, and E. H. Epstein. (2004). Discerning trends, contours, and boundaries in comparative education: A survey of comparativists and their literature. *Comparative Education Review* 48 (2): 123–50.

Crossley, M. (2000). Bridging cultures and traditions in the reconceptualisation of comparative and international education. *Comparative Education* 46 (3): 319–32.

Damrow, A. (2011). Navigating Multiple Worlds in the Twenty-First Century: Authoring and Editing the Story of One Japanese Kid. PhD diss., Michigan State University.

Dembélé, G. (2005) A Pre-service Teacher Learning to Teach Reading: A Case Study of Molly's Internship Journey. PhD diss., Michigan State University.

Dembélé, M. (1997). Making Teachers Full Partners in Their Own Professional Development. Paper presented at biennial meeting of the Association for the Development of Education in Africa in Dakar.

Dembélé, M., and J. Schwille, J. (2006). Can the global trend toward accountability be reconciled with ideals of teacher empowerment? Theory and practice in Guinea. *International Journal of Educational Research* 45:302–14.

Drake, T. A. (2011). U.S. comparative and international graduate programs: An overview of programmatic size, relevance, philosophy, and methodology. *Peabody Journal of Education* 86 (2): 189–210.

Drummond, T. (2014). *From Erickson to the World: A Review of Study and Learning Abroad Programming in the College of Education.* Unpublished report, Office of International Studies in Education, Michigan State University.

Fang, Y., and L. Paine. (2008). Bridging polarities: How Liping Ma's *Knowing and Teaching Elementary Mathematics* entered the U.S. mathematics and mathematics education discourses. *Pedagogies: An International Journal* 3 (4): 195–218.

Feiman-Nemser, S. (1996). *Teacher Mentoring: A Critical Review.* Washington, DC: ERIC Clearinghouse on Teaching and Teacher Education.

Foster, J., N. A. Addy, and J. Samoff. (2012). Crossing borders: Research in comparative and international education. *International Journal of Educational Development* 32 (6): 711–32.

Furlong, J. (2013). *Education—Anatomy of the Discipline: Rescuing the University Project?* London: Routledge.

Gallagher, J., C. Wheeler, M. McDonough, and B. Namfa. (1999). Sustainable Environmental Education for a Sustainable Environment: Lessons from Thailand for Other Nations. Paper presented at the Symposium on Sustainable Environmental Education for a Sustainable Environment, Seventh International Conference on Environment, Jerusalem.

Gilford, D. M. (1993). *A Collaborative Agenda for Improving International Comparative Studies in Education.* Washington, DC: Board on International Comparative Studies in Education, National Research Council, National Academy Press.

Glew, M. (2014). K–12 and International and Foreign Language Education: Global Teacher Education. Paper presented at Internationalization of U.S. Education in the 21st Century: The Future of International and Foreign Language Studies (A Research Conference on National Needs and Policy Implications). Williamsburg, VA, April 11–13.

Grenfell, M. (Ed.) (2012). *Pierre Bourdieu: Key Concepts*. 2nd ed. London: Routledge.

Halsey, A. H. (2008). Harry Judge and Oxford: College and university. *Oxford Review of Education* 34 (3): 275–86.

Hanson, J. (1984). *Report of the Task Force on International Activities*. East Lansing: Michigan State University, College of Education.

Hargreaves, A., and R. Dawe. (1990). Paths of professional development: Contrived collegiality, collaborative culture, and the case of peer coaching. *Teaching and Teacher Education* 6 (3): 227–41.

Henion, A., and N. Geary. (2009) MSU scholars help reform Pakistan's teacher-education system. *The New Educator* [MSU College of Education magazine]. Fall–winter issue.

Heyneman, S. P. (1993). Quantity, quality and source. *Comparative Education Review* 37 (4): 372–88.

———. (2009). The future of comparative and international education. *Newsletter of the Comparative and International Education Society* 151.

Hinckle, W., R. Scheer, and S. Stern. (1966). University on the make, or how MSU helped arm Madame Nhu. *Ramparts* [magazine], April 1966.

Ingvarson, L., J. Schwille, M. T. Tatto, G. Rowley, R. Peck, and S. Senk. (Eds.) (2013). *An Analysis of Teacher Education Context, Structure, and Quality Assurance Arrangements in TEDS-M Countries: Findings from the IEA Teacher Education and Development Study in Mathematics (TEDS-M)*. Amsterdam: International Association for the Evaluation of Educational Achievement (IEA).

Inzunza, V. (2002). *Years of Achievement: A Short History of the College of Education at Michigan State University*. East Lansing: MSU College of Education.

Judge, H. (1982). *American Graduate Schools of Education: A View from Abroad*. New York: Ford Foundation.

———. (1984). *A Generation of Schooling: English Secondary Schools since 1944*. Oxford: Oxford University Press.

Judge, H., M. Lemosse, L. Paine, and M. Sedlak. (1994). *The University and the Teachers: France, the United States, England*. Wallingford, UK: Triangle Books.

Kazamias, A. (1972). Comparative pedagogy: An assignment for the seventies. *Comparative Education Review* 16:406–11.

King, E. (1990). Observations from outside and decisions inside. *Comparative Education Review* 34 (3): 392–95.

Klein, A. (2014). Historic summit fueled push for K–12 standards. *Education Week*, September 24, 2014.

Kubow, P. K. and A. H. Blosser. (Eds.) (2016). *Teaching Comparative Education: Trends and*

Issues Informing Practice. Oxford: Symposium Books.

Kuhn, T. S. (1962). *The Structure of Scientific Revolutions*. Chicago: University of Chicago Press.

Lamont, M. (2009). *How Professors Think: Inside the Curious World of Academic Judgment*. Cambridge, MA: Harvard University Press.

Larsen, M. A. (2010). *New Thinking in Comparative Education: Honouring Robert Cowen*. Rotterdam: Sense Publishers.

LATTICE (2004). *LATTICE (Linking All Types of Teachers to International Cross-cultural Education): A Window to the World*. Video produced by Haslett MI Public Schools (TV channel 25, Brian Town, director).

Lemosse, M. (2008). *The University and the Teachers:* A cross-national experience. *Oxford Review of Education* 34 (3): 349–56.

Levin, H. M., and M. E. Lockheed. (1993). *Effective Schools in Developing Countries*. London: Falmer Press.

Lockheed, M. E., and A. M. Verspoor. (1991). *Improving Primary Education in Developing Countries*. Oxford: Oxford University Press.

Ma, L. (1999). *Knowing and Teaching Elementary Mathematics: Teachers' Understanding of Fundamental Mathematics in China and The United States*. Mahwah, NJ: Erlbaum.

Manzon, M. (2011). *Comparative Education: The Construction of a Field*. CERC Studies in Comparative Education 29. Hong Kong: Springer and Comparative Education Research Centre, University of Hong Kong.

Martin, M. O., K. Rust, and R. J. Adams. (1999). *Technical Standards for IEA Studies*. Amsterdam: International Association for the Evaluation of Educational Achievement (IEA).

McDonough, M. H., and C. W. Wheeler. (1998). *Toward School and Community Collaboration in Social Forestry: Lessons from the Thai Experience*. Washington, DC: ABEL Clearinghouse for Basic Education, Academy for Educational Development.

Merryfield, M. (1994). *Teacher Education in Global and International Education*. Washington, DC: AACTE Publications.

Michigan State University. (1998). *Academic Partnerships with South Africans for Mutual Capacity Building*. Report on a conference, October 1998, cosponsored by MSU, Committee of Technikon Principals, Historically Disadvantaged Institutions Forum, and South African Universities' Vice Chancellors' Association. East Lansing: Michigan State University.

Mishra, P., M. Koehler, and Y. Zhao. (2007). *Faculty Development by Design: Integrating Technology in Higher Education*. Greenwich, CT: Information Age Publishing.

Moore, K., N. Bryson, and S. Pinheiro. (1995). *Graduate Studies in Education Overseas: A Report on Faculty Participation*. Unpublished report from GSEO Office, Michigan State

University.

Moton, K. (2012). Habitus. In M. Grenfell (Ed.), *Pierre Bourdieu: Key Concepts*. 2nd ed. London: Routledge.

Paine, L. (1990). The teacher as virtuoso: A Chinese model for teaching. *Teachers College Record* 92 (1): 49–81.

Paine, L., and L. Ma. (1993). Teachers working together: A dialogue on organizational and cultural perspectives of Chinese teachers. *International Journal of Educational Research* 19 (8): 675–97.

Papanastasiou, E. C., and P. F. Conway. (2002). Teacher professional development through LATTICE, an international-intercultural project. *Studies in Educational Evaluation* 28 (4): 315–28.

Phillips, D., and M. Schweisfurth. (2008/2014). *Comparative and International Education: An Introduction to Theory, Method and Practice*. 2nd edition. London: Continuum Books.

Pérez, F. P. (2008). Voluntarism and Determinism in Giddens's and Bourdieu's Theories of Human Agency. *Essex Graduate Journal* 4: 12–17.

Peters, S., and R. Chimedza. (2002). *Disability and Special Needs Education in an African Context*. Harare: Open University Press.

Planel, C. (2008). The rise and fall of comparative education in teacher training: Should it rise again as comparative pedagogy? *Compare: A Journal of Comparative and International Education* 38 (4): 385–99.

Plank, D. N., and G. Sykes. (Eds.) (2003). *Choosing Choice: School Choice in International Perspective*. New York: Teachers College Press.

Porter, A. C., and A. Gamoran. (Eds.) (2002). *Methodological Advances in Cross-National Surveys of Educational Achievement*. Washington, DC: National Academies Press.

Pring, R. (2008). Teacher education at Oxford University: James is alive but living in Karachi. *Oxford Review of Education* 34 (3): 325–33.

Raby, R. L. (2007). Fifty years of *Comparative Education Review* bibliographies: Reflections on the field. *Comparative Education Review* 51 (3): 379–98.

———. (2010). The 2009 *Comparative Education Review* bibliography: Patterns of internationalization in the field. *Comparative Education Review* 54 (3): 415–27.

Raudenbush, S. W., S. Kidchanapanish, and S. J. Kang. (1991). The effects of preprimary access and quality on educational achievement in Thailand. *Comparative Education Review* 35 (2): 255–73.

Robitaille, D. F., and R. A. Garden. (1989). *The IEA Study of Mathematics II: Contexts and Outcomes of School Mathematics* (Vol. 2). Oxford: Pergamon.

Schmidt, W. H., S. Blömeke, M. T. Tatto, F. J. Hsieh L. Cogan, R. T. Houang, and J. Schwille.

(2011). *Teacher Education Matters: A Study of Middle School Mathematics Teacher Preparation in Six Countries*. New York: Teachers College Press.

Schmidt, W. H., R. Houang, D. Wiley, R. Wolfe, C. McKnight, S. Wang, and L. Cogan. (2001). *Why Schools Matter: A Cross-National Comparison of Curriculum and Learning*. San Francisco: Jossey-Bass.

Schmidt, W. H., D. Jorde, L. Cogan, E. Barrier, I. Gonzalo, U. Moser, K. Shimizu, T. Sawada, G. Valverde, R. Prawat, C. McKnight, S. Raizen, E. Britton, D. Wiley, and R. Wolfe. (1996). *Characterizing Pedagogical Flow: An Investigation of Mathematics and Science Teaching in Six Countries*. Dordrecht: Kluwer Academic Publishers.

Schmidt, W. H., C. C. McKnight, L. Cogan, P. Jakwerth, and R. Houang. (1999). *Facing the Consequences: Using TIMSS for a Closer Look at United States Mathematics and Science Education*. Dordrecht: Kluwer.

Schmidt, W. H., C. McKnight, S. Raizen, P. Jakwerth, G. Valverde, R. Wolfe, E. Britton, L. Bianchi, and R. Houang. (1997). *A Splintered Vision: An Investigation of U.S. Science and Mathematics Education*. Dordrecht: Kluwer.

Schmidt, W. H., C. C. McKnight, G. A. Valverde, R. T. Houang, and D. E. Wiley. (1997). *Many Visions, Many Aims: A Cross-National Investigation of Curricular Intentions In School Mathematics*. Dordrecht: Kluwer.

Schmidt, W. H., M. T. Tatto, K. Bankov, S. Blömeke, T. Cedillo, L. Cogan, S. Han, et al. (2007). *The Preparation Gap: Teacher Education for Middle School Mathematics in Six Countries*. East Lansing: Center for Research in Mathematics and Science Education, Michigan State University.

Schneider, A. I. (2003). *Internationalizing Teacher Education: What Can Be Done?* Washington, DC: U.S. Department of Education.

Schwille, J. (1993a). The Promise of Comparative Inquiry in Teacher Education and Teacher Development: Lessons to Be Learned from Non-Western Contexts. Paper prepared for conference Towards Education for All, Universiti Brunei Darussalam, September.

———. (1993b). Rethinking Comparative Education to Accommodate Nonspecialists and the Spirit of Reform. Paper prepared for annual meeting of the Comparative and International Education Society, Kingston, Jamaica.

———. (Ed.) (1993c). Teacher Collegiality and Professional Development: International Variation in Practice and Context. Special issue of the *International Journal of Educational Research* 19 (8): 669–74.

———. (2004). Comparative dissertation becomes bestseller in mathematics education. *Comparative and International Education Society Newsletter*, May 2004.

———. (2011). Experiencing innovation and capacity building in IEA research, 1963–2008.

In C. Papanastasiou, T. Plomp, and E. Papanastasiou (Eds.), *IEA 1958–2008: 50 Years of Experiences and Memories*. Nicosia: Kykkos Research Center.

Schwille, J., and M. Dembélé. (2007). *Global Perspectives on Teacher Learning: Improving Policy and Practice*. Paris: International Institute for Educational Planning, UNESCO.

Schwille, J., and M. Dembélé, with J. Adotevi, K. Bah, D. Fofana, N. Camara, J. Tinguiano, F. Camara, and H. Doumbouya. (1997). *Dignité en jeu*: Small Grants for Teacher Projects as a Catalyst for Professional Development in a Resource-Scarce West African Country. Paper prepared for annual meetings of the American Educational Research Association, Chicago.

Schwille, J., M. Dembélé, and G. Bah. (1999). Balancing Internal and External Evaluation Responsibilities for Teacher Designed Professional Development Projects in Guinea. Paper presented at annual meeting of the American Educational Research Association, Montreal.

Schwille, J., M. Dembélé, and M. Baldé. (2002). *Rapport de l'assistance technique fournie par l'Université d'Etat du Michigan dans le cadre du Programme de Petites Subventions d'Ecole en Guinée (1996–2002)*. Unpublished report prepared for submission to Ministry of Pre-University and Civic Education, Republic of Guinea.

Schwille, J., M. Dembélé, and A. M. Diallo. (2001). Teacher improvement projects in Guinea: Lessons learned from taking a program to national scale. *Peabody Journal of Education* 76 (3–4): 102–21.

Schwille, J., L. C. Ingvarson, and R. Holdgreve-Resendez. (Eds.) (2013). *TEDS-M 2008 Encyclopedia: A Guide to Teacher Education Context, Structure, and Quality Assurance in the Seventeen TEDS-M 2008 Countries*. Amsterdam: International Association for the Evaluation of Educational Achievement.

Schwille, J., and D. Roberts. (Eds.) (2014). *What the TPP Education Team Has Learned in Milola, 2006–2013*. East Lansing: Tanzania Partnership Program, College of Education, Michigan State University.

Shamin, F., and A. Halai. (2006). Developing professional development teacher. In I. Fareh and B. Joworski (Eds.), *Partnerships in Educational Development*. Oxford: Symposium Books.

Smuckler, R. H. (2003). *A University Turns to the World: A Personal History of the Michigan State University International Story*. East Lansing: Michigan State University Press.

Swartz, D. (1997). *Culture and Power*. Chicago: University of Chicago Press.

Tatto, M. T. (1996). Examining values and beliefs about teaching diverse students: Understanding the challenges for teacher education. *Educational Evaluation and Policy Analysis* 18:155–80.

———. (1998). The influence of teacher education on teachers' beliefs about purposes of education, roles and practice. *Journal of Teacher Education* 49:66–77.

———. (1999). The socializing influence of normative cohesive teacher education on teachers' beliefs about instructional choice. *Teachers and Teaching* 5:111–34.

———. (2011). Reimagining the education of teachers: The role of comparative and international research (Presidential address, Comparative and International Education Society). *Comparative Education Review* 55(4): 495–516.

———. (2013). *Teacher Education Study in Mathematics (TEDS-M): Technical Report.* Amsterdam: International Association for the Evaluation of Student Achievement.

Tatto, M. T., L. Ingvarson, J. Schwille, R. Peck, S. L. Senk, and G. Rowley. (2008). *Teacher Education and Development Study in Mathematics (TEDS-M), Policy, Practice, and Readiness to Teach Primary and Secondary Mathematics: Conceptual Framework.* Amsterdam: International Association for the Evaluation of Educational Achievement.

Tatto, M. T., H. D. Nielsen, W. C. Cummings, N. G. Kularatna, and D. H. Dharmadasa. (1993). Comparing the effectiveness and costs of different approaches for educating primary school teachers in Sri Lanka. *Teaching and Teacher Education* 9:41–64.

Tatto, M. T., J. Schwille, S. Senk, L. Ingvarson, G. Rowley, R. Peck, K. Bankov, M. Rodriguez, and M. Reckase. (2012). *Policy, Practice, and Readiness to Teach Primary and Secondary Mathematics in Seventeen Countries: Findings from the IEA Teacher Education and Development Study in Mathematics (TEDS-M).* Amsterdam: International Association for the Evaluation of Educational Achievement.

TC Community. (2009). Shaping education around the world: Teachers College, Columbia University. http://www.tc.edu/news.htm?articleID=7042.

Thomas, D. A. (2008). *Michigan State College: John Hannah and the Creation of a World University, 1926–1969.* East Lansing: Michigan State University Press.

Thomson, P. (2012). Field. In M. Grenfell (Ed.), *Pierre Bourdieu: Key Concepts.* 2nd ed. London: Routledge.

Tikly, L., and M. Crossley. (2001). Teaching comparative and international education: A framework for analysis. *Comparative Education Review* 45: 561–80.

Torney-Purta, J., J. Amadeo, and J. Schwille. (2010). IEA study in civic education. In P. Peterson, E. Baker, and B. McGaw (Eds.), *International Encyclopedia of Education* (Vol. 4, 3rd edition). Oxford: Elsevier.

Torney-Purta, J., R. Lehmann, H. Oswald, and W. Schulz. (2001). *Citizenship and Education in 28 Countries: Civic Knowledge and Engagement at Age 14.* Amsterdam: The International Association for the Evaluation of Educational Achievement.

Torney-Purta, J., J. Schwille, and J. A. Amadeo. (1999). *Civic Education across Countries: Twenty-Four National Case Studies from the IEA Civic Education Project.* Amsterdam: International

Association for the Evaluation of Educational Achievement.

U.S. Department of Education, National Commission on Excellence in Education (1983). *A Nation at Risk*. Washington, DC: U.S. Department of Education.

Valverde, G. A., L. J. Bianchi, W. H. Schmidt, C. C. McKnight, and R. J. Wolfe. (2002). *According to the Book: Using TIMSS to Investigate the Translation of Policy into Practice in the World of Textbooks*. Dordrecht: Kluwer Academic Publishers.

Wang, J. (1998). Learning to Teach Mathematics: Preservice Teachers, Their Collaborating Teachers, and Instructional Contexts. PhD diss., Michigan State University.

Wang, J., and L. W. Paine. (2001). Mentoring as assisted performance: A pair of Chinese teachers working together. *Elementary School Journal* 102 (2): 157–81.

Wang, J., M. Strong, and S. Odell. (2004). Mentor-novice conversations about teaching: A comparison of two U.S. and two Chinese cases. *Teachers College Record* 106 (4): 775–813.

Wheeler, C. W. (1975). *White Collar Power: Changing Patterns of Interest Group Behavior in Sweden*. Champaign: University of Illinois Press.

Wheeler, C. W., P. T. N. Hong, B. L. Chi, and H. T. T. Ho. (2007). Lesson Study, Vietnamese Style: Bringing Meaning to a Hollow Shell. Paper presented at the World Association of Lesson Studies International in Hong Kong.

Wiley, D. S. (2012). *Michigan State University Cooperation with South Africa: Forty Years of Partnership*. East Lansing: African Studies Center, Michigan State University.

Wiley, D. S., and R. S. Glew. (Eds.) (2010). *International and Language Education for a Global Future: Fifty Years of U.S. Title VI and Fulbright-Hays Programs*. East Lansing: Michigan State University Press.

Wiseman, A. W., and C. Matherly. (2009). The professionalization of comparative and international education: Promises and problems. *Research in Comparative and International Education* 4 (4): 334–55.

Zhao, Y. (2009). *Catching up or Leading the Way: American Education in the Age of Globalization*. Alexandria, VA: Association for Supervision and Curriculum Development.

———. (2012). *World Class Learners: Educating Creative and Entrepreneurial Students*. Thousand Oaks, CA: Corwin Press.

Index

A

Academy for Education Development (AED), 87, 103–4, 196, 106–8
Addy, Nii Antiaye, 10, 11–12
Aga Khan Foundation, 210–11
Algeria, 108–9, 240
Altbach, Phil, 10–11
Ambach, Gordon, 45, 56
American Educational Research Association, 231
American Institutes for Research, 103–4
American International Schools, 197–98, 201, 204, 221, 236, 246
Ames, Carole, 35, 38–39, 106, 135, 140, 156, 157–64, 186, 189, 198, 202, 215
Anderson, C. Arnold, 10–11, 34
Anupama, 123
Apol, Laura, 159, 184, 223

Archer, Jeff, 89–90
Austin, Ann, 120, 122, 218, 244
Australian Council for Educational Research (ACER), 69–70, 72, 76
Azim Premji Foundation, 121–22, 124–25, 240

B

Babcock, Jacqie, 214
Backman, Steve, 188, 193
Baker, Jean, 39
Bale, Jeff, 249
Banks, Vickie, 186
Bartz, Cheryl, 227–28
Beach, King, 241
Beeftu, Alemu, 86
Behar, Anurag, 124
Bell, Terrell, 54

Benham, Maenette, 139–40, 245

Benjalug Namfa, 92

Ben-Peretz, Miriam, 217

Berzina-Pitcher, Inese, 232–33

Bird, Tom, 109, 110–11

Blackman, Charles, 265n4

Blömeke, Sigrid, 74, 142, 159, 208, 218; profile, 213–16

Board on International Comparative Studies in Education (BICSE), 14, 55–57

Book, Cass, 215

Boston College, 57–58, 72

Botswana, 73, 164–65, 240

Bourdieu, Pierre, xvi, 3–7, 13–15, 30, 36, 50, 70, 140, 215, 240; his concepts of capital, 4–6, 9–10, 23–24, 169, 173, 217

Bowman, Mary Jean, 34

Brady, Nyle, 85

Brazil, 30, 144, 200, 243

Brembeck, Cole, 11, 20, 21

Bricker, Betsy, 105

BRIDGES (Basic Research and Implementation in Developing Education Systems), 49, 51, 59–61, 81, 84, 121, 217, 220, 247

Britton, Ted, 65, 66–68

Bryson, Sandy, 118, 198–99, 228, 245

Buchmann, Margret, 36, 243–44

Bulgaria, 70

Burke, Bruce, 198–99, 245

Burkina Faso, 176–78

Burstein, Leigh, 52

Burundi, 51, 59–61, 149, 240

Bush, George H. W., 54

Bush, George W., 57

Byun, Soo-Yong, 189–90

C

Cafagna, Al, 110–11

Cain, Joyce, 117, 190, 241

Cambodia, 240

Canada, 73, 141, 246

Cantwell, Brendan, 241

Carnoy, Martin, 242

Carolan, Aliah, 188, 192–93

Chikombah, Cowden, 117

Chile, 73

Chimedza, Robert, 118, 194

China, 30, 31–33, 37, 64–67, 133, 135–36, 137, 139, 141, 144, 145, 150–52, 170–71, 173, 200, 235–36, 240; doctoral study tours to, 162–64, 166

Choi, Jonathan, 150

Chudgar, Amita, 142, 159, 242

civic education, 57–58, 142

Claffey, Joan, 84

Clark, Chris, 172

Clause, Stacy, 233

Clinton, Bill, 45–46, 54

Codde, Joe, 108–9, 159, 245

Cogan, Lee, 53, 214, 245

comparative and international education (CIE): approaches to, 10–18, 25; arguments for, 22–25, 83, 163; international development approach to, 15–16; disabilities and, 125–27, 242; integration-infusion approach to, 11, 12–13, 20, 21–22, 25, 40–41, 50, 77–78, 97, 125, 173, 186, 235–40; K–12 schools and, 129–33, 142–44, 147, 152–53, 166, 203; resistance to, 9–10, 14, 18, 87, 119, 139–41. *See also* Michigan State University–College of Education

Comparative and International Education Society (CIES), xvi, 35, 40, 48, 174, 185, 223, 231–34
Confucius, 37
Conway, Paul, 144
Costa Rica, 240
Council of Chief State School Officers, 56
Craig, John, 34
Cranfield, Corvell, 193
Crespo, Sandra, 244
Crossley, Michael, 11
Cuba, 144
Cyprus, 164, 166, 217
Czech Republic, 144

D

Damrow, Amy, 203
Delany, Brian, 36, 140–41
Dembélé, Gaston, 192
Dembélé, Martial, 96, 98, 100; profile, 175–78
Dirkx, John, 159
Dominguez, Higinio, 245
Dominican Republic, 240
Drake, Timothy, 15–16, 17, 264n24
Drummond, Todd, 194
Duong, Tran Phuoc, 92, 95
Dzjimbo, Peter, 190

E

Educational Development Center (EDC), 87, 103, 106, 225
Educational Quality Improvement Program (EQUIP), 103–4, 106, 225
Education for Global Education (EGC) schools, 135, 150–51
Egypt, 102, 103–6, 200, 225, 240

Eisemon, Tom, 60
Elayan, Sakeena, 188
Elliott, Emerson, 56
England, 63–64, 87, 137, 171, 235
Engler, John Mathias, 45
Ethiopia, 102–3, 240
ethnocentrism, 10, 83, 169
Even, Ruhama, 159

F

Fang, Yanping, 174
Featherstone, Helen, 177
Feiman-Nemser, Sharon, 63–64, 66, 175, 217
Feltz, Deb, 164–65
Finland, 87, 247
Finn, Chester, 56
Floden, Bob, 68
Ford Foundation, 88, 209, 223, 224
Foster, Aroutis, 159
Foster, Jesse, 10, 11–12
France, 55, 63, 65, 67, 87, 143

G

Gallagher, James, 88, 92–94, 119, 200, 245–46
George Washington University, 103
Georgia, 73
Germain, Marty, 139
Germany, 70, 73, 76, 87, 143, 214
Gilford, Dorothy, 56
Ginsburg, Mark, 104–5, 106, 175
Giridhar, S. (Giri), 124
Glew, Margo, 162, 184, 227–28, 246
Global Educators Cohort Program (GECP), 161–63, 184, 227, 246
globalization, 15–16, 134, 136–37, 166, 198
Gowda, Chandan, 124

Graduate Studies in Education Overseas (GSEO), 198–202, 204, 225, 228, 247
Graham, Patricia, 63
Greenland, Jeremy, 211
Greenwalt, Kyle, 143, 246
Grenfell, Michael, 6–7
Grønmo, Liv, 75, 76
Gross, Karl, 141
Guinea, 96–102, 176, 177–78, 225, 235–36, 240

H

Hannah, John, 19
Harvard University, 59, 87
Hegarty, Martha, 125–26, 247
Heilman, Elizabeth, 246
Heyneman, Stephen, 16–17
Hollingsworth, Sandra, 200, 246
Holmes Group, 209–10
Holtschlag, Margaret, 149, 155–56, 181, 193
Houang, Richard, 53, 214, 215, 244
Hungwe, Kedmon, 191–92

I

India, 30, 114–15, 121–25, 144, 240, 242
Indonesia, 109, 110–11, 164, 182–84, 200, 240
Ingvarson, Lawrence, 69, 249, 250
International Association for the Evaluation of Educational Achievement (IEA), 14, 44–45, 51–58, 69–70, 73–78, 213–14, 226; Data Processing Center, 69, 71–72, 75
Internationalizing Michigan Education conference, 157
Iran, 144, 170
Ireland, 126, 200, 247
Israel, 144
Issac, Benson, 123

Izzo, Tom, 215

J

Japan, 55, 65–66, 67, 87, 139, 144, 170, 236
Japanese Saturday Schools, 197–98, 202–5, 225
Jita, Loyiso, 119
Johnston, Scott, 139
Jordan, 144, 146, 179–81, 240
Joy, Anu, 123
Joyce, William, 246
Judge, Harry, 62–63, 208, 218, 267n21; profile, 209–13
Junqueira Rodrigues, Eduardo Santos, 194

K

Kamata, Akihito, 203
Kang, San Jin, 61
Kauffman, Nils, 188, 194
Kazamias, Andreas, 11
Kearney, Phil, 157
Keeves, John, 53
Kellogg Foundation, 148
Kelly, Jim, 157
Kennedy, Mary, 121, 173
Kenya, 200
Khalifa, Muhammed, 246
Kifer, Edward "Skip," 52
Kinyanjui, Kabiru, 208–9
Koehler, Matthew, 115
Korea, 70, 144, 170, 189–90, 200
Kuhn, Thomas, 4

L

Lanier, Judith, 20, 22, 30, 85, 117, 136, 138, 186, 209, 211, 243

LATTICE (Linking All Types of Teachers to International, Cross-Cultural Education), 36, 130, 131–33, 143–50, 155, 157, 179–81, 183, 186, 223, 225, 239

Leahy, Mike, 40, 126, 247

Lebanon, 109

Lesotho, 188

Levin, Hank, 34, 243

Levine, Joe, 86

linkages, 95, 110, 116, 121, 125, 135, 222; LATTICE and, 148, 155, 221; online, 164; South African, 118–20; Wheeler and, 80–82

Lucas, James M., 195

M

Ma, Liping, 177; profile, 173–74

Mabokela, Reitu, 40, 107, 119, 160, 232, 244, 251–52

Madagascar, 200

Malawi, 144

Malaysia, 73, 109–10, 144, 193

Malete, Leps, 165

Maloff, Ashley, 184–85

Manzon, Maria, 13–15

Markle, Barbara, 50, 157; profile, 133–34, 136–37

Martin, Mick, 57

mathematics. *See* science and mathematics education

McClintock, Sally, 130, 143–44, 148, 150, 155; profile, 131–33

McDonough, Maureen, 92

McGinn, Noel, 34, 48, 59, 60

McKnight Foundation, 92, 94

McPherson, Peter, 39, 85, 153, 220

Melnick, Susan, 118, 199, 247

Metzler, John, 117–19, 153, 242

Mexico, 48, 70, 236, 240

Michigan State University–College of Education: awards of, 54, 166, 220, 239; beginnings of CIE at, 19–25, 171; doctoral study tours, 161, 163–66; faculty recruitment and development at, 29–41, 158–60; internationalization courses and requirements at, 138–43, 153–54, 161–62, 192–93; internationally oriented students at, 169–95, 222–23; listserv established at, 186–87; semester transition at, 138, 141, 153; support staff of, 227–28; visiting scholars at, 207–18. *See also* comparative and international education

UNITS: Center for Teaching and Technology, 134; Confucius Institute, 135, 151–52, 226; Institute for International Studies in Education, 20, 21; Institute for Research on Teaching, 21, 54, 61–62; International Student Association, 188; National Center for Research on Teacher Education (NCRTE), 48, 62; National Center for Research on Teacher Learning (NCRTL), 63, 64, 143, 173, 175; Nonformal Education Information Center (NFEIC), 21, 84–87; Office for Academic Outreach, 198; Office of International Studies in Education, 86, 187, 225, 227–29, 232; Office of Rehabilitation and Disability Studies, 126; U.S.-China Center for Research on Educational Excellence, 135, 150, 226

Mill, John Stuart, 36–37

Mishra, Punya, 39, 40, 113, 122, 124, 159–60, 172, 189, 226; profile, 114–16

Miske, Shirley, 202

Moldova, 188

Molosiwa, Annah, 188

Moore, Kay, 118, 200

Moran, Chery, 110

Mozambique, 240

MT21. *See* Teacher Education and
  Development Study in Mathematics

Mugabe, Robert, 116

Mullis, Ina, 57

Mungai, Anne M. N., 194

Myanmar, 144, 240

N

NAFSA Association of International
  Educators, 14

Nagappan, Rajendran, 109–10

National Academy of Sciences, 56

National Center for Educational Statistics,
  56, 57

National Science Foundation (NSF), 44, 54,
  56, 57, 69–71, 224, 226

Nation at Risk report, 54

Navarro, Richard, 34, 59, 242

Neisler, Gretchen, 105, 227–28

Nepal, 144, 241

Newman, John, 37

New Zealand, 44, 53, 65, 67

Nguyet Hong, Phung thi, 92, 93

Nigeria, 19, 79, 116

9/11 attacks, 35, 38–39, 145, 189

Norway, 55, 73, 87

Nyagura, Levi, 117

O

Ogisu, Takayo, 185

Oka, Evelyn, 165

Okwako, Betty, 233–34

Oman, 73

Ombonga, Mary Mokeira, 194–95

P

Paine, Lynn, 30, 36, 37, 40, 51, 56, 63–66, 68,
  69, 139–41, 159–60, 162–63, 172, 177, 215,
  232, 242; profile, 31–33

Pakistan, 59, 102, 103, 106–8, 210–11, 225

Palestine, 144

Papanastasiou, Constantinos, 217

Papanastasiou, Elena, 144, 217

Paraguay, 188

Peña Reyes, Maria Eugenia, 195

Pérez, Francisco P., 5

Peters, Susan, 34, 40, 118, 119, 160, 190, 232,
  242, 251

Philippines, 73

Phillipps, Roy, 53

Phillips, Kristin, 242

Pigozzi, Mary Joy, 84, 85–86

Pimm, David, 65

Pinheiro, Sandro, 200

Plank, David, 34, 40, 50, 118–19, 142, 232,
  242–43

Poland, 73, 76

Pongpaibool, Panom, 216–17

Porter, Andy, 21, 62, 85

Postlethwaite, Neville, 53

Prawat, Dick, 172

Premji, Azim, 121, 124

Pring, Richard, 210

Program for International Student
  Assessment (PISA), 14, 58

Progress in International Reading Literacy